DRAMATURGY AND DRAMATIC CHARACTER

Dramatic character is among the most long-standing and familiar of artistic phenomena. From the theatre of Dionysus in ancient Greece to the modern stage, William Storm's book delivers a wide-ranging view of how characters have been conceived at pivotal moments in history. Storm reaffirms dramatic character as not only ancestrally prominent but as a continuing focus of interest. He looks closely at how stage figures compare to fictional characters in books, dramatic media, and other visual arts. Emphasis is sustained throughout on fundamental questions of how theatrical characterization relates to dramatic structure, style, and genre. Extensive attention is given to how characters think and to aspects of agency, selfhood, and consciousness. As the only book to offer a long view of theatrical characterization across this historical span, Storm's dramaturgical and theoretical investigation examines topics that remain vital and pertinent for practitioners, scholars, students of theatre and literature, and general audiences.

WILLIAM STORM is a Professor in the Department of Theatre Arts at New Mexico State University, where he teaches dramatic literature, theory, and theatre history. He is the author of *After Dionysus: A Theory of the Tragic* and *Irony and the Modern Theatre* as well as plays and essays in literary criticism and dramatic theory. He was literary manager of the Mark Taper Forum in Los Angeles and was production dramaturg for many plays in workshop development and full production.

DRAMATURGY AND DRAMATIC CHARACTER

A Long View

WILLIAM STORM

CAMBRIDGE
UNIVERSITY PRESS

CAMBRIDGE
UNIVERSITY PRESS

University Printing House, Cambridge CB2 8BS, United Kingdom

Cambridge University Press is part of the University of Cambridge.

It furthers the University's mission by disseminating knowledge in the pursuit of education, learning and research at the highest international levels of excellence.

www.cambridge.org
Information on this title: www.cambridge.org/9781316509067

First published 2016

Printed in the United Kingdom by Clays, St Ives plc.

A catalogue record for this publication is available from the British Library

Library of Congress Cataloguing in Publication data
Names: Storm, William, 1949– author.
Title: Dramaturgy and dramatic character : a long view / William Storm.
Description: Cambridge; New York : Cambridge University Press, 2016.
Identifiers: LCCN 2015043646 | ISBN 9781107145757 (hardback) |
ISBN 9781316509067 (paperback)
Subjects: LCSH: Characters and characteristics in literature.
Classification: LCC PN56.C45 S76 2016 | DDC 809.2/927–dc23
LC record available at http://lccn.loc.gov/2015043646

ISBN 978-1-107-14575-7 Hardback
ISBN 978-1-316-50906-7 Paperback

For Adam, Dylan, and Madolyn Storm

Contents

Acknowledgments   *page* ix

Introduction: Dramatis Personae   1

1. The Art of Dionysus   17

2. Character, Form, and Genre   41

3. Character by the Rules: Neoclassicism and Beyond   62

4. Scientific Character: The How and Why of
    Naturalism – and After   84

5. How Characters Think   104

6. Anti-Character   130

7. Dramatic Character Today   153

Notes   183
Works Cited   211
Index   223

Acknowledgments

I honor the legacy of Bert O. States and his extensive writings on character in drama. I am grateful to James Phelan and colleagues at Ohio State University for hosting the "Symposium on Narrative, Science, and Performance" and publishing the collected papers from that conference. Parts of Chapter 4 appeared originally in *Narrative* 19:2 (May 2011): 242–252, with the title, "On the Science of Dramatic Character," and I am grateful to Ohio State University Press for permission to reprint. Many thanks to Steve Pinker for the discussion of consciousness, especially regarding David Chalmers's "hard problem," and to Rebecca Goldstein for email conversations on Plato, including the relation of dramatically presented character and real persons. My thanks also to Richard Powers for the correspondence on dramatic and narrative character and focalization in relation to *The Echo Maker,* and to Mark Rose for his commentary on Chapter 2 in relation to *Hamlet*. I am deeply appreciative of the opportunity to teach two new courses, "How Characters Think" and "Dramatic Character," in my home department at New Mexico State University Theatre Arts, and of the students who brought so much to our class discussions. I benefit once again from the exemplary editorial care at Cambridge, and am profoundly grateful to the editors there: Kate Brett, Fleur Jones, Clare Dennison, and especially Victoria L. Cooper who invited me to write my own book on dramaturgy and character.

Introduction: Dramatis Personae

Dramatic character is among the most long-standing and, by now, most familiar of artistic phenomena. In the ancient world, certainly, characterization was not conceived or understood as it is today, yet the onset of mimetic representations of persons through enactment – or, more elaborately, a dramatis personae conveyed through storytelling by performers before an audience – dates to the sixth-century B.C. in Greece. Evolving from the discoveries of that ancient populace and its theatre, characters in drama have conveyed their personalities, interrelations, and life histories under vastly contrasting circumstances: in different eras and cultures, on all manner of stages, and before widely disparate audiences in many languages. Today, we are so accustomed to the telling of stories and the portrayal of fictional persons through characterization and acting – on stage, on television, or in film – that dramatic characters can seem to be everywhere, and our ability to know and appreciate these fictive personages has long since come to be second nature. At the same time, though, such characterization is dependent, as it has always been, upon a magnificent, if necessarily disguised, trick of theatrical art.

Character, indeed, is a basis for the theatrical illusion itself – that is, the enacted pretense that a group of onlookers, in a collective accommodation of skepticism or disbelief, is pleased to accept as representative and truthful. To this end, the conjuring of a dramatist is focused on the persuasive delivery of a stage figure's lifelikeness, but not of completeness. The entirety of a dramatic character, comprising all that an audience must know in order for a play to function optimally and be comprehended in performance, must be conveyed within a conventional two or three hours of stage time, a strict but necessary limitation on the background information that can belong to any member of the cast. And yet, what would appear to be missing, those nonessential elements of background and experience that must be omitted in the stage presentation of personhood, go largely unnoticed by the observer.

I

An audience, willingly assistant in the playwright's legerdemain, tends to helpfully yet unconsciously fill in the blanks in characterization.[1] Thus, the observer is led to experience what is perceived through spectatorship as fully drawn stage personas that are complete with current activities and concerns as well as possibly intricate pasts that might well reflect an audience member's own life – or at least be accepted as plausibly so. Does it matter that a theatrical character once learned to ride a horse or a motorcycle or that he or she attended third grade or was ill at times with cold or flu? Perhaps so and perhaps not, but the spectator can assume such background as one might of most anyone, and without being told by the playwright. In literary narrative, by contrast, authors can describe at will and at length, editorial or budgetary considerations aside.

Indeed, this transaction between audience member and dramatic character is a qualitatively different means of engagement from that of a reader with characters in a novel or short story. The physical presence and immediacy of the actor, whose embodiment of a theatrical character is, by definition, abbreviated and made succinct by the limit on performance time, aids tremendously in an audience's ability to perceive both completeness and roundedness in the representation of a character in a play – that is, a fully realized stage figure. The observer is encouraged, ideally, to accept the depiction of character as reliable, and to behold therefore a person on the stage, as opposed to in the mind's eye of the reader. Or, to put this slightly differently, the audience collaborates with both the dramatist and the actor toward an artful thoroughness of depiction and reception.[2]

In this sense at least, dramatic character becomes a collaboration, even a fusion, between the design of the dramatist and the actor's own interpretation as created for performance and apprehended by onlookers. And clearly, the nature and composition of a theatrical audience are, in themselves, highly variable phenomena. Spectators in differing historical periods and geographical locales are distinguished and differentiated by factors as various as gender, race, class, or economic status, cultural manners and mores, civic or national traditions, or simply the popular trends of a particular day. That said, the collaboration to which I refer speaks specifically but also broadly to what is aesthetically basic in theatrical art and pertains fundamentally to the engagement of an observer with a story that is enacted through characterization. In fact, the relation of an audience to a play and to the performance of character has its own creative and protean aspects. An audience is not, one hopes, passive in the face of an artful portrayal but is, rather, drawn emotionally and intellectually to enter into partnership with the representation, whatever it may be. Herbert Blau speaks to exactly this proclivity when he observes that an audience "is not so much a mere congregation of people as a body of thought and desire. It does not exist before the play but is *initiated* or *precipitated* by it; it is not an entity to begin with but a consciousness constructed. The audience is what happens when, performing the signs and passwords of a play, something postulates itself and unfolds in response" (25, italics original). What Blau does not say is that a goodly part of these interactive dynamics belongs to the volatile relation between observer and those who are observed – the enacted characters who inhabit a given play at a particular time and before an assemblage.

This collaborative interaction, which occurs naturally but often unconsciously on the part of audiences, and which is by now so routinely familiar, has a genesis that is anything but commonplace. From a contemporary perspective, in fact, the beginnings of theatrical characterization are, though by no means inscrutable, extraordinarily foreign and distant to a modern sensibility. There is, to be sure, a relatively straightforward and conventional way of deciphering these beginnings. Within the Aristotelian tradition at least, it is believed that the birth of character in drama took place in the ancient world as part of an early development of tragedy, sixth century B.C., when the Greek tragedian and choral leader Thespis became not only a solo performer but also an actor, one who assumed a role in mask – perhaps that of a mythic hero or the figure of Pentheus or even the god Dionysus (although this is disputed) – and interacted with the chorus of fifty men who sang the dithyramb in the god's honor.[3] While the specifics of this impersonation remain in question, it is precisely this phenomenon, the depiction by a performer of an individual other than himself, deity or not, that is associated typically with the beginnings of Greek tragedy and also of acting – when the latter term is understood simply as a person's enactment of a fictive persona that is observed by others in the service of storytelling. Here, within this elemental relation of personal imitation to collective observation, dramatic character emerges also and concurrently as a variety of artistic representation that was heretofore unknown. The concept of an embodied fiction – that is, the visible manifestation of a personage other than the performer as a figure within a story – was, in the ancient Greek setting, radically new in spite of the Homeric tradition of orally presented poetic narrative that preceded it.

In addition, the exotic nature of the deity who was celebrated in the dithyramb – the changeable god Dionysus – taken together with the religious and performative aspects associated with the dithyrambic ceremony itself, add immeasurably to the complexity and fascination of this

initial onset of theatrical character.⁴ To refer to Dionysus as a god is accurate, certainly, in terms of his status in the Greek world and his range
of religious associations and visual forms. The god appears often, as on
a calyx krater, as a robed and bearded figure with thyrsus, but also, as
in Euripides's *Bacchae*, as a smiling young man with blonde curls, or in
such varied manifestations as a bull, lion, snake, the Stranger, Traveller,
or fire.⁵ And yet, even when one considers the phenomenon of the
Dionysiac apart from ancient religious beliefs – as a set of ideas rather
than something metaphysical or supernatural – this figure still evinces
a remarkable intricacy and, in fact, a strangeness. Dionysus is, after all,
famously paradoxical, a personified union of contradictions and opposi-
tions.⁶ With respect to theatre specifically, Dionysus is preeminently the
god of the mask, of acting as theatrical illusion and representation as
well as impersonation, and hence of dramatic characterization in its initial appearances. Or, perhaps more accurately, he is the god *within* such
phenomena, the spirit that gives rise to them, singly and in combination. The significance and impact of this generative theatrical spirit are
such that I begin my inquiry into dramatic character and its dramaturgy
with "The Art of Dionysus" (Chapter 1), examining this unique figure's
spectrum of associations with theatrical art in its moments of genesis.
Dionysus stands, in this connection, not only for a religious conception
but also for seminal ideas that led to characterization as a fictional impersonation that is given body and speech within a performance space and
before a collective body.

Under these very circumstances, the onset of theatrical characterization
is connected directly to the development of a play's overall design and dramatic shape, dating to early tragedy. Ancient dramaturgy, in its relationship to play structure and based initially upon a succession of exchanges
between the individual performer and a chorus, developed in the case of
tragic drama into a structural alternation of episode and choric ode, or
stasimon, beginning often with a *prologos* and *parodos* and ending with
the *exodos* of the chorus. For the ancient Greek dramatist and audience,
this established a template for dramatic interaction that was supremely
effective in placing an individual and a group in concert or in opposition, a pattern that found its analog, quite naturally, in the relation of
dramatic actions performed by individuals to the assembled observers – in
this case, the Athenian citizenry or body politic.⁷ Just as the purview of
Greek tragedy included political as well as historical, mythic, and religious
discourses, the counterpoise of character and chorus made for dramatic
situations in which the Athenian spectators participated, as if analogously,

as members of a civic forum as well as witnesses to a religious spectacle and theatrical entertainment.

A stage figure such as the Antigone of Sophocles would, in this view, be simultaneously a young woman who appears centrally in several dramas and also as one who stands before a public tribunal within the varying circumstances of her story. The Greek audience, knowledgeable in the myths and histories upon which the plays of Sophocles or Aeschylus (for example) were based, was well-acquainted with the stories that were turned into theatre at the City Dionysia – but they would not know how Euripides, say, or another dramatist, might choose to depict Electra, Phaedra, Medea, or even Dionysus by comparison with the same figure as imagined by another writer. In so richly generative a setting, the versatility of theatrical characterization – or, let us say, the mutability of the Dionysian mask, including as it does a mirror of the god's contradictory nature as an ingredient of conflict in drama – made way in the ancient Greek world for a burgeoning of theatre that was swift and vastly inclusive, a drama that could encompass the cosmic as well as localized and personal arenas.

In spite of these seminal, even definitive, aspects of ancient drama, Greek tragedy or comedy is, of course, only one (albeit astonishing) instance in which a fashioning of dramatic character is wedded directly and necessarily to formal aspects of dramaturgy and, in particular, to dramatic structure. My investigation of the ratio between characterization and dramatic form is advanced in Chapter 2, "Character, Form, and Genre," wherein this interrelation is examined from historic as well as aesthetic standpoints, with Shakespeare's Hamlet serving as prototype. Is Hamlet aware that he is a dramatic character? In one sense, of course, certainly not. He is a fiction, the invention of a dramatist, and his business is to ponder mortality, not the existential or ontological (or Pirandellian) implications of being a functional component in someone's play. And yet, at the same time – yes, absolutely. Hamlet is exquisitely self-conscious; he is consistently aware that he is a pawn – or player – in a larger and enigmatic game, and that some cosmic or malign duress has both fingered him and prompted him to performance along with actions taken or delayed. Hamlet is demonstrative and theatrical, an actor and enthusiast of acting, both. Indeed, Hamlet's self-consciousness as a performer – or, again, as "player" – makes him an exemplar of meta-characterization. He is also, to be sure, a figure of tragedy, as were so many of his Greek forbears. By Shakespeare's day, of course, the dramaturgy as well as the language of dramatic characterization and of tragic drama had shifted markedly from the ancient patterns. Even so, new and evolving theatrical forms could be rigidly deterministic with regard to character types, motives, and behaviors, in both the Elizabethan and Jacobean settings.

Given the potential rigors of a dramatic form, but in consideration also of Hamlet's versatility as well as intellect, can such a figure have autonomy? Does a character in drama have any quotient of freedom at all? Here again, one might respond quite reasonably with a "no" or a "yes." No, in that characters in plays are written; they are defined utterly, like Pirandello's rueful and introspective Father, by the contours of their respective dramas. And yet, at the same time, yes, because the resourceful actions and deliberations of characters, even as they arise from the imagination and inventiveness of the playwright, are what seem to engender such stories and structures in the first place. Here again, the theatrical illusion is such that a stage figure who appears to be like us, with our own ostensible freedoms regarding volition, will quite likely be perceived as having choice. That character's fate may be written, but choice in itself is dramatic and life-like and is provocative of suspense and engagement with a play's progression of events.

The issue here could scarcely be more crucial in its relation of structural considerations – elements of plot and the orchestration of scenes, chiefly – to characterization. Indeed, this relationship has, since Aristotle, provided for a sophisticated set of philosophic interrogations as well as aesthetic balances. The action of tragic dramas, for example, typically contains an intrinsic aspect that is directional, a fatality or destiny to which a character is bound, no matter any exertions to the contrary. From this standpoint, Hamlet can no more avoid a calamitous demise than Oedipus can foil the prophecies of gods. Comedy, on the other hand, often partakes of and thrives on the chaotic, with characters surviving through wit, guile, or plain dumb luck under apparently uncontrolled and at times perilously farcical circumstances. In either instance, however, there is the aspect of genre, form, or artistic philosophy that signals a corresponding dramaturgical tactic and an appropriate conception of character. Even as stage characters may be dependent fundamentally upon a practical assignation of traits, as Aristotle would advise, such qualities must be fitting and truthful not only to the particular individual and story but also to a play's formal and stylistic identity.[8]

Is it most pleasing or socially advantageous when the behaviors of a dramatic character provide the audience with an admirable, or at least useful, example – and if so, should such a model for characterization be a requisite for the creation of theatre? In Chapter 3, "Character by the

Rules: Neoclassicism and Beyond," a French Neoclassical ideal is consulted on this question, one that has implications well beyond the time of Molière, Corneille, or Racine. Within the stringent admonitions of French Neoclassicism as applied to theatrical art, guidelines of duration, location, action, genre, the depiction of violence or the supernatural, and the portrayal of individuals, including their deeds and outcomes, was followed exactingly. The unities should be obeyed; a play is either a tragedy or a comedy, with no cross-pollination; scenes of violence and horror must be reported and described verbally rather than shown onstage; characters who behave respectably should merit reward while those who are excessive or otherwise debauched must suffer – and often horribly, as in the case of Racine's Phaedra and Hippolytus. From the Neoclassical standpoint in general, the "character" qualities of a dramatic character are very much at issue, the simple reason being that the behaviors of fictional personas – and perhaps especially those who are visibly embodied upon the stage – can be so persuasive and influential upon the observer. And yet, by no means does this important concern belong solely to the Neoclassicists or to any one period in history. In fact, the conception of dramatic character as role model, or as object of potential imitation for an audience, endures and remains contentious to this day.

Even as controversy may center now on other dramatic media – the potential influences of filmed or televised violence, drug use, or sexuality, say – it was the theatre, and stage characters, where this attention was focused first, and with lasting and far-reaching effects. Moreover, the reference to stage characters as exemplars of behavior has contributed over time and on several occasions to instances of antitheatrical prejudice, whereby fictional personages are taken to task by critics of the theatre such as, famously, Jeremy Collier or Jean-Jacques Rousseau.[9] Significantly, a hallmark of dramatic writing in seventeenth-century Europe is a marked emphasis upon enlightened reason by comparison with the passions, with admonitory cautions regarding the latter. Given the centrality of this dialectic of rationality and high feeling, I pursue the question in Chapter 3 of how complete or fully rounded a character in drama can be if the emotions are stunted or if they are represented as dangerous or in need of modulation.

A quality of life-likeness, touched upon earlier in comparison with that of completeness, is of vital significance with respect to characters seen on stage, and a play need not be strictly realistic for this to be the case. In fact, the degree to which a dramatic character approximates a "real" person, and can be believable as such, is in many ways the primary basis for an audience's reception of such a figure and the success of the theatrical representation or illusion overall. In Chapter 4, "Scientific Character: The How and Why of Naturalism – and After," there is a shift in focus from the importance of behavioral standards or practical traits to the criterion of truthfulness in the depiction of persons on stage. Here, my initial point of reference is the naturalism associated with Émile Zola – and, in a closely related instance, August Strindberg – and the extent to which reasons that may underlie or account for a character's nature, behaviors, or motives are viewed as paramount in the story telling. Is environment the key, as Zola would propose? What importance is given to factors of economic status, heredity and parentage, psychology or physical health as formative and as basis for accuracy in depiction?

My intention in this chapter is to examine the avowedly scientific impulse that was characteristic of both Zola and Strindberg along with others in the late nineteenth century and afterward. Elaborating on that motive and extending its purview, the chapter inquires also into the manner in which the sciences and scientific discoveries have continued to shape not only the understandings of the human self but also the ways in which personhood can be represented in art in accord with what is known, say, of biology, physics, or neuroscience at a particular point in history. The recent popularity of the "science play" is referenced in this regard, as are differences between narrative fiction and drama with respect to a "real person" dilemma that arises in any art form as a ratio of representation to what is represented, but is particularly acute in the case of dramatic character.

A different intricacy results when factors of consciousness and cognition are introduced in ways that relate specifically to the depiction of a character's thought processes. In Chapter 5, "How Characters Think," the inquiry turns again to interiority and how it is revealed on stage, including a comparison to the representation of thought in fictional narrative, with Henry James's character of Isabel Archer serving as a ready example. In this instance, too, there is an innate relation of dramatic character to dramaturgy, due largely to the question of what is required for a portrayal of thought and how that is accomplished on stage as opposed to in narrative writing. A character's manner of thinking becomes, along these lines, a dramaturgical consideration along with matters of genre, scenic structure and focus, thematic considerations, or artistic philosophy per se. However, and while there are plays in which access to the mind of a character is germane and necessary, there are many others where it is of lesser importance in the storytelling. Indeed, there are innumerable situations in which a character in drama requires little interiority or presentation of thought whatsoever, not because the character's thinking is irrelevant to the action but because the playwright's emphasis is elsewhere – on events of plot, most likely, or performative or exteriorized behaviors, as in Restoration comedy. Do we need to venture inside the mind or emotional temper of Mr. Horner in Wycherley's *The Country Wife*, or are his intentions plain enough? There are occasions, too, where the portrayal of a mental state is enhanced by a corresponding style – as, for instance, in expressionist drama when a character's inner life and point of view are accentuated by theatrically stylized means, such as in Sophie Treadwell's *Machinal* or Eugene O'Neill's *The Hairy Ape*.

Interiority provides one perspective on thought, most typically of the reflective or introspective variety, while ratiocination, inference, intuition, attention, or observation offer other means of access to a character's way of thinking. The strategy of Chapter 5, therefore, is to analyze the mentalities, thought processes, and states of consciousness of representative characters in different periods, and to assess these comparatively, with reference to one another and also to narrative fiction. In this regard, the complexity of mind associated with Hamlet, for instance, or with Halvard Solness in Ibsen's *The Master Builder*, stands for one sort of theatrically represented interiority or self-consciousness, while a figure such as Arthur Miller's Quentin, in *After the Fall*, has not only a different mode of thought from either – one that foregrounds memory – but also a way of thinking that calls for a unique dramatic structure in which recollection itself prompts the order of events. In each case, though, the particular historical and geographical milieu in which a play is situated, with corresponding linguistic, scientific, and cultural understandings, is pertinent. One might wonder, in fact, if in consideration of such differences among sensibilities it is possible at all to draw meaningful comparisons, or if stage figures from contrasting eras might be too disparate for such analysis. For purposes here, again, the effort is to be inclusive, and to assess phenomena that have been most pertinent to the fashioning of dramatic characters over time – including their thought processes.

Psychoanalytic perspectives, as they apply to past or more recent times, are considered here also in relation to particular prototypes as well as more generally. In this regard, prominent archetypes of character (as, for example, in familial interrelations) are examined in conjunction with Freudian and Lacanian theory among other contextual frameworks. My primary aim, though, is to examine how consciousness is depicted in drama and literature in relation to theories of mind and cognition, and in philosophic as well as neuroscientific or psychological terms. Consciousness is investigated from both a standpoint of familiarity – as a phenomenon that is universal among human beings – and as mysterious in the sense of scientifically unexplained. Also problematic in this regard is the concept of "self," which has a natural, not to say innate, linkage to character as well as consciousness.

With respect to either dramatic or narrative character, what is to be understood by terms such as identity, personality, or selfhood? To what extent are these interchangeable, and in what cases not?[10] In this instance, too, the pertinence of such phenomena is wedded necessarily to historical situations and contexts – and, in particular, to levels of understanding of cognition and its processes and implications at given times, scientifically and in common parlance. Characters that are conceived for the stage or for the novel, while possibly sharing a similar object of imitation – the human mind, with all of its intricacies and vulnerabilities – can be strikingly different in the context of how thinking and state of consciousness are represented to a theatre audience as opposed to a reader. There are, in short, very different means of showing and of describing per se – a key factor in dramaturgy as well as theatre aesthetics. The significance and centrality, not to mention complexity, of this distinction is such that comparisons are necessary not only among plays but also with novels or short stories that feature a portrayal of thought. To that end, I refer comparatively in Chapter 5 not only to Edgar Allan Poe and Henry James but to more recent fictional narratives that share an emphasis on thought process and neuroscience.

Over the past hundred years especially, the fashioning of characters has at times included a reflection of the self and personality in disjuncture, as illogical, unreliable, or lacking a cohesive basis or definition. Naturalistic and other methods of unified or integrated depiction have in this context been countered or discounted in numerous ways, sometimes in response to a worldview that is similarly fragmented, disjointed, nonsensical, or absurd in the sense of inchoate or meaningless. The concept of a cohesive, unique, and definitive self has been queried repeatedly, not to say disproven, from more than a few psychological or philosophic standpoints. Just as a dramatic structure, when standing for a fragmented condition or situation, may need to violate the terms of a more balanced, synchronous, or unitary means of showing, so too a dramatic character may be fashioned to embody disassociation or a lack of empirical sense or meaning. Dramatic character and dramaturgy can, in this sense also, be consubstantial – an irony, perhaps, given the likely degree of discord that might underlie this particular complementarity.

Not surprisingly, a key point of reference in Chapter 6, "Anti-Character" is the Italian playwright Luigi Pirandello, including not only his *Six Characters in Search of an Author* – itself a rigorous inquiry into dramatic character and the theatrical illusion – but also his points of view on the vagaries of self, personality, and identity more generally. Plays by Eugene Ionesco and Samuel Beckett, among others, are consulted also in this regard with an emphasis on the ways in which dramatic structures and characters have been designed over the past century to reflect in varied ways a pervasive, rather than localized, specter of fracture, lack of meaning or sense, and uncertainty. By contrast with a naturalistic or scientific cohesiveness, this chapter entertains abstraction, alienation, dissolution, and permutation of character and situation, looking also at consciousness as a negative state as in the case of Beckett's *Happy Days*. The "anti-"dramaturgy of Ionesco is set comparatively alongside Pirandello's innate sense of opposition (the *sentimento del contraria*, or "feeling of the opposite").[11] There is an important distinction here, in that the effort is not to probe the ways in which a theatrical character can reflect mental illness or madness – subjects that have been featured in plays for centuries, even millennia – but rather to focus on comparatively recent instances in which characterization does not mirror an empirical reality and is revealed instead through a portrayal of mind, self, or consciousness that is subjective and mutable, reflecting an illogic or unpredictability or mysteriousness that are norms rather than aberrations.

The final chapter, "Dramatic Character Today," entertains the ways in which a lengthy ancestry of theatrical characterization has been formative with respect to a present time in which embodied fictional characters are ubiquitous and where stage figures coexist with those on film and television. This chapter opens, however, with a consideration of mystery and enigma in relation to Harold Pinter's *The Homecoming* and Tennessee Williams's *Cat on a Hot Tin Roof* as a means of examining how characters in drama may be drawn partially or more completely, and with what yield – especially in regard to suspense and its importance in characterization. The discussion here delves further into the phenomenon of meta-character, entertained earlier in relation to Hamlet and to the Pirandellian model in which figures such as The Father or The Stepdaughter in *Six Characters in Search of an Author* are so painfully aware of their ontological status as fictions, as creations for the stage, despite the reality they proclaim for themselves.

In fact, metatheatricality in relation to personality and selfhood can have a different sort of complexity and effect than Shakespeare or Pirandello might imagine or dramatize, and can suggest a broadened range of how characterization in the theatre can depart gainfully from the ostensible constraints of style or genre. In one notable example, the figure of Henry Carr, in Tom Stoppard's *Travesties,* has a markedly disrupted (and in this way comedic) viewpoint on events, in part through fallibility of memory and also through self-awareness and personal aggrandizement, each of which becomes eminently theatrical and self-reflexive in Stoppard's handling. Indeed, and with a variety of styles and voices, dramatists as various as Caryl Churchill, Luis Valdez, Tony Kushner, and Sarah Ruhl have used theatrical self-consciousness, self-reflexiveness, and meta-characterization for pictorial as well as thematic, ironic, or comedic effect. I attend in particular to Churchill's *Cloud 9* in relation to the portrayal of gender and race, and to Valdez's *Zoot Suit* as a play that combines meta-character with a slant on historical events, using representational and presentational strategies concurrently, including (like Churchill's play) the Brechtian.

Although characterization in the theatre need not always be tied to a genre per se, it is very often the case, historically as well as recently, that a dramatic character will have some sort of direct relationship to the category of play in which he or she belongs. The relation of character to theatrical genre is thus extremely pertinent, especially so in that the variety of play – whether it be tragic, melodramatic, naturalistic, comedic, farcical, romantic – can have so pronounced an effect upon the traits and qualities, individually and collectively, that are chosen by the dramatist in the creation of a cast. Pursuing this idea, I look to one familiar genre, the American family play, with an eye on how the demands of a form can impact the creation of a character and group of characters in familiar, and even archetypal, circumstances and relationships. To this end, the familial aspects of *Zoot Suit* and August Wilson's *Fences* are compared, providing a complementary assessment to the earlier one of Eugene O'Neill's *Long Day's Journey Into Night* and Tennessee Williams's *The Glass Menagerie* (Chapter 5), with emphasis in those cases on collective thinking among characters in a family context.

In direct counterpoint to this proposition, that genre types tend by their nature to emphasize particular traits in characterization, this chapter looks also at arguments that go precisely against such an emphasis. Particular attention is paid to Elinor Fuchs's proposal of a "death" of character and to Hans-Thies Lehmann's proposition of "post-dramatic" theatre which negates the idea of genre conventions and proposes a variation on characterization that is not based on fictive assumptions and would take the element of "drama" out of dramatic character. Fuchs's idea, in brief, is that just as dramatic character was at one time subordinated to plot (Aristotle's hierarchy), and just as character once assumed its own supremacy (the Romantic conception), that modernism initiated a move away from character as the primary point of emphasis and fascination. For Lehmann, the imperative is to avoid "fabulation" in pursuit of a reality that now belongs more to an alternative theatre tradition than to the ancestry of dramatic art or, certainly, to mainstream theatre of today. His argument is for praxis over mimesis, an aesthetic schism that, of course, implies a departure from basic precepts of imitative story telling and the theatrical illusion of "real," if fictional, characters altogether.

Assessing the status of dramatic character by comparison with such points of view can be highly revelatory with respect to the most basic of dramaturgical concerns, such as the need (or not) for a stage figure to be involved in conflicted or suspenseful situations in order to provoke and then sustain the engagement of the spectator – that is, the involvement of an audience through drama. To what extent has dramatic character remained at center stage, as it were, and to what degree moved to the periphery – and for what causes? How much have trends in alternative or performance theatre challenged the concept of mimetic character per se, not to mention a concept of "self" as self-enactment or self-construction? And, how might such phenomena relate to a "death" of more conventional models of character or even to a diminishment of the pertinence or import of drama-based characterizations? Such questions are vital, especially as they bring such baseline aspects of character and of dramatic structure into a bold relief.

I conclude the study with *Other Desert Cities*, by Jon Robin Baitz, a play that exemplifies not only the endurance but also the capabilities of a realistic and conventional dramatic structure, and of a traditional genre – here again, the American family play. In spite of such familiar associations, Baitz's play is very much in touch with its world; it engages with the politics, popular culture, anxieties, and tempos of the day, and does so largely through characterization, use of language, and the tensions within and among its people. Indeed, and perhaps ironically, the play is notably successful, in tone and pace and the stakes at hand, in capturing a current mood, similar perhaps to what Lehman refers to as the "desperately psyched up sense of life" that marks its time (118). In addition, the play connects with its era by referencing other media – film, television, and Hollywood generally – in ways that enrich, rather than detract from, what is purely theatrical: a story meant for the stage and built substantially upon the interior dynamics of one family with all of its shared, pained, and hidden history.

Throughout this book, and even as characterization in drama is examined with a long view – historically, and from a number of aesthetic, stylistic, and cultural standpoints – there are certain primary topics and motifs that are reiterated over the course of the entire discussion. Foremost among these, as my title suggests, is the relation of dramatic character and dramaturgy. Character is, after all, the product of a playwright's dramaturgical conception, strategy, and execution, even as the idea for a character may have prompted composition in the first place. Dramatic character is born with the ancient beginnings of a scripted theatrical art and has retained a centrality, even though embattled at times, ever since. The relation of a plot's agents to a dramatic structure has been a vital factor in dramaturgy from the time of Aristotle. Moreover, the innumerable methods of presenting characters on stage, from the presentational or representational to the abstracted or mimetic, connect a concept of character to dramatic theory along with aspects of play structuring.

Dramaturgy refers basically and traditionally to the art and technique of dramatic composition and theatrical representation, a definition that effectively bridges the structuring of plays with theatre aesthetics. The term does, however, have a broader range of definition and application, especially in the sense of analysis or interpretation of drama, or of an active process in rehearsal and production, perhaps in connection with the role of the dramaturg.[12] For purposes here, my concern is primarily with dramaturgy in its essential and practical relation to playmaking, and as an aspect of dramatic theory that includes the position of character in relation to other elements of writing and performance. What character *is*, in other words, is a theoretical as well as a dramaturgical question that remains central throughout this study. That said, however, I attend to dramaturgy as it includes the conformity (or not) of theatrical art to the conventions of a time – as, say, in the ancient world or in the case of French Neoclassicism – or to accepted ideas concerning proper "character" and how this is depicted on stage and approved or disapproved in different eras. Dramaturgy involves, from this perspective, the ways in which a play applies to, and engages with, the society or world of a given period and under particular circumstances. Why does a certain play, or even a character, have resonance in one place or epoch and not another? What are the optimal means, structurally and stylistically, through which a stage figure's experience can be conveyed? All of these factors, then, are within the scope of dramaturgy and together they comprise, in direct relation to dramatic character, this study's core discussion.

Relevant to that emphasis, once again, is the art and practice of presenting a "real person" to an audience or a reader, and the means by which this is possible through widely varying techniques. From this angle, dramaturgy pertains pointedly and even innately to what the stage can accomplish by comparison with other art forms. I consider both modeling and portraiture in this connection (Chapter 6), but a focus is maintained throughout this study on the differences between theatrical and literary characterization, with the corollary contrasts between the experiences of audience and reader. Similarly, the distinction between characters who are crafted from an essentially realistic premise as opposed to some form of stylistic abstraction or innovation is consistently germane. The chapters that follow are designed for sustained investigation, too, into the nature and the function of an invented character's interiority and how it is dramatized on stage or described through narrative. At the same time, a good deal of emphasis is given to external presentation and behaviors and to strictly performative aspects, as in ancient tragedy or style comedy. In brief, then, the historical yet inclusive framework that I work with enables a wide-angle view of theatrical characterization over centuries, but at the same time underscores key themes by revisiting critical points of commonality or contrast.

There is an important sense, once again, in which dramatic character is linked directly to performance and to the actor. A key distinction between character in drama and in narrative literature, to which I return repeatedly, includes both the factor of embodiment and the time limitation that is enforced upon live performance. Moreover, the individual actor's selectivity when it comes to the presentation of a given role can alter the apprehension of a stage character markedly from one performer or performance to another, even as the text is identical. Thus, and while the focus of this study of character will remain on dramaturgy in its foremost relation to a play's text and the aesthetics of theatrical representation generally, I am mindful throughout, not only of the performance element per se but also of how actors have chosen to approach their roles at various times in history. In this relation, the testimony of, say, Benoit Constant Coquelin or Michel Baron or Henry Irving is illuminating with regard to what actors themselves have found to be telling about characters – or at times disputatious, as in Irving's letter arguments with Coquelin concerning performance techniques. The Lady Macbeth of Sarah Siddons will not be that of Ellen Terry or Dame Judy Dench – even as the written character may remain the same over time.[13]

A fundamental assumption, and one that informs this book overall, is that a person today is likely to be extensively involved and invested in the depicted lives of fictional characters who are presented by dramatic means, and that this proposition has an intricate set of implications. This discussion inquires, for example, into the factor of surrogacy – in the audience-character rapport and by comparison with fictional narrative (i.e., one's identification through reading about, rather than observing, a character's experience). In what situations and under what circumstances do dramatic characters become our imaginary stand-ins or extensions of ourselves, our surrogates in experience or thought, and what is the potential range of psychological or sociological outcome from such transactions? Or, how might the presence of the actor accentuate this identity? Whether a character in drama is called upon, or needed, as surrogate or as model for behavior, the transaction is indicative of a profound identity between depicted personality and observer. Even without such considerations, though, the significance of character in drama remains a constant. For any play, and at any time, dramatic characters have a basic commonality: to wit, the dramatis personae are latently the story itself. They are the persons of the drama, the agents in the action, the figures that compel our care and attention, those who deliver all of a story's interactions, conflicts, and experiences. This, in essence, is the reason for the primacy of dramatic character and for why characterization in the theatre has mattered so vitally, beginning with its inception in the ancient world and continuing into our own.

CHAPTER I

The Art of Dionysus

Now
I shall go and costume Pentheus in the clothes
which he must wear to Hades when he dies, butchered
by the hands of his mother. He shall come to know
Dionysus, son of Zeus, consummate god,
most terrible, and yet most gentle to mankind. (193)[1]

Among the several extraordinary sequences in Euripides's *The Bacchae* is the interaction between Dionysus and Pentheus as the latter is costumed as a woman by the god, just prior to his doomed journey to observe the maenads on the mountain. Pentheus, as accustomed to manly associations as he is to ruling the city of Thebes, at first cannot imagine such an incongruous possibility – "*What?* You want *me*, a man, to wear a woman's dress? But why?" (191) – but then he changes his mind, or rather, he undergoes an elaborate series of alterations, having to do with perception and sense of identity as well as external image. In fact, this doubled sequence, which has an ostensibly simple and straightforward progression – Dionysus must convince, enthrall, and then dress Pentheus prior to the young leader's maenadic journey and travail – is actually one of seemingly endless complexity, due in part to its layered implications concerning dramatic character and theatre art more inclusively. Dionysus, or the Stranger, is in this instance a character in a play, yet he is also the god of character – of the mask, of impersonation and illusion, of theatrical performance itself.[2] Or, more precisely, he is the god *within* these phenomena, the spirit and the energy that creates, enlivens, and sustains them. More so than any other passage in *The Bacchae*, which is among the most theatrically spectacular of all the extant Greek tragedies, these final moments between Dionysus and Pentheus conjure and embody that spirit, even as they enact the effect, of a purely theatrical illusion.

Dionysus, significantly, is already costumed – he is disguised so as to avoid recognition, to be a "god incognito" as he pursues the vindication of his mysteries (155). Further, the appearance he assumes in *The Bacchae* is androgynous, a young and softly contoured Lydian male with long blond hair, smiling continually in mask. Pentheus must be costumed now as well, in a way that will transform utterly his self-conception along with clothing and manner of outward show. Dionysus says that he will dress him in a "wig with long curls," as well as "robes to your feet and a net for your hair." And Pentheus must don the garments and adopt the indicia of the maenad: "a thyrsus for your hand and a skin of dappled fawn" (191–192). By the time the first part of this encounter is over, when Pentheus exits as if in need of time to ponder what Dionysus has proposed, the movement from one identity to its opposite is already underway.

When the transfigured Pentheus reenters following a choral interlude, he is entranced, completely in thrall to the god's power. He appears now in the costume Dionysus has fashioned, but that is not all that has changed. His personality and behavior are altered as well, and to diametrical extremes. Now the manly leader of the city is worried about the straightness of his hemline and for a wandering strand of hair, which "must have come loose when I was dancing for joy and shaking my head" (196). Moreover, and in a condition of Dionysiac *ekstasis* – the state of apartness from the self – he is able to see through the outward image of Dionysus to the god himself, as an incarnation of a bull with horns. Pentheus is sent off to death by dismemberment at the hands of the maenads and his own mother Agave, but not before the god has issued an ironic farewell: "You are an extraordinary young man, and you go to an extraordinary experience" (199).

The God of Character

These remarkable scenes in *The Bacchae* refer to, and are built upon, a set of basic theatrical elements including role-playing, costuming, use of props and indicia, change of identity, and other signals of inward or outer appearance and transformation. In much the same way that an actor becomes, or at least signifies, the character that is portrayed, these encounters are very much about an alteration of exterior show and persona, with the added factor of performance before an observer. Pentheus turns into a parenthetical version of himself – "Pentheus" – and then into a would-be maenad with a self-image and awareness that has been transfigured into the feminine.[3] Froma Zeitlin reads the scene as having a ritualistic component as well as a theatrical one, with both qualities in complementary relation. That is, Pentheus must be dressed in ceremony as the sacrificial victim, but the scene's performative quotient mixes such early ritual with drama ("Playing" 64–65). And yet, this final duet between Dionysus and Pentheus has a considerably broader and more profound range of theatrical references and implications than its allusions to dramatic or ceremonial fundamentals would imply, and this intricacy pertains in large part to theatre as a domain of the god himself.

Dionysus is, famously, the god of wine, the vine and the grape, and intoxication as well as the theatre. As a nature god, his domains include fertility, the growth and ripening of plants, and specific wild animals (including the bull, which is the image that Pentheus, in his transformed state, beholds).[4] His spirit is reflected in the *orgia* as both *ekstasis* and *enthusiasmos* – dissociation from the self and being imbued with the god's spirit – as well as through *sparagmos* and *omophagia*, the tearing apart and ingestion of the sacrificial victim in worship and ceremony. *The Bacchae* incorporates many of these associations, especially the transformative ones, into its dramatic structure as well as characterization. To observe that Dionysus is the god of character is accurate, in that an illusory depiction of personhood is central to theatrical performance and to the mask. And, the association of the god to the ancient theatre generally, although exceedingly complex, is also direct.[5] As Ruth Padel notes, the theatre is the god's "own art form," and all tragedies are under his auspices (*Gods* 29, 89). Even so, a crucial distinction must be made between the god who presides and the god who is within and who animates – gives life to – a phenomenon, which is a core point of differentiation with regard to dramatic character and its ancient invention and presentation.

When the Greek actor – such as he who depicts the god or Pentheus or Agave in *The Bacchae* – dons the mask and takes on the appearance or signification of a character, he is entering into the art region of a god who represents and misrepresents, who is there, suddenly, and then is not, who deals in paradox, conflict, and recognition, and who is deeply invested in identity and its permutations. With reference to a god who is "present in the particular," Steven H. Lonsdale writes of a Dionysus who resides "in" phenomena – "in the mask, in the dances of the maenads, and in his cult hymn, the dithyramb" (81).[6] This apparently minor adjustment – from "of" to "in" – is in fact critical as an aesthetic, if abstract, aspect that asks to be included along with the more fundamental theatrical attributes or conventions that are also innate to the god.

Thus, the "character" of Dionysus embodies, and is at the same time within, the performative necessity not only of masking per se, but of deception, antithesis, alteration, and reversal.[7] The drama of Pentheus is, along these lines, a miniature of theatrical means, procedures, and effects. As Charles Segal describes this effect, Dionysus, as the "patron god of theatre," stands for the "power of fictional representation and illusionistic drama, the power that makes us believe that a masked actor is Pentheus or that a stage-front is the royal palace at Thebes." In Segal's formulation, indeed, Dionysus in *The Bacchae* "exists both as a character among characters and as a symbol of the very process that makes the dramatic fiction possible at all" (233).[8] Here, then, is a god spirit who is of, and is in, the mask, the portrayal of self and other, the principle of conflict and opposition, the dramatic action and its observation, the perceptual illusions of character and of story. This, in essence, comprises the centrality of the deity's relation to theatrical art, as both a genesis and an ongoing source of creation. If, as in Segal's portrait, Dionysus is "the god of fusion with nature's energies," he is also the one who can enable, infuse, and animate the transformative components of performance (*Tragedy* 197).

Dionysus and the Dithyramb

Dionysus precedes theatrical enactment, even as his ceremonies allow for the theatre's ancient genesis. And, in the same way that the god of the mask can be viewed as intrinsically multiform, so too must the name of Dionysus be understood as connoting multiple presences and functions at varying times and in differing situations. My intention here is not to enumerate these incarnations, which is likely impossible, but rather to look at current understandings of how a form of godly worship led to the genesis of dramatic character. Here one is mindful that the prehistory of tragic drama is sparsely documented and has been productive of extensive controversy, particularly among classical scholars over the past century. Indeed, there is scarcely an interpretation of this art in its ancient beginnings that does not have a variation or a countering assertion. As Gerald Else has remarked, "anyone who deals with the origin of tragedy is theorizing. Aristotle theorized, and so must we; he had too few facts to do otherwise, and so have we" (*Origin* vii). Complicating this situation is a range of disagreements over the initial, actual, and ongoing relevance of Dionysus, especially by the fifth-century B.C. when the scope of tragedy – in all of its political, religious, and philosophical aspects – rapidly attained so embracing a purview. Still, and given this array of cautions, a series of assumptions do remain that may be open to question but are difficult to negate entirely, which retain a general acceptance in spite of disputatious challenges and despite the remoteness and all but inaccessible qualities of drama's originating circumstances.

In broad contour, there is a tendency to trust (or at least not be overly skeptical of) Aristotle, who in the *Poetics* identifies the dithyramb and its choral leaders as the source of tragedy, and to accept, in generalized terms anyway, the Dionysian character of the early dithyrambic odes and ceremonies.[9] For purposes here, emphasis is placed not on historical agreement or lack of same but rather on the dithyramb as representative of the progress from a collective presentation to one that produced and then featured individual performances – to wit, the movement from choral activity with a Dionysian theme toward individual characterization. In brief, this ancient ode, sung by a group of fifty men, can be described as an increasingly formal, poetic, and choral composition, concerned often with the god's origin (as the son of Zeus and a mortal woman, Semele), his life and sufferings, and finally his own dismemberment followed by reconstitution of parts, or resurrection. Even in such a context, though, the dithyrambic poet was not constrained to any single theme (Kerényi 317–318). A dithyramb could be Dionysian, in performative style as well as subject, but its form and purpose were available to broader content and to other characters.

In further elaboration of this distinction, it is essential that the god's own mysteries, ceremonies, and retinues – maenadic dancing, depiction of satyrs, sparagmos and omophagia, and transportative aspects (as in *The Bacchae*) – be distinguished from subject matter and practices associated with the dithyramb only. Dionysian religion is ecstatic in its nature.[10] The maenadic votary of the god is, through worship and ceremony, transported into states of consciousness and physicality well beyond the normal confines of self and of ordinary perception – as reflected in *The Bacchae*. Quite apart from Euripides's play, though, and aside from other works that deal specifically with the story of Dionysus and Pentheus, there are ways in which the ecstatic and participatory worship of the god, as well as the dithyrambic ode, are associated intimately with the origins of theatre and, by extension, of dramatic character. Margarete Bieber's contention, in fact, is that Dionysian worship was the only possible religious source for theatrical performance in antiquity. Identifying the beginning of acting directly with Dionysian ecstatic transport, she argues that the "practice of representing someone other than oneself grew out of the ecstasy and led to the development of the mimic art of the actors" (1).[11] Dionysus was, along these lines, aligned intrinsically not only with the subject of dithyrambic worship but with the earliest methods, style, and spirit of ancient performances.[12]

Writer, Actor, Character

Upon the occasion when a solo performer first pretended before observers to be another person in the service of ceremony or story or both, we find the beginning of acting and thus of dramatic character as a seemingly obvious corollary. That is, if there is acting, then there must be a personage to be imitated and represented – hence, character. And yet, here again there is an array of variables having to do with the basis of characterization itself, its connection to theatrical representation, the respective roles and interrelations of actor and writer in the ancient Greek environs, and the perception of both onlooker and participant regarding fictional enactment and its reception. In this regard, the identity and the innovations of Thespis, the person generally credited with the introduction of acting, are more nuanced than might be expected. Thespis was, first, an author of early tragedy. As such, his primary business was to convey through means of the poetically fashioned dithyrambic performance the stories of ancient figures of Greek history or myth. Until well into the fifth-century B.C., in fact, it was expected that the writer of tragedy would also perform in his work, a practice associated, for example, with the early plays of Aeschylus and even with Sophocles. At the time of Thespis, however, in the early sixth-century B.C., the concept of character, even in rudimentary form, was not what came to be associated with depictions at the City Dionysia of renowned figures of, say, the Houses of Thebes or of Atreus that Aristotle identifies among the ideal familial models for a dramatist to consult (due to their tendency toward murderous internecine violence, among other appeals).[13]

Thespis conceived of, and introduced, the idea of actor in relation to a dramaturgical structure as well as performance – although he would not have referred to the components of his invention as such. As a writer, he incorporated into a collective performative style the function of an individual who would question, or answer, and thus interact verbally with the choral body and its leader (*exarchon*). In other words, Thespis wrote the actor, and thus himself, into the enactment, the result being a form of dramatic exchange between a recognizable figure and the choral body, coexisting with an incantatory delivery of song – an early basis for the alternation of episode and stasimon that would later characterize all of Greek dramaturgy. Historian Alois Nagler identifies Thespis as "the genius who accomplished the transition from dithyramb to drama" and as one who "seems to have evolved the protagonist (*hypokrites*, the 'answerer') destined to face a tragic dilemma and forced to answer the ever-questioning chorus..." (3). When a second actor was introduced by Aeschylus, of course, the opportunity for dramatic exchange was greatly enhanced, along with the delineation of one individual performer, or mask, from another.

While the early dithyramb could depict, say, maenadic or satyric or other celebrant behaviors collectively, the individual actor is needed to portray the circumstances of a particular personage, most likely a figure of epic or myth, who is shown in some situation, one assumes, that is provocative with respect to story and, perhaps, to dramatic conflict. Exactly what constitutes this variety of "impersonation," however, calls for some fine distinctions. Roy Flickinger asserts that, "the early dithyramb did not require impersonation," in that the "performers may sing words which are appropriate to characters and yet make no attempt by costume, gestures, or actions to represent those characters. Thespis changed all this" (16–17). Perhaps so, but since the dithyrambic participants were performing not as themselves but as votaries of various sorts, the distinction has more to do with the portrayal of a personal versus a group identity than an absence of impersonation per se – or, one might say, with the first individualization of a dramatic character.

Who, then, were the earliest characters in drama? What sorts of figures were portrayed by Thespis, and what can be deduced of the style, not to mention any dramaturgical features, of his performance? Arthur Pickard-Cambridge, whose *Dithyramb, Tragedy, and Comedy* retains authority, allows that it is "probable enough" that Thespis "introduced an actor who impersonated a legendary or historical character, and gave him a prologue and set of speeches to deliver" (78). It is also likely that Thespis brought the participation of this actor into a "pre-existing lyric performance" and, in doing so, effectively created tragic drama in its rudimentary but seminal form. And yet, there was likely some choral member prior to Thespis, "presumably the leader or *exarchon*," who also set himself apart from the group and entered into lyric question and answer. Finally, and as a crucial point with regard to the genesis of any dramatic impersonation of individuals, Pickard-Cambridge proposes that, in line with Aristotle's sense of tragedy developing over time from the leaders of the dithyramb, the role of *exarchon* might have evolved into that of an actor "impersonating a definite character" (86). This is the basis, then, for what might be extrapolated, even in these early initiating circumstances, with respect to acting as it became more commonly understood. In James H. Butler's scenario, for example, Thespis could perform as an "epic hero" while the dithyrambic chorus and *exarchon* would "react to his sufferings." From this angle, Thespis would be acting within a dialogic pattern, representing a personage other than himself, "substituting it for his own personality, expressing the feelings that thoughts of this imagined character to others publicly, and in turn reacting to their feelings and ideas" (5–6). Bieber, who refers to Thespis as the "true founder of Attic tragedy," tells us that he placed the "hypokrites" (actor) opposite the exarchon, the two appearing in "the most widely differing costumes." With respect to what can now be seen as an early but evolving dramaturgy, Bieber offers that the "spoken dialogue between the actor and the exarchos was developed by interpolations between the songs of the chorus, and therefore is called Epeisodion, an episode" – in other words, the dramatic scene that would continue to alternate with stasima throughout the development of Greek drama (18–19).[14]

One wonders, of course, what compelling personage or mythic story provided Thespis with the inspiration for so radical an imitation, and which others may have brought about a further refinement of his innovation. Here it is well to remember that even in these early performances there are key dramaturgical components that go together with personification, having to do with details of character and story and with the rudiments of a theatrical prologue or introductory segment followed by the episode-stasimon alternation.[15] Else, who exalts the contributions of Thespis and Aeschylus in particular with respect to tragedy's invention, believes that the prologue, as initiated by Thespis, included the hero's description and the background for the story, but may also have featured the portrayal (i.e., the impersonation) of such a hero (*Origin* 60). Moreover, Else argues, it is precisely this figure who becomes central in early tragedy, not in terms of a roundness or complexity of character as we know it, or even of a dramatic action or conflict with which the figure is associated, but rather in terms of his "pathos," his "moment of disaster or failure: death, loss, humiliation." Greek tragedy began, Else asserts, as "a self-presentation of a single epic hero" (65).

In *The Birth of Tragedy*, which has exerted inestimable influence upon modern conceptions of how tragic art began from a theoretical perspective, Nietzsche names Dionysus as the seminal and the archetypal dramatic character – as the original, and indeed, the consistent figure that prompts tragic drama:

> It is an unimpeachable tradition that in its earliest form Greek tragedy records only the sufferings of Dionysos, and that he was the only actor. But it may be claimed with equal justice that, up to Euripides, Dionysos *remains* the sole dramatic protagonist and that all the famous characters of the Greek stage, Prometheus, Oedipus, etc., are only masks of that original hero. The fact that a god hides behind all these masks accounts for the much-admired 'ideal' character of these celebrated figures. (65–66)

Such an assertion must, of course, be understood in the context of Nietzsche's renowned opposition of the Dionysian and Apollonian, which for him provided the fundamental aesthetic condition and counterpoise that prompted the ancient drama. Nonetheless, there is a way also in which Nietzsche can be taken quite literally on this point. There is a "one true Dionysos," he writes, that "appears in a multiplicity of characters…The god ascends the stage in the likeness of a striving and suffering individual" (66). In a sense that would later be called Platonic, then, there is a Dionysian truth or essence that is always there, but that only becomes manifest in the specific and particular incarnations – the stage figures themselves – in ancient tragic characterization.

Some have suggested, by contrast, that Dionysus himself was in actuality the earliest character, likely portrayed by Thespis, who, it is suspected, performed in a Pentheus play (Pickard-Cambridge 28) – although the point is widely disputed.[16] Thespis began, most likely, with the portrayal of prominent figures of myth and history, and not the god (although, of course, when Dionysus is considered not as character per se, but as the god of character, mask, and impersonation, then his spirit must, of necessity, embody the very earliest of dramatic characters, much as Nietzsche would suggest). Ironically, in this regard, it is also Pentheus who has a claim on the title of the earliest dramatic character.[17] Still, and apart from the particular names or situations or antagonisms of specific figures, it is indeed the advent of the actor-writer that points directly to the phenomenon of tragic drama in the ancient setting, in no small measure because of the give-and-take, the question and answer, the dialogic language that was initiated among the earliest represented figures. This, for Hardison, is what "created the basis for the plot, characters, and dialogue of formal tragedy" (101–102). Here, then, is where we locate a fundamental relation of dramatic character to acting, to original modes of presentation, and to a developing dramaturgy in terms of scenic structure and modes of interaction.

With that said, however, one must keep in mind that what Thespis did was not to discover character as we know it, or to replicate a human being as such and in accord with any modern understanding of performing a role. Rather, he assimilated through speech, costume, and mask a replica, an image, a recognizable imitation of a fictional personage who was known already from the context of myth or history. Thespis would "be" that figure by way of standing in for him and delivering appropriate introduction and contextual reference. Yet character, in the sense of personality or behavior or thought or consciousness, is not within this purview. Significant in this regard is the array of differing words that are used as if interchangeable in the situation. Nietzsche, for example, refers in the excerpt quoted earlier to actor, dramatic protagonist, character, mask, and hero – with the implication that all of these are in some way synonymous, the supposedly connective presence of the Dionysian notwithstanding. In light of the fragmentary evidence, it is particularly difficult to delineate a relation between actor (as introduced by Thespis) and dramatic character – which is a more elusive phenomenon than, say, "hero" might imply – and it can be tempting to read more into the evidence than is justified.[18] The image of Thespis as a protean actor representing a succession of roles is, after all, markedly different from that of one who simply opens a performance with an introductory set speech, appearing as he does so as a figure of legend and providing the background for that person's story and situation. More certain, however, is the idea that Thespis became accomplished in the use of the mask to represent a fictive persona and to differentiate one such representation from another.

The Mask of Character

Thespis began by painting his face with white lead and later shifted to the use of a linen mask.[19] And, by contriving various masks, he was able to present a variety of faces or personages to the onlooker. From this perspective, the association of masks with the ancient actor seems not only direct but also familiar: one could easily relate such a connection to contemporary practice, or so one might imagine. Yet again, though, such an understanding is belied by complexities having to do, first, with the nature of the association in the Greek setting between mask and character and, second, by the profoundly Dionysiac spirit of masking, including the theatre god's powers of change of identity, deception, conflict, and confrontation. An issue that recurs throughout these chapters, and that alters significantly according to historical age, is the concept of interiority by comparison with external show – and how the two are combined or balanced in the performance of character. The ancient mask symbolizes this opposition and underscores its significance, being both external and expressive of a figure's dominant trait or predilection, at once. The mask, in short, is a phenomenon of considerable nuance and sophistication, in spite of its ostensibly simplified and deliberately vivid aspects.

"In dramatic and historic fact," writes John Jones, "Aristotle's stage figure is the mask" (43). The author of the *Poetics* would, of course, be familiar *only* with the actor in mask, as primary among theatrical conventions of the fifth-century B.C. In addition, though, Aristotle's conception of character, based as it was on faithful representation, practical traits, and moral choices, would derive directly and strongly from the succinctness and even the reductive quality that masking affords. To what extent can any character in drama be reduced to a single, if commanding, facial image? Or, conversely, through the skills, expressiveness, and physicalization of the actor, is the mask more versatile than its apparently staid aspects might imply? Jones points out that, "Prosopōn, the Greek word for mask, also means face, aspect, person, and stage figure (*persona*)" and argues for an assimilation – that "we should allow mask and face to draw semantically close together, and then we should enrich the face far beyond our own conception, until it is able to embrace (as it did for Greeks from the time of Homer) the look of the man together with the truth about him. The face is the total aspect; it presents the human individual, the person" (44). For Jones, the actor-mask relationship is intricate indeed, and is absolutely at odds with any concept of individual interiority. The mask has, in fact, "no inside." The concern, therefore, is not with "inwardness" but rather with the face of action and of deed, a distinction that Jones links directly with the "central argument of the *Poetics*, that tragedy is an imitation not of human beings but of action and of life" (46).[20]

And further, the mask is Dionysian. The god is of, and is in, its contours, purposes, and effects. The mask unused, in a state of rest, is replete with potential for the representation of personality and passion. The mask in play, and with the capabilities of the actor enlivening that potential, is actively embodying the Dionysian double – the fictional persona that is to be recognized as real, the identity that is not the one of the person enacting the portrait, the very essence of change and alteration of self. In "A Show for Dionysus," P.E. Easterling links the mask directly to an understanding

of the god of theatre. The mask, for her, "must be one of the most important clues for anyone trying to understand 'the Dionysiac'." And further:

> As worn in drama, the mask enables individual performers to assume mul-
> tiple identities: each actor will play different roles from one drama to the
> next, and often enough within a single play, and each chorusman will have
> four different identities, one for each tragedy and one for the satyr play.
> So the Pentheus is also Agave and the Furies of *Eumenides* are also satyrs.
> While the performers take on these different roles, the masks themselves,
> fixed and unchangeable, are a visible reminder to the audience of the fictive
> nature of the dramatic events. Yet paradoxically the mask in performance
> may create the illusion of facial movement and fluidity of expression, as
> viewers have often noticed in modern performances of masked drama. This
> exciting complexity perhaps helps to explain the reverence that perform-
> ers evidently felt for their masks, shown, for example by the fact that the
> masks were dedicated to the god after the performance was over and hung
> from the temple in his sanctuary. (49, 51)

Easterling describes the capabilities of the character mask in terms of the
performer's identity with a sacred aspect of the art, and one that enables
versatility along with performance. The facial mask, abiding in the precincts of Dionysus, emerges through and for the actor, ensuring the requisite theatrical illusion along with impersonation. Walter Otto, by contrast,
emphasizes the linkage of mask and god rather than actor, and connects
the face of the deity – as seen on the vase paintings of Dionysus in which
large, staring eyes are frontal and prominent – with immediacy and confrontation.[21] In the domain of the Dionysian, there is always opposition,
always the strange, the extraordinary, and an "other" that will contradict
the known and the expected.[22] Much as the actor evokes the image of a
fictive personage, the capability of the mask is to conjure what Vernant
and Vidal-Naquet call "the presence of one who is absent" (*Myth* 383).

Aristotle, Character, and the Theory of Traits

Between the time of Thespis and of Aristotle lies the Greek fifth-century
B.C. and the glory of the tragic drama with which most of the *Poetics* is
concerned. Aristotle refers, in the brief treatise that Wayne Booth once
described as "a puzzling fragment" (387), to several names from the dramatis personae of the tragedies – Oedipus, Thyestes, Iphigenia, among
others – by way of illustrating what a reader today might be likely to
think of as "character." Famously, Aristotle identifies six elements that
are basic and essential in the construction of plays, and character (*ethos*)

is one of these, second to plot (*muthos*) and prior to thought (*dianoia*) in his hierarchy of dramaturgical and performative necessities. Through various brief chapters in the *Poetics*, he parses the qualities of dramatic character in detail, at times drawing exceptionally fine distinctions between the qualities of one sort of stage figure and another, as in the delineation of hamartia (chapter XIII) in relation to the characterization of the protagonist and the fortunes that relate to, or arise from, this frailty or vulnerability to error. He advises the reader – or, one should say, the aspiring poet/dramatist – that a character in a play should be acceptable to the audience and also believable – or, as he puts it (XV), good, appropriate, "like" reality, and consistent.[23]

If character in Aristotle's sense were more congruent with any idea of character in other aesthetic or literary contexts or in eras subsequent to his own, this "fragment" would perhaps not be so puzzling or controversial. This, however, is not the case, and Aristotle's vision of character is in fact quite remote from our own. This is not to say that the *Poetics* is not, or has not been over time, exceptionally relevant and contributory in the understanding of character in drama or, for that matter, in narrative fiction. It is simply to observe that when Aristotle looked back upon the century prior to his own, deliberated over the evidence for why the plays of Sophocles and others were artfully successful and capable of affecting audiences in particular ways, his definition of character was not of a fully rounded, psychologically or emotionally complex figure that conveys, through intents and behaviors as well as actions, the impression of a "real" person. This is a concept that is not only subsequent to the Greek era, but does not arise for centuries. In fact, as Simon Goldhill points out, there is no word in ancient Greek for character as it is commonly understood in modern criticism. "Ethos" is not, per se, character according to contemporary or even long-standing definition. Although it does imply, notes Goldhill, "a set of attitudes or a particular disposition, there is an important difference between *ethos* and the common sense of 'character'....*Ethos* does not attempt, as 'character' often does in modern usage, to express a whole personality or the make-up of a psyche" (172). This does not mean, though, that character in the ancient Greek world was fashioned without an awareness of human interiority, deliberative mental process, or temper of feeling. Obviously, this is not the case, as Euripides's Medea or Phaedra or Iphigenia or Orestes clearly demonstrate with regard to emotion, psychological response, or contemplative insight.[24]

While the Aristotelian concept of *ethos* may bear some resemblances to character by other sorts of measures or reckonings and in different epochs, it would be a mistake to conflate what Jones calls Aristotle's "stage fig-ure" of the mask with any type or variation of realistic depiction of per-sonhood. And, significantly complicating this picture is the fact that the *Poetics* interconnects three if not four of the six basic elements, making them all but inextricable from one another, in spite of Aristotle's differen-tiations, which are often extremely specific if not always clear. Indeed, the scientific nature and means of his analysis takes the reader through mul-tiple lines of argument from an identification of the vital components in drama to descriptions of their functions to conclusions about their com-parative levels of importance.[25] And yet, aside from Aristotle's provocative notion that a play can be without characters but not without plot (VI), his more consistent line of explication, or at least of implication, is that character and thought are aspects of one another, that thought is known through character and language (*lexos*), and that character and plot are a unity – at least to the extent that the former enables the latter. However, since these assertions are not necessarily reflective of what Aristotle advises directly, it will be useful to look more closely at how these fundamental yet ostensibly disparate factors can be understood as unified.

Aristotle's conviction that plot, the "soul of tragedy," at the top of his hierarchy is now among the more contentious of his findings, and justifi-ably so. In dramaturgy more generally, the ratio and interrelation between structural factors and the persons or objects of imitation could scarcely be more important to how plays are fashioned. In one sense, of course, the controversy may be productive of a chicken-and-egg debate in which neither component can be deemed more significant if only because they are so interdependent and with such equal claims on what impels action and engages the attention of an audience. Moreover, the ratio is directly related to balances within a particular work or type of play. Still, what good is a plot with no people, or vice versa? What would Euripides's story of rage, betrayal, and vindication be without the particular intensities of Medea's emotions as well as her ambivalence at the thought of murder-ing her sons? But, of course, the question is thornier than that, especially with respect to what exactly it is that character contributes to plot, from Aristotle's point of view.

Here we encounter, and for the first time in history, one of the most enduring and significant baseline issues in the study of dramatic character – to wit, the creation, delineation, and function of personal and behavioral traits in characterization. While a modern dramatist, Tennessee Williams, can say that a play such as his *Cat on a Hot Tin Roof* begins with an idea for the portrayal of people – "My characters make my play"

(*Live* 72), such a belief, including its practice, is completely foreign to the Aristotelian view. In the *Poetics*, characterization is what allows the plot to function optimally. As Aristotle says (VI): "By Character I mean that in virtue of which we ascribe certain qualities to the agents."[26] To understand character as "agent" is, naturally, to prioritize functionality, and this is precisely Aristotle's standpoint. Hardison succinctly captures the nature of this Aristotelian ratio, noting simply that "character is something added to the agent after the plot has been worked out" (199).

In consideration of one familiar character (and one of Aristotle's favorites), might we infer that Oedipus, for instance, is short-tempered, incestuous, a gifted leader, fatherly, and oblivious? Or, to slant the question a bit differently, is he simply the type of person to have such traits among others, or *must* he be this way because Sophocles needs for him to murder Laius, marry Jocasta, be King of Thebes, care deeply for his daughters, and be oddly blind to the whole situation? And, are the traits ascribed to character (agent) by the playwright aligned more with the qualities of individual identity and personality or of behavior – including a moral sense? This, in fact, is a question that can elicit a whole variety of answers depending on the changing aesthetic sensibilities as well as situational factors having to do with historical or cultural contexts – and, as such, it will be revisited in subsequent chapters. From Aristotle's point of view, as in life, "character" exists and is revealed by what one chooses to do in a situation – through moral or ethical choice – a reduction that neatly combines elements of personality, or at least personal values, with actions taken.

That Oedipus is a talented leader might, in this perspective, pertain more to plot (how he came to Thebes in the first place and will now set forth to discover the cause of the plague on the city), just as the character's blindness may relate most to the Aristotelian idea of hamartia. The "good" character has a moral sense that informs decision, choice, and action. Hardison argues that, "there should be a necessary and/or probable relation between the actions an agent performs and the type of characteristics assigned him. When such a relation is established, the reader or spectator has the illusion that the character of the protagonist is the 'cause' of his actions, as in real life" (199). Along these lines, again, Aristotle's insistence that tragedy is an imitation not of men but of action and of life (VI) is absolutely reflective of a dependency on believable traits that will be useful in establishing a convincing arrangement of events (i.e., plot). Else, in his commentary on the *Poetics* (XV), in which Aristotle likens the ways in which a character behaves (according to what is necessary and probable) to a play's orchestration of events, asserts that, "the principle is stated to hold good for character and plot concurrently *and interdependently*. So far as the hero of the play is concerned, at least, plot and character ought to be not merely parallel structures but one structure, subject in both aspects to the law of necessity or probability" (*Argument* 468).[27]

And, just as character and plot achieve a synchronicity through selection and demonstration of traits that are structurally and sequentially practical, so too can character, thought, and language (speech) be read as co-dependent. Thought (*dianoia*) might be understood – simply, capaciously, and along modern lines – as thematics, the ideas that a play is concerned with, what the drama has on its mind, as it were. This is not Aristotle's sense, however. In the *Poetics*, thought is linked to character (*ethos*) through language – that is, via speech and dialogue. Else is clear and precise on this interrelation, again with respect to Aristotle's argument (XV), when he identifies "the conception of both character and thought as being speech, or conveyed through speech." Else's finding, indeed, is that there is "a close affiliation between character and thought, as joint or reciprocal aspects of what is said by the dramatic persons in their speeches" (*Argument* 266, 270). From one angle, of course, such interconnection seems not only necessary but also obvious – how else do we know characters except by what they say and the manner in which they say it? That point of view would, however, miss what Aristotle actually means with regard to a combination and synergy of character, thought, and speech.

Character and Thought in *Agamemnon*

In the *Agamemnon* of Aeschylus, the magnificent scene of the title character's return from the war with Troy to Argos must rank among the most intensely charged encounters in all of Greek drama. It is a scene for three characters – the king, his wife Clytemnestra whom he has not seen for ten years, and the captive Trojan princess Cassandra – and it functions on multiple levels, including the daimonic and the godly as well as the personal and familial. I will return to this finely wrought interaction later on in the chapter with a focus on Cassandra, but for purposes here it is Agamemnon who is exemplary of a linkage of speech, choice, and character as *ethos*. The action during the scene's first half is, on the face of it, straightforward: upon the king's arrival, Clytemnestra wishes for her husband to step down from his chariot and walk upon sacred purple tapestries that have been laid out before him, presumably in his honor. Agamemnon knows better than to do this, as such tapestries are reserved for divinities, not mortals – and he says exactly that: "I am a mortal, a man; I cannot trample upon these tinted splendors without fear thrown in my path. I tell you, as a man, not god, to reverence me" (63).[28] The speaker here is cautious, knowledgeable, and appropriately humble – or so it would seem. Moreover, he has declared his independence – "My will is mine. I shall not make it soft for you" (63). And yet, within moments, he has reversed this decision and given way to his wife's own will and power of persuasion: "Now since my will was bent to listen to you in this my feet crush purple as I pass within the hall" (64). Agamemnon steps down upon the tapestries and heads into the palace where his murder, about to be envisioned vividly by Cassandra, is imminent.

Here I am simplifying, obviously, what is in fact a dramatic sequence of considerable elaboration, in which Agamemnon's choice is layered with all manner of impacting factors that would argue against the king's will being anything close to his own.[29] That said, however, the scene is also a highly succinct representation of speech in relation to moral choice – and, even as it tersely demonstrates Agamemnon's situation and his possible options, it is suggestive also of a psychology, a mind at work, and of internal turmoil in the face of a dilemma. Character, from this angle, is not simply fictive personhood but is also "character" in the ethical sense, as demonstrated through choice in a conflicted situation and in accord with the qualities given by the playwright to an "agent" in the plot. As Else puts it, again with respect to the *Poetics* (XV), " 'Character' will be present, says Aristotle, when a speech or action reveals a choice, whatever it may be, and a good one if it reveals a good choice" (*Argument* 457). The relative goodness of Agamemnon's decision may, here, be open to debate, while such critical options available to other characters in tragedy are perhaps more clearly definitive. Oedipus determines resolutely to discover the reason for the plague on his city; Antigone will not waver from her integrity or determination to bury her brother Polyneices; Electra and Orestes cannot be dissuaded from the achievement of vengeance for their murdered father – all of these are exemplary of character as ethical imperative.

The "Mind" of Greek Character

One might say that in the midst of the confrontation with Clytemnestra (which is laden, among other factors, with a refusal on her part to forgive her husband's sacrifice of their daughter Iphigenia as well as the queen's adulterous relations with Aegisthus) Agamemnon is faced not only with choice but also with mental conflict. Yet how much do we know of his mind or his thinking, and by what means? In performance, Greek character presents the observer with an exterior – a mask – and in one sense this factor stands rigidly between onlooker and a stage figure's interiority. Jones draws a comparison to Hamlet ("I have that within which passes show"), in order to emphasize that "within" is precisely what the Aristotelian stage figure does not have.[30] And yet, the border between the mask figure and the mind is more ambiguous than definite. To the reader, as opposed to the observer, of the homecoming scene in *Agamemnon*, the characters may seem very much akin to theatrical figures over time, in that their thoughts, motives, and behaviors are conveyed through dialogue and interaction. To what extent, however, can one truly attribute thought – as interiority, consciousness, a brain – to these portrayals?[31] Indeed, the nature of "mind" as ascribed to dramatic characters is another baseline issue that, as it remains consistently important over time, will be examined in these chapters in several historical settings and within different contexts including the scientific. For now, though, it will suffice to assess how a stage figure who is designed (in Aristotle's view) to facilitate plot, but who must offer the convincing representation of a personage nonetheless, can or cannot be psychological or exhibit aspects of a cognitive process as part of the characterization itself.

It would be instructive, and possibly amusing, to know what Aeschylus or Sophocles or Euripides would think of the *Poetics*, had the puzzling handbook been available to playwrights a century earlier. Given that Aristotle derives the definitions and principles in his treatise from observations of the drama of the fifth century, it is of course not the case that the dramatists of that age were conceiving plays in accord with Aristotelian prescriptions. At the same time, one might infer that plot, or at least story, was a foremost consideration for the writer of tragedy, if only because the tragic plays were based on existing myths and histories. Character, however, presents a much more ambiguous face – and its manifestations vary significantly among these three playwrights and others. To be deliberately simplistic, the figures of Sophocles are seen often as grandly idealized – as Antigone is, to be sure. For example, as A.O. Rorty writes, "Tragedy represents protagonists who are recognizably enlarged and simplified versions of what is best in us, presented without the multiple extraneous purposes that confuse our actions. They are what we would be if we could undergo an alchemy, a purification of the elements that compose us" ("Psychology" 91). Fair enough, perhaps, for Sophoclean character as it is evidenced, say, by the extraordinary portrait of Theseus, that "best of men" in *Oedipus at Colonus* or, again, of Antigone, in the same play.[32] But such idealization doesn't apply equally, or perhaps at all, to the plays of Euripides or even of Aeschylus. In the tragic drama of Euripides especially, characters are far from ideal in their motives and behaviors, do not conform to classical balances or symmetries, and are driven to large degree by violent or sexual passions and by psychological manias or confusions. Euripides's Phaedra may be aggrandized by her regal stature and desire for *sophrosyne* in the face of shame, but her mental state is deranged, horribly torn, and suicidal.

What, then, is to be made of the disparity between character as *ethos*, or as facilitating agent, or as individual, personal, and psychological? Passion, of course, is intensely experienced by characters and conveyed by dramatists throughout the history of tragic drama – as, for that matter, is madness. But, in the Greek context per se, does the fixed mask of exteriority exclude a depth or intricacy of thought on the part of stage figures, apart from emotional intensities? Or, is it the case that while a character may be interpreted psychologically or in accord with a later standard by a reader or an observer, the characterization would not originally have been fashioned from that perspective? Jones, in his discussion of the Greek stage figure and "Human Beings" from the Aristotelian perspective, insists that character "must be denied even the most primitive autonomy" (31). Or, from Jean-Pierre Vernant's standpoint, a character's free will is, in the ancient setting, ambiguous, not fully defined or developed, and it is precisely this factor, together with the amount of distance between a heroic past and the present life of the city and its theatre, that contributes to the "moment of tragedy" – in other words, to the rare and extraordinary conditions of its inception.[33] Without the factor of psychological agency or independence, as opposed to motive as an exigency of plot, it would appear that character for the Greek playwright would not have been imagined as introspective or even cognitive by design.

And yet, there are characters that would belie that conclusion. To refer once again, and not surprisingly, to Euripides, the figures of Phaedra or Medea (if not Hippolytus or Jason) speak and behave from the standpoint of revealed mental suffering. That each of these characters is given opportunity, in their respective plays, to address a chorus of women and to share intimate feelings with a confidante, is no accident. The playwright isolates these women by gender and sexuality, and also pathology, identifying them as utterly apart from the surrounding norms and from their respective male antagonists. Each is driven to thoughts of suicide, as when Medea speaks to the Women of Corinth:

> But on me this thing has fallen so unexpectedly,
> It has broken my heart. I am finished. I let go
> All my life's joy. My friends, I only want to die.
> It was everything to me to think well of one man,
> And he, my own husband, has turned out wholly vile.
> Of all things which are living and can form a judgment
> We women are the most unfortunate creatures. (*Medea* 66)

Or, Phaedra, to the Women of Troezen:

> At first when love struck me, I reflected
> How best to bear it. Silence was my first plan.
> Silence and concealment. For the tongue
> Is not to be trusted; it can criticize
> Another's faults, but on its own possessor
> It brings a thousand troubles.
> Then I believed that I could conquer love,
> Conquer it with discretion and good sense.
> And when that to failed me, I resolved to die. (*Hippolytus* 180)

How not to understand the plight of either woman psychologically? In each case, the tone is intimate, confessional, and desperate. Each character is intent on making her own thoughts, experience, and reasoning clear – and this is accomplished by describing mental process. Goldhill, in *Reading Greek Tragedy*, attends to the apparent contradiction that, in the ancient setting, there is no "character" by modern understandings but that interest remains in "the internal life of its personae." There is, he says, a "considerable focus on the words which express such an internal existence, attitude of mind, disposition" (174). Using Sophocles's *Ajax* as revelatory of the title character's mind, Goldhill argues that even as one might not be satisfied with "the notion of an inclusive psychological personality to be discerned behind the words of the text, we have seen that it would be misplaced totally to repress a sense of 'character' in this play" (197).[34]

Greek characters can, of course, be read in ways that stand for an array of psychological archetypes, including the Freudian or Lacanian, even as they precede such articulations and in spite of whatever component of consciousness or interiority may be missing from their original compositions. Such characters are available, too, for psychoanalytic criticism. Segal, in *Interpreting Greek Tragedy*, adopts such a standpoint (including Lacan's "discourse of the Other") – to probe *The Bacchae*. Pentheus may

not have interiority but he does have sexuality – together with a very limited self-understanding. Dionysus does understand, however, and Segal
highlights the full awareness of the god and his "hidden knowledge of
Pentheus' unconscious or repressed desires" (300). In sum, the matters of
thought, mind, and interiority with respect to ancient characterizations
do, Aristotle notwithstanding, present a conundrum with respect to both
the composition and the reception of depicted persons – and the complexities do not end with the purely psychological.

Cassandra and Apollo

In the scene described earlier, the centerpiece of *Agamemnon*, the figure
of Cassandra, captured princess and seeress, is utterly silent throughout
the encounter between the returning king and Clytemnestra. She is quiet
as the king decides finally to step down upon the tapestries and enter
the palace. Imagining the scene now, one will remember that the ancient
stage picture was not of a regal young woman atop a chariot but of a male
actor in mask who is, in effect, demonstrating the role of that woman.
Earlier, that same actor, one among three, would have been available for
the roles of Herald or Watchman. Nonetheless, this spectacular scene,
in parts and in its entirety, is unique in both content and interaction, as
well as in its dramatic effects. Cassandra's silence is profound in itself,
particularly as it tacitly conveys a forceful tension, expectation, and
potential for the unleashing of powerful feeling. Cassandra is a person in
the scene, just as Agamemnon and Clytemnestra are. At the same time,
though, she is a prophetess, doomed by Apollo to see into the future but
not be believed. When she does speak, in fact, her first utterance – what
Kitto calls "one of the most astonishing moments in all drama" (28) – is
an imprecation against the god who is destroying her. Prior to that, however, she is characterized amidst her silence by Clytemnestra, who says
that Agamemnon's captive, called a "stranger girl" by the chorus, is "in
the passion of her own wild thoughts" (67), an insight that provides a
telling – and also truthful – unification of a character's thinking with
emotional and visionary urgency.

Cassandra's thoughts, and more so her visions, are represented as wild
indeed. Nowhere in the scene is she depicted as remotely "like" anyone or
even as susceptible to ordinary human experience or feeling. Rather, she
is portrayed as horribly bereft, estranged from anything familiar, torn in
temporary equipoise between earthly life and imminent death, and caught
in an excruciating fashion between the realms of humans and of gods. Her

character cannot be reduced to Aristotelian *ethos*, although a moral sense underscores her diatribe. Her traits may aid or complement the sequence of events, but her thought and speech surge forth in a series of relentless, rending arias. She envisions the deaths that have brought doom on the House of Atreus, including those of Thyestes's children; she sees the killing of Agamemnon as though performed before her very eyes; she prophesies the vengeance of Orestes and foretells her own murder, degrading as she does so her own person and status as "a small thing, lightly killed" (78).

Cassandra has no interiority, no "thought" linked to consciousness or cognitive process in terms anywhere close to a modern understanding. And yet, her mind is at work and is given by Aeschylus a potent, startling demonstration – and it is a mind connected directly to the god realm. Apollo is brought into the scene as if corporeally present. When Cassandra speaks to him, it is as if he were there to listen. As she tears away her prophet's indicia ("these mockeries upon my body, this staff of prophecy, these flowers at my throat"), it is a performance of inconsolable misery and terrible wrath, inwardly directed yet played out before the god who has brought her to this end (75). Greek dramatic character, along these lines, is not only affected or influenced by larger powers, but is wedded to those powers, inseparable from their domains. Cassandra is tied to Apollo, to the god's curse, and to the fatality that comes at his instigation. Aristotle does not remark upon this unity of character with deity, but it is an essential aspect of these ancient characterizations.

Returning now, in this vein, to the figure of Agamemnon – and to the king's confrontation with Clytemnestra and the decision to descend from his chariot and walk on sacred tapestries – I noted earlier that in this brief scene he faces a mental conflict as well as a contest of wills. Yet that offers only a partial, and quotidian, view of the remarkable array of factors that impinge on his autonomy and, indeed, upon his character. Here, as in the case of Cassandra, is a stage figure with profound linkages to the gods, and particularly to the implacable will of Zeus. In addition, the scene of his homecoming is one in which not only gods but also other abstract or supersensory forces – Ate, daimon, Dike, the embracing curse of blood vengeance that dooms the House of Atreus – are at play in the situation, and to these must be added the king's palpable limitations, his own hubris and hamartia.[35] Even as Agamemnon may appear to struggle internally with his decision, the choice he makes is, in Lloyd-Jones's assessment, due to the fact that "Zeus has taken away his wits" – yet another manifestation of the blight on Agamemnon's House. Indeed, argues Lloyd-Jones, the events leading up to Agamemnon's death, tracing back to the king's decision at Aulis (the sacrifice of Iphigenia on behalf of Artemis, in trade for propitious winds for his armada) and the war on Troy itself, has "been in accord with the will of Zeus" (69, 71–72).

Agamemnon and Cassandra are each exemplary of a tendency for characters in Greek tragedy to be connected, for good or ill, with some transcendent order or supersensory realm. Hippolytus, allegiant only to Artemis, must suffer the consequence that Aphrodite brings down upon him and Phaedra.[36] Antigone, following the dictates of her father's legacy, must honor family and the gods of earth above all else. Orestes fulfills his mission of vengeance only because of the participation of Apollo. Again, it is not only that characters such as these honor a deity or act at a god's behest. Rather, each one is coupled inextricably with the divine even as he or she goes about an ostensibly autonomous business at hand. In *Myth and Tragedy in Ancient Greece*, Vernant and Vidal-Naquet describe this linkage as existing necessarily between a character, expressed as ethos, and daimon, with the figure thus "constituted within the space encompassed by this pair, *ethos* and *daimon*" (37).[37] "The true domain of tragedy," they write, "lies in that border zone where human actions are hinged together with the divine powers, where – unknown to the agent – they derive their true meaning by becoming an integral part of an order that is beyond man and that eludes him" (47). Even when the tragic figure's action seems commonplace – a step taken from a chariot – the resonance is with a cosmic, and also enigmatic, sphere and duress.[38] Agamemnon's ruin (Ate), together with the will and justice of the gods (Dike), are alive in this scene, woven into this character and built into the total situation, one that must include the *daimon* along with participatory divinities per se. In ancient tragedy, even as a play's events appear to arise naturally from the motives and interactions among its dramatis personae, the vision of mortal character cannot be truly separated from the macrocosmic dimension. As Vernant and Vidal-Naquet indicate, "Each action appears to be in keeping with the logic of a particular character or *ethos* even at the very moment when it is revealed to be the manifestation of a power from the beyond, or a *daimon*" (37).

There are later epochs, certainly, when characters in drama will be fashioned with a cosmic dimension, or at least with the implication of such an embracing context and of abstract or metaphysical powers. Yet the Greek theatre is unique in the ways that character and cosmos are conjoined, in the manner in which this union is evoked, and the intricacy with which each is related, in turn, to a play's pattern of events. Aristotle's dictum, once more, that tragedy is an imitation not of men but of action and of life, may be read as point of view rather than a fact – and there are times, to be sure, when individual character will take precedence as object of inquiry over events, community, or even a core action. No matter what the case, figures such as Agamemnon or Cassandra or Phaedra or Orestes were drawn with a complexity of background and a debt to divinity (including the audience's recognition of that realm) that concepts of ethical choice or even of traits or of thought cannot fully capture. The ancient Greek stage figure is eternally Dionysian; there is always a debt, not only to Zeus or Apollo or Aphrodite but also originally and fundamentally to the god of the mask, of theatrical impersonation – of dramatic character.

CHAPTER 2

Character, Form, and Genre

These indeed "seem,"
For they are actions that a man might play;
But I have that within which passes show,
These but the trappings and the suits of woe. (26–27)[1]

Characters in drama can be recognized by a status that is innate and obvious – but also paradoxical. To wit, a dramatic character must appear to be alive and autonomous, free to exert his or her own agency and personality in a variety of situations, and yet that same character is necessarily constrained, and even defined, by the dramaturgy – that is, by the structure, style, form, or genre of the particular play in which he or she appears. In other words, there is a fundamental contradiction that belongs to the performance of drama: the need for an illusion of a character's freedom coupled directly with that which prevents it. Figures such as Agamemnon or Cassandra may, as we have seen, be indebted to godly influences as well as to traits or to demonstrations of *ethos*, in the Aristotelian sense of moral standpoint. Yet each one is fashioned by Aeschylus in accord with stipulations of what came to be called a genre, in this case the ideological, religious, structural, and formal tendencies of early tragedy. While Aeschylus would be aware, as a regular winner of prizes at the City Dionysia, that his plays were celebrated, he could not have known that he was instrumental in creating what would be regarded later as an embracing category of dramatic writing, a tradition of tragic drama that would outlast his era.

Even so, the evidence of what did become major genres dates to theatre's beginnings, including for that time the rigor of their separation, one from the other. On the Greek stage, the characters of Euripides's Medea and of Aristophanes's Lysistrata are approximately contemporaneous, with their first performances roughly twenty years apart. In further relation, both have powerful attitudes on gender relations (to put it very mildly). Yet the two are of different worlds, the one tragic and the other comic, with no possible commerce in between. Each character belongs not only to a story, but also to the form of the telling – to the orchestration of events and interactions that fulfills but at the same time delimits the potentials of a character. Such is the case, in fact, with virtually any stage figure. They must be like us, more or less, and even represent our autonomy (or illusion of same), but none can be free of the stories or types of stories they have been fashioned to tell. The play in question may be comedic, tragic, symbolic, farcical, expressionistic, melodramatic, "well-made," naturalistic, absurdist, or postmodernist, but the characters tend, no matter what, to march in step to the dictates of a form, genre, or philosophy – even in cases where a deliberate attempt has been made to be independent of such stipulations. In such cases, the departure itself can become the defining, and thus restrictive, factor. The tendency of form and genre is to be prescriptive with respect to dramaturgy and, by extension, to both enable and be restrictive upon characterization, simultaneously.

Still, the aesthetic issue is more ambiguous than it might seem. For example, Luigi Pirandello's perspective on characterization, including its genesis as well as composition and ontology, is famously complex, and in key ways contradictory, and we shall return to his philosophy in a later chapter. Suffice to say here that with respect to a character's origin, Pirandello's contention (which proceeds from his own experience as a playwright and writer of fictional narrative) is that a character is "born," that he or she comes to life in the author's imagination, and from that birth such an existence is lifelike and to some degree autonomous. Here, then, is a theory of fictional characters, as in *Six Characters in Search of an Author*, who have been imbued with life but can still be at large and in need of authorship – or, of a completed drama and a structure of relations and events within which they can exist. "Born alive, they wished to live," recalls the dramatist in his "Preface" (364). Further, Pirandello describes a state of limbo, or irresolution, between the creation of those six characters and their realized form or function. In their case, he recollects, there was "'being' without the reason for being" (368).[2] This particular play, of course, may be seen as the exceptional case, in that its entire conception and story is dependent upon this very irresolution. Even in so specialized an instance, however, Pirandello underscores the tension between characterization as an idea and as practical dramaturgy: or, put differently, as the idea of a reality invested in personhood that is not entirely belied by artistry or by the fictive element per se.

The playwright, and indeed the theatre as a collective enterprise that includes the actor, may go to substantial lengths to ensure that dramatic characters are perceived by an audience (or reader) as "real," and the real person dichotomy, noted earlier, attends in this respect to problems in narrative fiction as well as drama. The dialectic in *Six Characters* that is voiced principally by The Father and the Director is concerned in large part with an issue that is obviously problematic in ontological as well as aesthetic terms. On the one hand, the Characters are fixed in their reality; and, as such, they are "truer and more real" than the Actors, Director, and others involved with the performance. And yet, concurrently, they are seemingly free to rove in search of their dramas, and indeed, of their identities. The Director has never encountered a fictional character who can "get out of his part and go about expounding and explicating it," but The Father, in doing exactly that, assures him that characters, as opposed to authors, can be the generative agents of their own existence: "When a character is born, he at once acquires such an independence, even of his own author, that the whole world can imagine him in innumerable situations other than those the author thought to place him in. At times he acquires a meaning that the author never dreamt of giving him" (61–62).

Agency and Autonomy

To what degree, then, can a character in drama be liberated from an author's conception or, perhaps more significantly, from the dramatic structures that define the action and guarantee the coherence of a story? Is there any way for a character in a play to exist, even imaginatively, apart from the drama to which he or she belongs? The relation of a character's personal autonomy to dramaturgy is the central issue of this chapter, and who better than the figure of Shakespeare's Hamlet to tease out its intricacies and nuances? Hamlet offers, in fact, the quintessential, if extreme, case of a dramatic character who exhibits a remarkable individuality, autonomy, and agency (even while he balks at action) but who is still restricted, not only by plot but also by other exigencies having to do with form and, especially, genre. To a large extent, of course, Hamlet's apparent freedom arises from the display of his mind at work, notably his introspective yet mercurial genius. Together with this perceived freedom, Hamlet is the exemplar of interiority, and of an inner "self" in that context. Not only does he possess "that within," but he is also intensely self-aware, forthright about his train of thought, absorbed with his own states of consciousness, and determined to chase down ontological puzzles and conundrums.

Hamlet embodies, in other words, a radical difference from the Greek model of character, even given such allowances of psychology and complexity of mind or thought that were associated with figures of ancient tragedy in the previous chapter. Along with his ideation, however, Hamlet is also theatrical, with a proclivity for "show." To say that he is contradictory is, needless to say, to understate one of his primary and, for his part, intentional traits. For the purpose here, Hamlet's contrariness is especially opportune, given the array of questions that his example raises implicitly regarding character in relation to a dramatic scheme. Even as Hamlet must ultimately step to the structural tempos of the play that bears his name, he comes awfully close to transcending them – in no small part because he is so miscast in his own role, burdened with a plot that is so out of joint with his own nature, self, and sense of intention.

In many ways, no doubt, Hamlet has outgrown *Hamlet*, the text that holds him in even while enabling him. His name has long since passed into the language; his inventive yet contemplative nature is a touchstone for self-inquiry; he is the archetypal ponderer – or, as William Hazlitt would put it, "the prince of philosophical speculators" (Bate 325). In his mournful sables and with characteristic associations of vengeance and melancholy, Hamlet is at once utterly familiar and quintessentially enigmatic. He is emblematic of the theatre and of acting, even as he embodies philosophic or psychological questioning and is renowned in literary as well as theatrical realms. Yet fame and a breadth of dramatic or literary association do not, in themselves, suffice to reify a fictional character, and despite appearances of vitality and life-likeness, Hamlet cannot truly trespass the "real person" barrier. Still, and to the degree that any character can be independent of the text that frames him or her, it is Hamlet's vividness, alienated superiority, and the capaciousness of an impassioned intellect that would argue persuasively against being text-bound, especially in performance. In his case, certainly, such qualities of character must belie the Aristotelian mandate for a practical functionality of traits with respect to plot and perhaps even to tragedy.

In *Shakespeare: The Invention of the Human*, Harold Bloom fashions a portrait of Hamlet that would be nigh impossible for any other figure in drama, save perhaps for Falstaff, another of Bloom's favorites. For both characters, in fact, the aspect of freedom is highlighted (403). And here once more, as with Pirandello, there is a conflation of author and character. Bloom's contention is that Hamlet, a "more metaphysical dramatist than Iago," shares with his creator not only a power of intellect but also the conscious fashioning of a destiny (386). Thus, he is Shakespeare's surrogate in more than the usual way of a stage figure who stands in for the writer with respect to thoughts as well as actions. Yet, even for Hamlet, it is this very merging of an author and a stage figure that can intensify the strain between a character's autonomy and the dramatic structure. Indeed, the initiating situation of a father's murder and a mother's "frailty" are more than enough, given Hamlet's nature, to yoke him to a destiny, no matter the freedom that his nimble resourcefulness seems at times to conjure.

Is Hamlet free to marry Ophelia, or not – or kill Claudius or Gertrude, or not? Can he be free of his own obsessiveness? He is most certainly not free to avoid killing Polonius, even in so rash and thoughtless a moment. Such avoidance would stop the play in its tracks, and Shakespeare needs for the tragedy to bear the full freight of that murder. Yet still, Bloom has a point, and his angle on Hamlet embodying a dialectic of what is "free" and what is "bound" rings true, even for a figure who, despite his worldly excellence, was created for this one play only. And, when Bloom adds that "we cannot find the balance" in this opposition, he identifies a key, if rare, point of structural equipoise and tension, not only for this unique character but also for the singular dramaturgy that allows for the ambiguities of his portrayal in the first place (406).

Situating Hamlet within tragedy, where he seems oddly at home in what for him is a natural genre, is what allows for his existence and dooms him, at once. The quality of Hamlet's consciousness is such, though, that unlike his ancestors in the tragedy of the ancient world, he is self-aware with respect to both the texture and the contours of his destiny. Agamemnon, by contrast, is not conscious of his tragic fate, and only vaguely aware of the range of godly and daimonic exertions that contribute to his end. The same can be said for most figures in Greek tragedy, with the possible exception of the blind and elderly former king in *Oedipus at Colonus*, who in his own way has unwittingly written his fate and recognizes his predestined end in a sacred grove outside of Athens. Regarding Hamlet's self-awareness, Bloom fashions a provocative, if cryptic, statement with its own Pirandellian overtones.[3] "What Hamlet could tell us," he writes, "is his achieved awareness of what he himself represents, a dramatist's apprehension of what it means to incarnate the tragedy one cannot compose" (422). Hamlet cannot, of course, tell us anything beyond *Hamlet*, but perhaps that is enough. His metatheatricality is so engrained that an "achieved awareness" might indeed be construed as a product of his personal drama itself – in other words, the tale of what this title character suffers alone, linked to but still set apart from the plot that does not suit him. In the manner of The Father in *Six Characters*, Bloom's Hamlet cannot truly be author, but must still embody the drama – in this case the tragedy – that finally belongs only to him.

Pirandello says that a dramatic character must have his or her drama, and Hamlet certainly has his share, and extravagantly so, within himself as well as without. In fact, the extent to which external obligation and internal duress are balanced is a direct correlate, in the case of *Hamlet*, of the ratio of plot to character, the balance of a scenic structure with a portrait of interiority. And here, as an aside to Bloom's empathetic reification of Hamlet, the character does indeed seem to mastermind this particular balance, or at least convey the illusion that such a thing is possible. In the scheme of what James Calderwood has called the "explicit metadramatism" of *Hamlet*, the title character's self-regard is but one mirror of the play's inclusive consciousness of its own means, the employment of a knowing theatricality and performative dissembling (30).

Hamlet is, himself, a keen observer of character (in the sense, at least, of the personalities and motives of others) and an enthusiast of acting, a seeming master of his own stage and audience. However, these traits, apparently coherent and complementary, can nonetheless be at odds. Calderwood sees Hamlet as aware of his "dual identity" as character and actor, a combination that cages him within the play even as it sets him strangely apart from its interactions and scenic momentum (32). In the theatre, of course, this duality is magnified as the audience not only beholds an actor performing it but can be especially aware of the layering of roles.[4] Yet even when Hamlet is a body at rest, or in repose, or an apparent bystander, he is still in service to a playwright's will and design and to what is unavoidable as a tragic progression.[5]

Hamlet may, in his self-preoccupation, want to break from an authorial template, and need to do so, but he can only push the restraints of the tragic genre so far. If he does enjoy, or appears to, a greater autonomy or talent for self-invention than do most other characters in drama, it is due largely to Shakespeare's plot rather than to tragedy. Hamlet can, as it were, make room for himself in the irregular and at times outlandish succession of events, but he cannot do likewise for what are certain innate properties of tragic drama. Francis Fergusson may propose, with respect to such freedom, that Shakespeare is sufficiently reliant upon the "inherent and theatrical interest which this character has apart from the story" to allow Hamlet his time to one side, the occasional "cadenza on his own" before returning to the story line per se (113). But this cannot be the case for the tragic momentum, which in fact must include the time that the character spends on leave from the plot trajectory per se. The tragic exertion must, in other words, be at work all the way through, inexorably, even while Hamlet is allowed the room to speculate upon his own existential circumstances – which is to say, in this instance, his own tragedy or, as A. W. Schegel would put it, his "tragedy of thought" (Bate 307).

Character and Cosmos

At the same time, and with respect to the author as opposed to the authorial character, how much was Shakespeare himself beholden also to a tragic pattern and, in direct relation, to what is finally a one-directional succession of incidents in his play? Such a question entertains philosophical and aesthetic considerations as well as historical and structural ones, and perhaps cannot be answered beyond the evidence of, say, the playwright's debt to an existing Hamlet story, to other tragedies of the day, and to Seneca. How Shakespeare might have conceived the relation of, say, King Lear or Macbeth to an ancient tradition including the Greek is much less knowable. In reference to his own time, however, the revenge tragedy as a staple of English Renaissance drama is probably – apart from the Ur-*Hamlet* – the most familiar formula that can be applied to the Shakespeare *Hamlet* in the context of a genre with which its author would be exceedingly familiar. From this perspective anyway, Hamlet's infamous delay in accomplishing vengeance is what provides the space for his ruminations – but the revenge plot is merely slowed by the speculations and not finally disrupted.

Vengeance as a motif in tragic drama dates at least to Aeschylus if not to an early Pentheus story – with Dionysus as avenger. Yet to situate this play, this character, and even this era in relation to an ancient revenge motif is a more challenging proposition than the motive itself might suggest. My point here is not to join in the worthy inquiry into whether tragedy, as an ancient idea, has or has not proven to be transhistoric.[6] My interest, rather, is in looking at Hamlet's built-in indebtedness to form and genre per se, as a phenomenon that is likely to include an element of philosophy along with formal shape in relation to a character's identity, agency, and behavior. Agamemnon, as noted, cannot truly be regarded separately from godly influences, and is unaware of his tragic plight. As he steps down from the chariot at Argos, he is largely ignorant, during the discourse with Clytemnestra, of all that weighs down upon him in this vital moment of decision that appears (to him) to be his own. Hamlet, by contrast, is unsusceptible to such pantheistic or daimonic associations and is intensely cognizant of his circumstances. Even so, each figure inhabits a cosmos that can meaningfully be called tragic, and these realms bear certain key resemblances along with stark differences. George Steiner finds that "absolute tragedy," the pure and extreme instances of the genre, is "very rare," defining it as "dramatic literature (or art or music) founded rigorously on the postulate that human life is a fatality" (*Passion* 129). Steiner admits neither *Agamemnon* nor *Hamlet* to his society of the "absolute" in relation to this genre. Even so, is the life experience of either Hamlet or Agamemnon not a fatality, progressively and consummately so within the purviews and the structures of their respective plays? What is more certain, perhaps, is that in each case there is a linkage of character and cosmos, and in both instances the cosmic impression is all-embracing and, from first to last, malign.[7]

The cosmos of the *Oresteia* is, to be sure, not that of *Hamlet*, even as both are tragic. In the former, the presences and the interventions of Artemis, Zeus, Athene, and Apollo are essential to both the action and the outcome of the trilogy. In the latter, there is no pantheon, and formal religiosity as a feature of destiny is moot. Steiner's argument is that, "the agnosticism of Shakespearean drama in respect of the theological and the metaphysical is undeniable" – yet, in a seeming paradox, "the assumption that human destiny suffers constraints and interpositions of an order beyond the empirical and the rational is imperative" (*Passion* 136). In such a context, then, to what extent is Hamlet's character shaped by, and in debt to, some larger, metaphysical tragic frame, and in turn, how does this relate to genre and also to one with ancient beginnings? A tragic cosmos assumes a macrocosm, and this assumption need not apply to any particular age. In "Absolute Tragedy," for example, Steiner points to a transhistoric "myth content" that concentrates on "mortal encounters with supernatural agencies of fate, with transcendent visitations, with 'other than human' interventions of an ambiguous or destructive order" (136).[8]

Hamlet's display of consciousness, and Shakespeare's emphasis on the character's precise deliberations, cannot of themselves set Hamlet apart from a cosmic – and for him, a tragic, setting. In tragedy, the aspect of cosmos, variable though it may be historically, does provide a connective fabric. The sighting of a Ghost, by Horatio and others along with Hamlet, guarantees the supernatural. What Hamlet shares with Agamemnon or Cassandra, then, is not the Greek pantheon but another sort of macrocosmos, the totality of a manifest order that in tragedy oppresses and then, most typically, eradicates. Moreover, there is generally a factor of logic in this configuration; the fatality that is visited upon both of these characters is by no means random but arises rather from discernable, if abstract or not completely knowable, patterns. If there is an "absolute" in Hamlet's destiny, it is that tragic cosmos in which humankind is neither the sum or the measure.[9] Even as Steiner, in *The Death of Tragedy*, or Lionel Abel would exclude Hamlet from pure tragedy, it cannot be modernity alone, or conscience, or hyperawareness that sets him apart.[10] Hamlet is wedded, in fact, to a cosmos that is evinced not only by his own self and circumstances at Elsinore but also by other tragedies before and after his own.

Hamlet and Aristotle

Even though the *Poetics* is germane with respect to drama long after Aristotle, it is naturally impossible to know what the Athenian would make of Hamlet as a dramatic character – although, conversely, the prince's formal education could plausibly include Aristotle's philosophy. What would the philosopher think of a tragedy in which the plot is sufficiently pliable to admit an intense and sustained inquiry into a character's mental state and train of thought – not to mention the numerous departures from what he advises the poet concerning appropriate, believable, and practical characterization? The answer is unknowable, but the question itself is relevant precisely because it queries the basis of the plot/character ratio and weighs the value of a character's inner life in a balance with revealed behaviors. As a model of dramatic character, Hamlet strays far from the Aristotelian prescriptions. Still, as a figure that is exemplary with respect to so many theatrical attributes – in characterization, performance, and portrayal of interiority – he is especially well-suited for the comparison of the Greek sense with Shakespeare's own. Indeed, Hamlet varies from, and enlarges upon, the profundity of the Greek model of dramatic character to such an extent that a literal reconception of artistic latitudes and capabilities is the result.

In truth, Hamlet represents a challenge to almost all of Aristotle's dicta, and the departures that he stands for illuminate several aspects of dramaturgy, including story structure and the achievement of verisimilitude along with basic capabilities that belong to the fictional representation of people in general. There are stage figures of the Elizabethan and Jacobean eras that, even when classically based, represent a qualitative difference in the method of portrayal from those of the ancients, and in fact embody an evolutionary leap in character depiction. Lear, Faustus, or the Duchess of Malfi (or, for that matter, Webster's Duke Ferdinand) can serve as epitomes alongside Hamlet, but dramatic characterization in the English Renaissance is reflective often of such a newfound sophistication. A means of portrayal, coupled with inquiry, that probes thought and consciousness along with emotive state and volitional motive is a primary marker of this development. In that regard, what Fergusson calls Hamlet's "cadenzas" are among the chief factors that alter the balance of plot, character, and thought as Aristotle would conceive it. Shakespeare's allowance of what amounts to a regular leave time for Hamlet from the major plot lines, and the play's emphasis on thought process per se, finally guarantees this alteration of Aristotle's hierarchy and prioritizes the portrayal of mind over deed. In fact, the emphasis is shifted so markedly toward self-awareness that Hamlet comes to act out a subplot of his own, parallel to, yet oddly apart from, the main events of the story – and the practicality of this subplot would, from Aristotle's perspective, be questionable, to say the least. Aristotle does not, in the *Poetics*, comment on the utility of the tragic chorus, but Hamlet's soliloquies are most akin to stasima in this respect: they can inform the action even while standing apart from it. Hamlet is individually choral, as it were, with his speeches probing and standing for his and the play's *dianoia*, Aristotle's conception of thought, or the ideas that are conveyed through language, especially, and in actions undertaken.[11]

To what extent, then, do Hamlet's traits have a utile or functional value with respect to the revenge motive, which provides the play's overarching line of action? Or, in what particular way does *ethos*, as a demonstration of moral or ethical predilection, or of one's behavioral response in a given situation, serve this particular play? On the face of it, *Hamlet* is a tale of morality questioned and then enforced – at least with respect to the actions of Hamlet's mother and uncle, the prince's reactions to same, and the consequences.[12] At the same time, though, Hamlet's nobility, which is a result of ancestry and privilege, education, a refined nature, and intellectual brilliance, is presented in uneasy relation to the moral sense – and, as a consequence, to his behavior on the spot, or in the situation. Hence we have the delay, and also the abrupt and reckless murder of Polonius. Hamlet belongs at Elsinore, but is incongruent with its society. For Hamlet, in fact, solipsism has a way of intruding on, and at times supplanting, what might under different circumstances be closer to the Greek sense of character as an individual within community. Hamlet is prideful, to be sure, but often in the sense of isolation, of aloofness or apartness, rather than the ancient manner of hubris.

Aristotle prizes function and practicality, especially with respect to the relation of the character agent (*ethos*) to the arrangement of events (*muthos*). To create dramatic character is thus to "ascribe certain qualities to the agents," as the *Poetics* (VI) puts this, and the purpose is utilitarian with respect to the plot's efficacy. To refer once more to Else, Aristotle's conviction is that plot and character are not meant to be parallel, but should be comprehended instead as a unity (*Argument* 468). And, with reference again to Jones, dramatic character in the Greek setting "must be denied even the most primitive autonomy" (31). Thus, the cognitive sub-plot in *Hamlet*, together with the character's seeming freedom of move-ment in the main plot, are utterly foreign to the classical model – with the exception, that is, of the soliloquy's kinship with the choral stasimon.

The philosopher's recommendation of a connection, or even a unity, among character, thought, and language, is a dictum that might well apply to *Hamlet*, in that a presentation of self is so closely linked with an artic-ulation of philosophy. Or, from a slightly different angle, the ontology of this character is alive in words and thoughts, even as he so disparages a surfeit of the former. The intricacy with which Hamlet is drawn, and the range of his knowledge and insight, give him an over-abundance of traits and place him, in effect, at the polar opposite to what the *Poetics* would recommend. There is, in brief, an impracticality of traits (in relation to conventional plotting), coupled with a solitude that is at odds with com-munity and even with *ethos* (as personification of an ethical motive), that makes for this disjuncture between the ancient and Renaissance notions of what a character can, or should, be. Or, to turn Aristotle on end once more, *Hamlet* delivers more imitation of a man than of action and of life.

To speak of traits in connection with any dramatic character, a sub-jective endeavor at best, is an especially elusive enterprise in the case of Shakespearian as against ancient characterization, if only because of the psychological complexities and contradictions that a figure such as Hamlet can stand for, and indeed epitomize.[13] Moreover, there is the play-wright's procedural method to consider, and it is quite feasible, as Eric Bentley suggests in *The Life of the Drama*, that Shakespeare was "less inter-ested in attributing qualities to people than in providing a demonstration that they are alive, that they are in the world" (61). Be that as it may, my aim here is not to add to the multitude of analyses of Hamlet's character, which refuses categorization anyway. My interest, rather, is in probing the ratio of a stage figure's characteristic qualities to storytelling, genre type, and the form of a plot structure – with the intention of setting Hamlet distinctly apart from Aristotelian fundamentals and weighing the implica-tions of that contrast.

In the spirit of such inquiry, then, one might reasonably infer that Hamlet is observant, philosophical, ironic, indecisive, self-regarding, intellectual, and so on – and could readily find textual evidence to support such a portrait. Yet none of these qualities is particularly useful, apart from texture and resonance, with respect to the revenge plot – or, for that matter, for the motif of madness or mental instability that *Hamlet* also shares with an ancient and tragic ancestry. Only the quality of indecisiveness truly relates to plot as the series of shown events that Shakespeare has orchestrated, as against story, which could include Hamlet's emotional and intellectual life more generally. By contrast, a character such as Antigone or Oedipus is written with so marked an economy that individual qualities stand out prominently and affect the progress of events in immediate ways. The opposition of Antigone and Creon, with respect to the burial of Polynieces and attendant laws or beliefs, is set forth directly, and Sophocles gives overt attention to the precise beliefs and qualities of character that bring about such a divergence. For Shakespeare, on the other hand, the balance itself is skewed in the direction of full embodiment of a complex mind and personality. Hamlet may, to be sure, have an excess of traits by the Greek norm and by Aristotelian reckoning, but it is this very surplus, impractical as it may be by the ancient standard, that brings with it so tremendous a yield.

Plot, Pathology, and Genre

Contrasting Hamlet with the classical conception of *ethos*, in the sense of an individual or shared ethical tendency, must attend to the drama of his mental state and the depth of his psychological agitation – and to how these factors affect the ability to take action or to engage with community. Again, my interest here is not in venturing too deeply into Hamlet's thoughts, which are sufficiently probed, but rather in investigating how the revelation of his condition affects the course of events as part of a dramatic structure. For argument's sake, then, one might infer that Hamlet's depression has taken him inward, with a marked dissociation from the norms to which he was once accustomed. And, this dislocation has a performative dimension, at times intentional and at other times not so voluntary. "Madness" in the play becomes an pervasive, if elusive, catch-all motif that subsumes not only a loss of mirth but also grief, despair, disorientation, and deceptiveness – to name just a few of Hamlet's modes of feeling, thought, and presentation of self. Ophelia recalls the Hamlet that was – "the glass of fashion and the mold of form" (III, 1, 167) – but that is not the person with whom we spend the hours upon the stage. In fact, Hamlet's recent maladies shift the ground of story structure and at the same time provide a key point of adherence between the cognitive subplot

(Hamlet's mind at work in soliloquy on both immediate and macrocosmic conditions) and major lines of action wherein varied attempts are made, by Polonius and others, to decipher Hamlet's moods.[14] The relation of pathology and dramaturgy is not new, of course, and the coherence of mind (or mental consistency, at least) has been a part of tragedy's heritage since the gods would deprive humans of sense and sanity before bringing them to ruin.

In certain ways, ironically, it is Hamlet's depressive illness, or complex of ills, that can add to his reification. For Bloom, as we have seen, powers of intellect, acumen, and inventiveness are foremost in creating the illusion of independent thought and, by extension, freedom of action. A century earlier, A.C. Bradley, in the lectures collected as *Shakespearean Tragedy* (1904), also has an empathetic way of talking about Hamlet as if he were alive and complete with a past life, if not a future. For Bradley, Hamlet's "intellectual genius" is contributory also to an impression of life-likeness – although Bradley situates that quality in relation to the variable means that Hamlet has of performing his brilliance (98). Together with that virtuosity, however, there is Hamlet's "melancholy," which directly affects the play's dramatic pattern as well as this character's fluctuation in moods and, perhaps oddly, the related impression of versatility and freedom. Indeed, Bradley posits a fundamental connection of pathology – for him, Hamlet's "disease" or "melancholy" – and dramaturgy.[15] Hamlet's mentality, as Bradley sees it, is such that no "exertion of will" can heal what has gone amiss (404). With such power of volition lacking, agency is compromised, and along with it the conventional imperative to demonstrate and impel action. Hamlet cannot, however, be deemed "irresponsible" due to mental cause. In such circumstances, argues Bradley, one would be "too keenly conscious of his responsibility. He is therefore, so far, quite capable of being a tragic agent" (104–105). From a strictly dramaturgical standpoint, though, the result is a prospective agent with highly compromised agency – and a plot that must contain, and act out, that paradox.

In this total situation, therefore, it is the nature, intelligence, and personality of this famed character, together with his afflictions of mind, that affect and even determine the dramatic structure in *Hamlet*, by contrast with traits and qualities that are, as Aristotle would have it, appropriate, workable, believable, and functional. From Bradley's point of view, both the plot and the rhythm of events are set to the tune of Hamlet's mercurial persona – to the fits and starts of character in tempo with the structure of action.[16] Melancholy, from a psychological perspective, is for Bradley the "center of the tragedy," a direct line between character pathology and genre (109). And yet, the connection of such a character's thoughts and moods to the tragic can be stressed further, and precisely so in the direction of "absolute" fatality. The impression, contradictory as it may be, that Hamlet is wrongly cast in a plot that is nonetheless his, is here again underscored in connection with pathology along with intellect. Even if miscast, however, Hamlet brings a considerable energy, much of the time quite effectively, to a turning of events his way.

Indeed, Hamlet's command is such that his very presence can tug at the dramatic form through force of personality, acuity of intellect, and through ills that are expressed, alternately, as depressive, mercurial, alienated, attenuated, or sudden – to name only a few variations in a figure that G. Wilson Knight calls "an ambassador of death walking through life" (32). In truth, though, Hamlet is not so much an ambassador from any undiscovered country as an agent of immediate and pressing mortal fragility. And, if he has "held converse with death," as Knight would have it, this serves largely to bring such discourse to bear on the cognitive line of action that, through this dramatic character's compulsive preoccupations, gravitates continually to center stage (38). While the major plot trajectories of Hamlet are conventional, at least in terms of machinations, madness, ghostly directives, revenge, and so on, the title character is able consistently to turn the focus of attention to his own obsessions and his means of articulating them. Even so, such a positioning center-stage of the drama of cogitation and consciousness can, in the case of Hamlet, have an effect of nearly derailing the play's fundamental vectors of story line and development.[17]

The dissonance between the more conventional dramaturgy of *Hamlet* and Hamlet's own combinations of mental agility, depressive symptoms, and self-dramatization is reflected in the contradictions and paradoxes within the character himself, sometimes resulting from his own contrivance, and sometimes not. There is a burden of awareness that rests uneasily upon him, conveyed at times as a portrayal of consciousness together with conscience, that at times does threaten to upstage other events. As a supreme irony, Hamlet must be rashly inconsiderate at the same time as he is brainy and hyperconscious. In order for the progression of incidents to unfold optimally, in fact, Hamlet needs to be thoughtless (with Ophelia, mostly) as well as unthinking (with Polonius, disastrously) in alternation with the introspective subplot. Such a contradiction of knowledge and ignorance is usefully productive, if not essential, in the turn of events – ultimately prompting the madness and suicide of Ophelia and the counter-revenge of Laertes. At the same time, such polarities are refracted into conflicting images of character as representative of ontological worthiness or its opposite: the world as empyreal or as an "unweeded garden that grows to seed" (I, 2, 135–136). And then there is Hamlet himself, vacillating between these self-cancelling images as the play scurries to catch up to his moods.

Hamlet is constructed, as many tragedies are, upon a set of dynamic oppositions between order and disorder, cosmos and chaos. Hamlet's ideation, including fixations and abrupt changes of thought (as in the soliloquies), comprises a microcosmic realm of cognitive dissonance that, mirroring its larger environs, is out of joint. While Shakespeare's dramaturgy, in terms of the orchestration of events anyway, is able to welcome Hamlet's deviations into the rhythm of action, it can do so largely via soliloquy or through performative behavior that is often demonstrative of aberration or illogic (as the encounter reported by Ophelia; II, 1, 99). Hamlet's fancies and variations may be accommodated, more or less successfully, into the wanderings of Shakespeare's plot, but there are levels of order that bear on the action of *Hamlet* that can be stricter and less admitting of such inconsistency or autonomy, especially with respect to a depiction of cosmos and, yet again, of the tragic genre itself.

Even as he is all too aware of his mission and of his stature, Hamlet is only marginally cognizant of where he fits in the order of things – and a vision of cosmos, changeable as it is historically, must figure nonetheless in any appraisal of such a systematic realm.[18] Here once more, Hamlet presents the contradiction that arises from opposing versions of what constitutes mankind as created within a cosmic structure ("this goodly frame, the earth, seems to me a sterile promontory," II, 2, 322). And, this opposition is fundamental with respect to the play's design. As E. M. W. Tillyard has pointed out, the play is "largely animated by Shakespeare's consciousness of man's being in action like an angel, in apprehension like a god, and yet capable of all baseness" (76). Cosmos implies, in such an instance, not only a system and an orderliness, but also what is antithetical within that order. From this standpoint anyway, Hamlet's dialectic of healthiness and disease, nobility and baseness, is situated within a cosmos that is bifurcated fundamentally and completely. The polarities are, in fact, stringent: the Elizabethan chain of being is a formal hierarchy, and one founded upon gradients, purportedly in nature, of that which is immediate and abstract, inferior to superior.[19]

Hamlet and the Tragic "Sense"

The factor of sense, as distinct from order, is among the more elusive, puzzling, and yet essential attributes of a tragic cosmos – and here one is cautious of anachronism, as there is considerable variation among understandings of this quality. Cosmos, signifying orderliness along with universality, is imagined in tragic drama as mysterious, usually malign, and even unfathomable – a heritage from inscrutable gods. And yet, what can appear initially as lacking in logic, as random or chaotic – especially in connection with violence, high passion, or events that appear haphazard – may come to be viewed instead as sensible and even foreseeable in the totality of the circumstances. Wrongly geocentric or heliocentric, the astronomical cosmos as understood in Shakespeare's day may have seemed to make sense with all of its balances and analogies, even while fundamentally misguided with respect to spheres beyond the earthly, not to mention the place of humankind in such a realm. The tragic cosmos, by contrast, is never delineated fully or understood completely. Rather, it is powerfully enigmatic. And yet, there is generally an underlying force or presence of the kind originally aligned with ancient gods or with daimon, and it is this very exertion that can, ultimately, deliver the quality of sense, often through a portrayal of an intrinsically developing fate, a prevailing fortune of good or ill, or a seemingly destined progression.

With tragic drama, there are three questions (Aristotelian in the sense of a beginning, middle, and end) that are pertinent to this apparently orderly yet contradictory and possibly malign factor of sense: what initiates a tragic progression, what sustains it, and what is the termination? And, perhaps most significantly, what is the root source and cause for this dynamic and of such inevitability? The story *Hamlet*, as far-fetched as it can be, finally delivers precisely this type of logic and of sense – not in terms of the plot's wayward accommodations of Hamlet's introversion, but through a succession of occurrences that turns into something intrinsic with respect to the central character.[20] The tragic action is instigated not only by the edict of the Ghost but also by the fact of its appearance coinciding with Hamlet's rage over Gertrude's marriage. Indeed, the temper of that emotion, and Hamlet's inability to fully comprehend let alone surmount it, contributes substantially to the perpetuation of an action that culminates in the murder of Polonius and, in turn, points directly to the play's *telos*, which is the only termination possible given the play's (and its central character's) death obsession.[21] I have written elsewhere about the tendency that is common for characters in tragedy to suffer in the manner of the tragic god Dionysus – that is, to be subject to sparagmos, as a rending of spirit or of selfhood if not the body per se.[22] In this context, too, Hamlet's experience not only aligns him with tragedy in general and with a tragic progression in the play's actions, but is the logical result of the fault lines that lie within his bifurcated nature. What befalls him, therefore, does so within a prevailing and finally readable system, with qualities of logic and of sense emerging and becoming apparent from within this tragic pattern.[23] This is not to say that Hamlet himself finds such intelligibility prior to his silence, but rather that the dynamics of tragedy, even Steiner's "absolute tragedy," can be read in accord with the genre's long-standing belief systems and through an internal logic that, in its turn, is reflected in its dramaturgy.

Actor, Character, and Agency

Hamlet is famously performative. And yet, given that he is among the most famed of dramatic characters, it is ironic that he is more familiar with what it means to perform by comparison with embodying an identity and a self through representation – that is, with character. The associations of Hamlet with acting are, of course, many, and his histrionic proclivities are sufficiently demonstrated. Is he performing a role in scenes with Ophelia in which he seems not to recall the essence of their past relations, or with Polonius when he is so nimble with ironies at the elder's expense? These are standard examples (among several) of when Hamlet is not the same man that he is with, say, Horatio. Whether he is playing a part or not, Hamlet knows actors and he knows some plays, including "The Murder of Gonzago," to which he would like to add a dozen or so lines to suit his purpose.[24] He knows audience and he knows genre, including tragedy – as does Polonius, in the satirical riff on theatrical typology (II, 2, 420–426).

Yet the question of character, apart from his own persona and in its especial relation to performance, is something else again, and is not truly in Hamlet's purview. He is a keen observer of others, and he has much to say to the Players about acting style, but not much at all about how to convey an essence of character. The irony here is delectable, in the sense that given the prominence of interiority in his own composition and self-conception ("that within that passes show"), Hamlet himself views dramatic characterization and its performance with respect to others as predominantly, nigh exclusively, exteriorized. In a way, though, this should not be surprising. Both the setting and the society of Elsinore are given to theatrical "show" so extensively and in so many guises that acting and spectatorship are coin of the realm. As Bruce Wilshire remarks, "The actor who plays the part of Hamlet plays the part of one who has already adopted the techniques of theatre as a way of life" (71).

Hamlet's isolation, or studied apartness, or requisite solitude with respect to the soliloquies, is ironic also in precisely the sense that he is so in need of the dramatis personae for survival even as he scorns or condescends to so much of the company at Elsinore. We have noted the several ways in which the title character seems out of place in *Hamlet* or, at best, out of synch with the play's more familiar conventions. Concurrently, however, Hamlet is absolutely wedded to the fundamentals of the play's dramaturgy, having mostly to do with factors of motive and agency – the very aspects of storytelling, in other words, that are questioned typically with respect to the delay in taking action. And, he is bonded to his fellow cast members – to what Kenneth Burke would call, in *Perspectives by Incongruity*, the "character recipe," the idea that traits are not strictly individualized but are interactive with the traits of others who comprise the dramatis personae (176).[25] Burke's idea is that, "the *dramatis personae* should be analyzed with reference to what we have elsewhere called the agent-act ratio. That is, the over-all action requires contributions by the characters whose various individual acts (and their corresponding passions) must suit their particular natures. And these acts must mesh with one another, in a dialectic of cooperative competition" (167). Hamlet can only be or act alone for so long, and the demand is inviolate for coparticipation, and indeed consubstantiation, with those who populate the story along with him. From this angle, anyway, Hamlet is more indebted through characterization to Gertrude, Claudius, Ophelia, Polonius, and Laertes (to name his primary partners) than to his revenge project per se – which, after all, can wait.

The perennial question of Hamlet's delay relates directly to that of agency and to its corollary, the dramatic character as agent. In Chapter 1, attention was given to the Aristotelian concept of character as agent, in the sense of utility in relation to plot. Here, we have contrasted the characterization of Hamlet as agent with the classical model, highlighting his abundance of traits that would belie a strict usefulness, at least with respect to the play's central lines of action. There is another perspective proposed by Burke, rooted also in functionality and featuring the capacities of agent and agency in dramatic action – or, to use Burke's term, in "dramatism." Burke's proposal is that an effective model for delineation of "motives" in a sociological context can be based on a pentad that reflects the basic dynamics of drama: act, scene, agent, agency, and purpose. Among all the terms, interactive ratios are possible – as, for instance, a scene/act correspondence. While Burke's pentad is, ironically, not often consulted with respect to dramaturgy (although there are notable exceptions), its component parts can serve to point up a number of intrinsic ways in which Hamlet and his situation are delimited, thus establishing a further constraint on the character's potentials for autonomy.[26]

On the one hand, Hamlet's "purpose" can be understood objectively, at least insofar as a revenge plot demands it – yet "purpose" in the existential or ontological sense is, in *Hamlet*, far less clear. With that said, however, Hamlet's motives and behaviors are available still to the dramatistic model. Most notably, of course, Hamlet is the agent who occupies the play's center and is the action's prime motivator. And he contemplates agency as well as purpose within the embracing "scene" of Elsinore – a physical locale but also an abnormal climate and, in today's parlance, a crime scene. Several ratios are not only apparent in this configuration but are also prominent, including scene/act and agency/purpose. How is an action to be taken, by whom, where, and to what end? – an ostensibly uncomplicated question that can apply to most if not all drama.[27]

With respect to this title character especially, it bears noting that Burke's ratios are expressive of more than relationships among terms. They also imply levels of necessity with respect to one another. In other words, and in consideration of the pentad as a dramaturgical as well as sociological construct, Hamlet is obligated to act; and moreover, he must do so within the boundaries of these particular environs and in a way that will bring about the completion of that action as a total yield. The dramatistic formula is implicit but also strict, and in this regard Hamlet cannot stray too far from what Burke would call the motive. Even as Bloom reiterates (and counters) the assertion made by Samuel Johnson with respect to the difference between agent and instrument, the model of dramatism clarifies the distinction (*Invention* 412). "Hamlet is," says Johnson, "through the whole play, rather an instrument than agent" (112). There are several ways to interpret this contention, including a view of Hamlet as his deceased father's instrument of revenge, the character as a tool of fate or of tragedy, or simply as the playwright's most optimal vehicle for storytelling. Burke's theory, however, disallows the possibility for drama without agent and corresponding agency, and situates dramatic action in a figure who instigates and also executes action, just as Hamlet does.[28]

Hamlet and "World Character"

Uneasily situated as he might be in the story line of *Hamlet*, Hamlet is, as it were, completely at home with the dramatis personae at Elsinore and with the complex of intentions and interactions that this highly select group creates together at Shakespeare's behest. This is not to deny, certainly, that Hamlet is at odds or in conflict with many, if not most, of the others. It is rather to notice that, even with his superiority and apartness, he is a part of this unit and is, in fact, its reason for being. Hamlet is, in other words, centrally participatory in what Bert O. States refers to as the play's "world character." States's theory, advanced in *Hamlet and the Concept of Character,* is that figures who make up the casts of plays are, in his words, "made of each other." The perception by an audience or reader of a character's individuality arises actually from "the relationships among and between characters" (xx).

In this scenario, Hamlet is who he is because of those who are not simply his reflectors but who provide the opportunities for him to be realized as himself – whether it be Ophelia, Gertrude, Laertes, Claudius, or Horatio within a given relationship. And, as a logical corollary, it is Hamlet's personality and behaviors that determine the actions and identities of the other cast members who, in States's view, "behave in terms of Hamlet: they possess a personality designed to maximize Hamlet's opportunities for displaying a distinct character" (59). The standpoint here bears some kinship with Burke's "character recipe," and even with the Aristotelian emphasis upon traits in relation to action. The proposition is, however, more inclusive, finally implying a "super-character" or "world-character" that, with a necessarily cumulative quality of its own, transcends the notion of individuality and, even in so extreme a case as Hamlet's, of apartness (xx, 62).

If Horatio were a Neoclassical raisonneur instead of a Senecan confidant, he might inquire as to why Hamlet cannot be more reasonable or temperate. In doing so, Horatio would be enacting precisely what is expected, and indeed mandated, by his role as a consistent voice of reason. If Ophelia were a Romantic heroine instead of a primary reflector of Hamlet's mindset and, through her death, instigator of Laertes's vengeance, a rescue from drowning would be at least possible if not likely. But the mandates of *Hamlet*, and of Elizabethan tragedy, are not these. Characters in Hamlet participate both individually and collectively in an unruly plot that makes abundant room for speculative sidebars. They abide within Renaissance tragedy as a genre template that, as stringently as any other factor in the dramaturgy, delimits the characters' freedom and severely constrains any possibility for action that departs from what, in the tragic progression, is intrinsic and unavoidable. While Shakespeare has fashioned a scenic structure that can emphasize a demonstration of intellect and insight as symptoms of autonomy, even that portrayal of thought as action must be delimited by what belongs to this play as tragedy, with its ancient roots. Hence, Hamlet's "motive," in the context of Burke's dramatism as a five-part cluster of necessarily interactive terms, must finally be a tragic one: to weigh the nature of his mortality and then arrange for, and engage with, the proof of it.

CHAPTER 3

Character by the Rules:
Neoclassicism and Beyond

With all respect for your exalted notions,
It's often best to veil one's true emotions.
Wouldn't the social fabric come undone
If we were wholly frank with everyone?[1]

The contrast is stark indeed between English Renaissance and French Neoclassical characterization motifs in drama. Among the notable differences are constraints that are placed upon a character's behavior and the severity with which the passions are depicted and, often, judged. Under the more restrictive circumstances of this later age, particular principles and guidelines (in France, *les regles*) contribute to a fashioning of characters that, in many cases, are not allowed freedom of emotion without commentary or even censure. The result, paradoxically, can be a diminishment yet also an exaggeration of predominant traits and emotional tempers, concurrently. In this chapter I center on three well-known stage figures that are not only representative of this phenomenon but are also models for particular styles of theatrical characterization: Alceste and Phaedra in the French Neoclassic comic and tragic traditions, respectively, and Mr. Dorimant, a notable truewit in Restoration comedy. Molière's Alceste, the title character in *The Misanthrope* (1666), is from one angle a concentrated embodiment of animus toward humanity, a man who focuses adamantly on the rejection of spurious societal customs, especially the hypocrisies that mar the world of his paramour, the admired but flighty Célimène. From another perspective, however, Alceste transcends his singular type and is actually various: tragical yet romantic, comedic and pathetic, volatile but consistent. And yet, his character is not, and cannot be, as dimensional as Hamlet or of Shakespearean characters of less intricate design than the Prince. Within the jurisdiction of French Neoclassicism, the prescriptions regarding a character's composition and behaviors, in comedy or tragedy, are too precise and too regimented for that to be possible.

In both the French and English theatrical settings of the mid-to-late seventeenth century, either a suppression of emotion or a depiction of passion's ill effects can strongly affect the balance of feeling and reason in the figures represented, with a consequent impact on the fullness with which a dramatic character is designed – here again, a potentially impactful factor with respect to "real person" characterization. Whereas Hamlet appears at times to have a remarkable autonomy, characters wrought by Molière or by Jean Racine may have no such license, and certainly not by comparison to the versatile and embracing dramaturgy that was fashioned by playwrights of the Elizabethan and Jacobean periods. The point here is not to isolate free will as a marker of lifelikeness, but rather to demonstrate how stringent the limitations can be, in different historical and geographical settings, on the quality of freedom that characters in plays may or may not enjoy. Philinte, Alceste's close friend and confidant, is good-natured in his cautioning against the display of strong emotion or even of directness (as in his admonition quoted earlier), yet his message is far from dilute. It is, rather, a genially delivered version of what is in fact a rigorous – and preventative – guideline regarding the social good: that which benefits a society, providing a guarantee of social cohesiveness in the face of individual passions or departures from prescriptive norms.

Molière's dramaturgy in *The Misanthrope* is, of course, exemplary of French Neoclassical style and, in spite of Alceste's ravings, decorum. At the same time, however, the play enacts a rebellion against *bienséance*, or accepted propriety, through this character's rejection of what may appear suitable as social conduct but is actually false.[2] Indeed, Alceste's indignation goes against just about everything that constitutes his world – to wit, the society around Céliméne that includes Philinte and Eliante along with the would-be poet Oronte and the members of Célimène's admiring circle. For Alceste, their pretensions are simply too rampant and their hypocrisies too easily assimilated into what passes for an acceptable, if at times mean-spirited, set of social behaviors and graces. Thus, the play's exquisitely wrought dramatic form, with all of its symmetries and internal balances, also contains intrinsic contradictions – and Alceste, in his self-torture over the impossible Célimène, is made to embody them. Severely out of step with others, he cannot be tamed into conformity to a society that he loathes – but which is personified by the woman he cannot help but adore.

The "Character" of the Misanthrope

Perhaps the most striking contradictions in *The Misanthrope* arise from the ambiguity with which Molière renders his central figure's standpoints and beliefs. This is not to say that one does not understand Alceste's arguments – indeed, the opposite is true – but that one is unsure of what to make of Molière's presentation of them. Ostensibly, a comic dramatist in the tradition of the age is compelled to satirize aberrant behavior and in so doing guide a wayward character toward the mainstream, thus obeying the Neoclassical mandate to entertain and instruct – that is, to promote a good example for an audience in a pleasing way. Molière engages with this mandate, but ultimately flouts it through Alceste. This result is both magnitude and enigma, in that Alceste's refusal to be brought to heel lends him stature but at the same time there is uncertainty and, again, contrariness. Does Alceste truly set a good example? Assuredly so: he is a paragon of truthfulness, honesty, directness, and purity of motive. And, at the same time, absolutely not: he is irascible, incorrigible, bilious, and of a type that could not possibly be borne by society if more among us were like him. Molière's own point of view on this is difficult to read. Surely he must have recognized, as dramatist and as actor, that Alceste was extraordinary, but what about the character's own attitudes, by comparison especially with Philinte's?

The voice of the raisonneur is so vital in Molière's dramaturgy – as brought to bear by Philinte in his consistently temperate advice to Alceste or, in *Tartuffe*, by Cleante's steadily voiced moderation – that it is difficult to imagine an authorial disagreement with so persuasive an argument for reason. As Philinte counsels his friend:

> Let's have an end of rantings and of railings,
> And show some leniency toward human failings. (23)

Even as Philinte argues for what is moderate ("Good sense views all extremes with detestation"), it isn't easy to wholly condemn Alceste's manic idealism, even with its intractable and solipsistic aspects, without qualification as to the high ground to which he would have everyone aspire. Martin Turnell, in "Le Misanthrope," refers to Philinte as "Molière's spokesperson in places," but does not believe, for example, that "the whole of the play is behind his words" (273). Here, then, is another of the play's more notable oppositions or, in this case, a dichotomy: the dramaturgy of characterization that is demanded by the even-tempered raisonneur, coupled with the possibly outlandish but equally imperative aspects of Alceste's beliefs and values. Indeed, the splendor of this play resides in part in this very opposition. *The Misanthrope* is steadfast in its apparent adherence to a comedic principle of the era – the imperative to ridicule an oddball into conformity – while at the same time featuring a character who would sooner abandon humanity for good than be cowed into submission to its ways.

Of course, if Alceste were only misanthropic, the play would not have the magisterial scope, agelessness, charm, or consistency of application that it does. Alceste is a person of feeling, matched with an alluring woman without sincerity and a man, Philinte, of both feeling and reasonableness. Alceste may suffer the agonies of the condemned over the incorrigibly coquettish Célimène, but he believes nonetheless that his love is reciprocated: "I wouldn't love her did she not love me" (28). "Love," for Alceste, can be profoundly romantic as well as intensely frustrating, and his embodiment of that contradiction is extreme to the point of parody. In this instance at least, the predicament of a misanthrope with a heart is certainly comedic, but is oddly endearing, too. When Alceste recites for Philinte the love poem that for him is "the purest gold," a model of expression from "a loving heart," it is hard to disagree, if not with the lines themselves, at least with the conviction of the speaker. The poet (and, we see, Alceste) would not trade away all of Paris, the king's citadel and gift, for his paramour:

> My darling is more fair, I swear,
> My darling is more fair. (40)

And yet, to what degree actually is *The Misanthrope* concerned with emotion as against reason, and to what extent are feelings expressed and approved of, or tempered and possibly condemned? Alceste may seem, from one standpoint anyway, to be a romantic, if a foiled one. But the sensibility of the play itself does not align at all with values that, at a later time, would be a basis for Romanticism as a philosophy of art. Alceste may be a man of feeling, but *The Misanthrope* is finally a play of reason, and certainly one of societal cooperation. It is, after all, Philinte, in his union with the "honest Eliante," who comes away happy. For these two, the marriage of reason and candor is truly blessed. Alceste, for his part, cannot avoid being a social rebel and a crank. His integrity is forever at stake – no matter that Eliante would have been a much better match than Célimène, who would rather keep a host of admirers around the house than sign on for Alceste's staunch but less than alluring idealism.

Feelings, for Philinte and Eliante, are warmly and appealingly moderate, as they should be in the dicta celebrated by French tradition at the time. Eliante is never duplicitous, much less treacherous, and Philinte is a loyal friend – to the point of not competing openly with Alceste for the lady's hand – as well as an unfailing advocate of what is temperate and prudent. This is not to say that Philinte and Eliante do not share an attraction, and perhaps even a love for one another. That is far from the case, and each one is delighted, if not effusively so, to discover a mutual interest in the other. The example they provide in duet is undeniably pleasing – for them and, one expects, for anyone save for Alceste and the hypocrites around him who can only play at frankness. As Andrew Calder observes, the two of them offer "social strategies that work" and the audience is glad for their mutual discovery of one another (104).[3] And, Eliante allows that audience access to, and even a sympathy for, Alceste. In short, she admires him for his qualities, and justifies the audience's reasons for appreciating his candor if not his less than attractive behaviors.[4]

Here, then, are two characters that provide in performance a shared paradigm and a model for reciprocal feelings. It is not Philinte's talent for reasoning that leads him to Eliante, but rather his responses to her appearance, manner, and personal qualities, including her generosity of spirit. Yet still, their feelings for one another must be modulated, partly to provide a contrast with Alceste but also to recommend by example. In the Neoclassical view, Alceste is the epitome of a personal sense of balance and decorum gone amok, a status that Turnell describes simply: "There is something wrong with Alceste, and most of the play is devoted to discovering what it is" ("Misanthrope" 269). But there is nothing simple about what is wrong with this figure, which is one reason why the play's enigmatic and contradictory aspects endure and why actors over centuries have been able to bring such very different interpretations to the role, some more caustic and some more vulnerable, some more satiric or romantic or pathetic than others.

For the actor, indeed, Alceste over time has been a barometer for the moods of a particular age, dating to Molière's and, later, Michel Baron's performances of the role. From the standpoint of Philinte, though, or in accord with the politeness of his own day, what is "wrong with Alceste" is his irrationality, his rage, his extremism, his fits, his inability to compromise on issues that, in his view, only he can be right about. He must, however, and in spite of it all, be superior and attractive – and indeed he is so, to Célimène, Eliante, and Arsinoe, all at once. What, then, is recommended, and what advised against with respect to social behaviors?

Neoclassical prescription calls on theatre for an instructive point of view, to be delivered through the portrayal of characters and their behaviors and attitudes on stage. Does Molière truly hold back judgment concerning Alceste, or is it rather the polarities within Alceste himself that elicit the ambiguity?

The Misanthrope extols honesty, rationality, and truthfulness, qualities that are assuredly embodied in Philinte and Eliante – but also, to a large extent, in Alceste. Who, after all, could be more forthright? Alceste is unreasonable, but in a just cause, we might say. The root cause of his feelings are not the issue, however, and Molière's drama is not so much concerned with psychology as it is with placing an epitome of principled but unacceptable honesty in direct juxtaposition with one of hypocrisy and deceptiveness. This is the brilliant premise of Molière's matchup of Alceste with Célimène. Alceste becomes, naturally, the embodiment of this opposition – which is partially the cause for what Turnell calls his "lack of balance," a taboo in French Neoclassical art ("Misanthrope" 274). Yet Alceste, in his own way, finally transcends the dramaturgy of Neoclassical principles. He's simply too outsized for its edicts concerning character – in other words, for its models of behavior including the consequences of given actions or attitudes. In Molière's world, this misanthrope is neither Harpagon nor Orgon, and he is assuredly not a cat's paw or a fool. Alceste is, needless to say, one of the great roles in the French theatre. He is a supremely effective dramatic figure, not only because he is volatile, or because his distilled feelings for humanity are timeless, but also because he is so self-dramatizing with regard to his own emotions:

> Why, why am I doomed to love you?
> I swear that I shall bless the blissful hour
> When this poor heart's no longer in your power! (53)

It is this very passion that, in effect, makes of Alceste a fuller representation of personhood than Philinte. Alceste can never be as thoroughly rendered or as autonomous as Hamlet (what character can?), but he stretches the limits of his age's sensibilities nonetheless. His emotive intensities can be read, in this view anyway, not as unhealthy extremism that had best be moderated but as authentic expression of a largeness of spirit that cannot be squelched.

These very attributes, when taken in the context of the play's unhappy (for Alceste, at least) ending have contributed to a long-standing assertion that Molière's play borders on the tragic while skirting, and at times exceeding, the boundaries of French comedic stipulations. But *The Misanthrope* is no tragedy, certainly not formally, and Alceste is not a tragic figure. His experience comes nowhere near the ancient and terror-invoking visions of Molière's compatriot, Racine. At the same time, it is true that in his self-dramatizing, Alceste conceives of his circumstances as not only sad, deplorable, and undeserved but also tragic – which becomes part of the humor. As Calder puts it, it is in the context of Alceste's hopeless chasing after Célimène that "the discrepancy between his view of himself as a tragic figure and the audience's view of him as a comic one is greatest" (101–102).[5] In this relation, the factor of genre merits attention once more, given that Neoclassical dramaturgy admits no admixture of comedy and tragedy. Neither Molière nor Racine would have license to cross that divide, and neither would think of doing so. But in this play at least, the writer of comedy engages with seriousness of a different sort from any of his other works. His play does admit a stark and unsettling view of a man who is so discontent with the human lot that he is prepared, in effect, to cancel out his humanity.

Rousseau and Molière

The separation of comedy and tragedy is necessarily stringent, and so are the stipulations of the Neoclassical ideal with respect to the unities, in particular. I will not, here, revisit the seriousness with which these and other principles of drama were conceived in seventeenth-century France (including the rule of the Académie francaise) or look into the particularities of the "Querelle du Cid" that accentuated those guidelines to such a degree.[6] My interest, instead, is in the implications of the Neoclassical sensibility in relation to characterization – including the portrayal of traits and behaviors – and, by extension, the impact of such a delineation upon audiences. Of particular interest, with respect to both dramatic characters and spectators, is the expressed need, even the directive, to "moderate," or "correct" the emotions, especially by contrast with reason.

Nearly one hundred years after the first production of *The Misanthrope*, Jean-Jacques Rousseau wrote about the play and its creator in his famed "Letter to M. D'Alembert" (1758), a treatise that is unequivocal with respect to the purpose of drama and the relationship of characterization to such a mandate. To query the purpose of art is, naturally, to entertain a grand subject in its own right. In the case of theatrical art, the particular ways in which the characters are shown – including any conception or ideology of how they *ought* to be seen – is germane indeed. Again, the Neoclassicist sensibility would prescribe that theatrical works deliver an edifying as well as entertaining experience. It is commonplace, of course, for a hero or heroine in drama to stand for qualities that can be affirmed by the onlooker. A fundamental concern for Rousseau, though, is not merely the designing of individual characters for the stage, but how such depiction, as a part of theatrical performances collectively, can influence a community – in his case, Geneva – for better or worse. For him, significantly, the representation of passion, as against reason, is critical:

> Do we not know that all the passions are sisters and that one alone suffices for arousing a thousand, and that to combat one by the other is only the way to make the heart more sensitive to them all? The only instrument which serves to purge them is reason, and I have already said that reason has no effect in the theatre. (21)

The point is clear: representation of high feeling is a perilous enterprise, and is inherently contagious – one emotion will likely set off another, and the best way to curb or eradicate such inbreeding is by rational means of the sort not encountered in the theatre.[7] To imagine a theatre without reason is, of course, to ignore the very basis and purpose of the raisonneur – but Rousseau himself is thoroughly acquainted with the plays of Molière, including what he acknowledges as the playwright's masterpiece, *The Misanthrope*.

Rousseau's point of view on Alceste is that Molière betrayed his own title character by making his rare and remarkable traits laughable. Whereas Alceste should offer audiences the chance for a lauding of virtue, those opportunities are sacrificed by an author who prioritizes the observer's laughter. "You could not deny me two things," argues Rousseau, "one, that Alceste in this play is a righteous man, sincere, worthy, truly a good man; and, second, that the author makes him a ridiculous figure. This is already enough, it seems to me, to render Molière inexcusable" (36–37).[8] Rousseau does not worry so much about Alceste's passions, in other words, as the manner with which they are presented. For him, in fact, Alceste is a champion against vice and is not misanthropic at all. He "loves his fellow creatures, hates in them the evils they do to one another and the vices of which these evils are the product" (37). A minority view, certainly, and one that doesn't jibe at all with the more usual understanding of Alceste as almost wholly unsympathetic to the shortcomings of others.

More characteristic of Rousseau's treatise overall is the contention that human passions need to be "moderated" or "regulated" for the social good, lest there be undue influence upon audiences – thus, a society – that may be impressionable and persuadable by dramatic storytelling.[9] Here once more is a recommendation that, if actualized, serves to diminish rather than expand the potentials of characters in drama, restricting the range of emotion that may belong naturally and properly to a person of strong if perhaps contentious feeling. Alceste is not so diminished, and Molière does not dismiss him as laughable or trade on his strength of character for a laugh. Instead, the playwright matches through friendship a man of feeling with one of reason, with the impassioned one (ironically, to be sure) offering at last a fuller rendition of personhood than the reasonable other. Whether or not Alceste sets a good example is a question of belief and of perspective – as is the aesthetic question of whether he *must* do so or not, and according to whose sensibility and authority.

The "Character" of Mr. Dorimant

In theatre, the familiar but uneasy relationship of passion and reason presents an art problem with a long and significant history, dating as it does to the ancient world. In this regard, the Platonic, or Socratic, view is that artistic representation is deceptive by definition and, as such, needs to be guarded against. Artistic depictions of the passions, in particular, should be regarded with suspicion, as feelings can be exploited for cheap effects. Indeed, the imitation of strong emotions, in place of the real thing, may be damaging to an observer's own sensibilities.[10] The standpoint here is not only venerable but also has had enduring implications – as in Rousseau's "Letter" along with other instances of what Jonas Barish calls the "anti-theatrical prejudice." In a related vein, there is Jeremy Collier's inflammatory treatise, "A Short View of the Immorality and Profaneness of the English Stage" (1698), an attack aimed directly at plays of the high Restoration. Collier's target is not so much the passions and their depiction as it is an alleged celebration of libertine behaviors, as evidenced by, say, Mr. Dorimant in George Etherege's *The Man of Mode* (1676) or Mr. Horner in William Wycherley's *The Country Wife* (1675). For Collier, the latter is "horribly smutty," and the former an epitome of Collier's "fine gentleman" who is in fact a debaucher without conscience or scruple (499–500).

In Etherege's comedy, which appeared ten years after Molière's, Mr. Dorimant is shown to care little for an emotional life and a lot for a sex life – in addition to long afternoons at the Mall or the Exchange partaking of witty banter with such good friends as Medley and Young Bellair, prior to their diverting evenings at the theatre where they might well be in attendance with a "mask." Etherege's masterful opening scene, which concerns itself almost exclusively with Dorimant's preparation for his day, dressing and preening and entertaining friends as he does so, draws the audience up close to this character's social circle and to the intricacy of his assignations. It is a scene of elaborate comedic manners along with performative raillery and rites of personal comportment. Together with its ornate and extravagant showiness, though, *The Man of Mode* also introduces a realistic strain that penetrates startlingly behind the masks and public faces of its cast. The result is a scenic dramaturgy that divides cool machination from heartfelt response and, in doing so, probes the character, or lack of the same, of the man who, along with Sir Fopling Flutter, is the play's title figure.

Mr. Collier's admonishment, that "the business of plays is to recommend virtue and discountenance vice," tells us, first, that the author has a conviction of what theatrical art ought to concern itself with and, second, that he would almost certainly disapprove of Mr. Dorimant as a role model (493). Never mind that plays may have other, less moralistic, business or that characters in drama are not always called upon to be upstanding, or to set an example, by necessity.[11] In this respect anyway, Dorimant and Alceste have an important trait in common: neither figure is subordinated to what, ostensibly, are the rules that prescribe the contours of characterization in a given social milieu. Alceste will not, on principle, be cajoled into the ranks of social custom; hence Molière's dilemma in fashioning such a figure in the context of the Neoclassical rulebook. Dorimant, for his part, is so much the quintessential type, the truewit, that he seems an unlikely candidate for reform, even given the charms, graces, and persuasive allure of his new love interest, Harriet Woodville.[12] How could so thoroughgoing a rake possibly give up his coterie of friends with all of their fashionable diversions, not to mention his diverse sexual liaisons and the elaborate games that attend them? It is this very doubtfulness, or ambiguity, that underlies an ongoing question concerning Etherege's intentions in *The Man of Mode*. Was it to satirize, and thereby "correct" the behavior of his licentious wit figures, or to applaud their cool and elaborate style, amorality, and libertinism?[13] For Barbara A. Kachur, the answer is clear, even in consideration of Dorimant's possible future with Harriet at the play's end. Etherege, Kachur asserts, "deliberately shows Dorimant not as the libertine converted, but rather as the libertine confirmed" (122). Alceste will not be tamed into conformity, and Dorimant will not change his spots – which is to say that he cannot alter his own character type, or the dictates of what constitutes fashionable truewit behavior.

Dramaturgically, the nature of this phenomenon – that is, the particular qualities and behaviors of this character type – results in precisely the sort of play of which *The Man of Mode* is so superb a model, in which a stage figure's sense of irony and power of observation, expressed as uncommon wittiness, and of seduction, manifested as intricate romantic machinating prior to what is very often adultery, dictate scenic structure along with character relationships. In this prescription, and for this play, scenes feature witty badinage (as the initial one does), or romantic encounters such as Dorimant enjoys alternatively with Loveit, Bellinda, and Harriet, or they display the intricacies of deceit, pose, and contrivance – as in Dorimant's plan to jettison Mrs. Loveit from his calendar. As an especially clever turn, Etherege satirizes the very content and performance of such scenes, not through Dorimant and Loveit or Harriet but with the latter and Young Bellair as they enact, purely for show and deception, how lovers should behave with each other while courting, and for the benefit of others who may be watching (56–57). The scenic detail of this encounter, with minute attention given to the drawing of breath, exchanges of look and attitude, a modest heave of the bosom or deployment of a fan, is a perfectly executed sketch of Restoration manners and social conventions in action. Yet it is Dorimant himself who most fully embodies the mode and method of the newfound comedy of manners, with all of its theatrical splendors, arch libertinism, badinage, and self-conscious spectatorship.

While Alceste has an abundance of attitudes, he has no interiority. The audience is never allowed entry behind the alternation of diatribe and self-dramatizing display, even in one-on-one scenes with Philinte or Célimène. With Dorimant, the case is similar but with an important qualification. Even as he is a figure of elaborate external pose (but, unlike Alceste, to the near exclusion of forthrightness) Etherege's play contains scenes, especially between Dorimant and Bellinda, of such atmospheric detail that a texture bordering on the realistic is achieved. Still, and although Dorimant claims a readiness to join Harriet in marriage and in the country, it is difficult to trust so drastic a change. He has enjoyed the public life of artifice and manner too much for his promises to her to be taken at face value. He may say, "I will renounce all the joys I have in friendship and wine," and claim that his "passion knows no bounds" – but Harriet is justifiably skeptical (132–133). For Alceste, honesty should be a coin of the realm; for Dorimant, it is largely to be avoided – and, with respect to this character's interiority (such as it is), honesty with one's self can be included in such an assessment. Dorimant is smart, but if he thinks at all it is mostly about his clothes, his wit, his friends, his wine, and his trysts. These are the concerns of his type, and they absorb his mental time to the near exclusion of reflection.

For Dorimant, in fact, there is a notable schism between the social and the personal that his character both represents and enacts. As a theatrical figure, Dorimant is almost completely frontal in his presentation. Comedy of manners during the Restoration demands an elaborate showiness of self – as personalized in the play by Sir Fopling, even more of a fashion plate than Dorimant, who becomes agitated when a room has no mirror in which he can regard his image. The presentational and mannerly style also foregrounds spectatorship – an emphasis upon watching and being watched, among the characters as well as between actors and audiences, reflexively. In this connection, Kachur refers to Dorimant's life as an "unending performance" – a factor that may also encourage skepticism about any possible marriage (108).[14] Alceste, too, is performative to a fault, but in his case the personal show is designed not to deceive but to underscore the importance of undiluted frankness. For him, performance can be a display of intense emotion – vexation, rage, rancor – but for Dorimant, the very act of performing a contrived version of himself serves to disguise or to disavow feeling of almost any kind.

Despite the prominence (and the enactment) of deception in *The Man of Mode*, the carefully wrought masks that are assumed by characters do not always remain securely in place. Mrs. Loveit, among the cast members, is the most likely to lose her cool and betray high emotion, as when she rages over Dorimant's blasé unfaithfulness. Dorimant, for his part, mourns the passing lull in his affairs, as he remarks to Medley:

> Most infinitely; next to the coming to a good understanding with a new mistress, I love a quarrel with an old one. But the devil's in't, there has been such a calm in my affairs of late, I have not had the pleasure of making a woman so much as break her fan, to be sullen, or forswear herself, these three days. (18)

If Alceste had a fan, he might very well tear it up in a pique, whereas Dorimant would never be so demonstrative of feeling. Neoclassical characterization is typically concerned with advancing the cause of moderation; but Dorimant is immoderate, and the comedy of the high Restoration does not commend reason or temperance by any means close to the manner of Molière or the strictures under which he operated.

Theatricality, in *The Man of Mode*, implies a decorative visual style based on conventions of gesture and physical expressiveness, an absorption with costuming and props (cane, fan, snuff box) that can amount to a fetish, an up-tempo pace in the character's raillery, and the versatile use of masking as object, identity, and idea. "Mask," in Etherege's play, signifies a literal aspect of costuming, a female character type of low repute, and the false- ness with which one's face to the world is expected to be presented. The mask, then, is here again a key attribute of dramatic character – though in a very different way than, say, in Greek or Asian dramatic styles. Whereas the Greek mask was meant to convey an essential or dominant aspect of character, the Restoration mask is by nature a falsification and a façade, and one that belies interiority and even individuality. One's invented outer image is what calls for presentation, not one's inner thoughts or feel- ings. Indeed, the private self is so camouflaged, or devalued, in a play such as this that an impression can be conveyed that there is little if anything beneath the show, the clothes, the mask. With reference to a society that was "obsessed with the outward show of forms and manners," Kachur's view is that "despite the attractive or seductive lure of the mask, there is actually nothing behind it" (100).

Again, and with all of that said, *The Man of Mode* stands also for a sur- prising and almost naturalistic departure from such fakery and vacuity – itself a notable aspect of Etherege's dramaturgy. I refer here not to naturalism as it is investigated in the following chapter, but rather to occa- sions when Etherege's scenic approach renders his characters – Bellinda in particular but also Dorimant – an uncommon sensitivity to realistic detail and to authentic, if passing, feelings. Bellinda can be open, unassuming, and without guile – although Dorimant has no scruple about using her as a tool in his romantic games.[15] While Mrs. Loveit flies into snits and rages at Dorimant's gaming and deceit, Bellinda is genuinely hurt by his ways. When they are together in Dorimant's lodgings late at night after love- making (IV, ii), her appeal is for constancy, especially regarding his ploys with Loveit. And, even though she knows that Dorimant cannot recip- rocate her feelings, she cannot imagine herself without him (105–107). Finally, in the last act (V, i), she recognizes the depth of her plight: "I knew him false and helped to make him so. Was not her ruin enough to fright me from the danger? It should have been, but love can take no warning" (127).

In sum, Dorimant is not only unfeeling; he is incomplete as a dramatic character. He is the essence of a Restoration truewit and a superbly effec- tive theatrical personage; his sense of style and his insight into the social moment is without match among his circle; he is well-versed in fashion as well as the best places to dine, converse, and see plays – and yet the view is partial, and the impression of humanity that his character imparts is stilted. In this case, it is not the strictures of Neoclassical prescription that limits a perception of personhood, but the dictates of genre and of what constitutes truewit cool – a reflection of the anti-Puritan, liberated (or libertine) aspect of the historical moment itself. The showing of emotion, in particular, is taboo in this culture. Powell refers to "the emptiness of this life of isolation" with respect to Dorimant, and makes the point that the character is alone even in his social circle and in relationships with the three women especially. The picture that Etherege draws of his central character is one of "lovelessness and boredom," with associations that are "scarcely worthy of the name relationship" (79). Even Harriet Woodville, who can match Dorimant wit for wit, bases much of her assessment and mistrust of him upon theatricality, artifice, and masking – so much so that even near the end of the play (V, ii), she can wonder as follows: "Did you not tell me there was no credit to be given to faces – that women nowadays have their passions as much at will as they have their complexions, and put on joy and sadness, scorn and kindness, with the same ease they do their paint and patches? Are they the only counterfeits?" (132). Dorimant, who is manifestly adept at switching faces, donning disguises, and conveying his character through a deliberate, even automatic dissembling, finally confounds the idea of an actual or meaningful sense of selfhood.[16] He is imminently theatrical and entertainingly so; he is arguably, in all of Restoration comedy, the model of truewit acumen and modishness; yet he is bereft of emotional depth to the point of a handicap.

The Passion of Phaedra

There could scarcely be a starker vision of passion as a power that will overwhelm reason than in Jean Racine's portrait of Phaedra, who embodies an even more extreme polarity between emotion and rationality than her namesake in Euripides's *Hippolytus*. French Neoclassical prescriptions (*les regles*) are enforced so exactingly in *Phaedra* that there is no possible way for the title figure to escape the turmoil that consumes and then kills her as a result of an illicit lust and love for her stepson. For Racine's part, there is obedience to the maxim of the day that tragedy must demonstrate for an audience and society the dire results of immoderate or misdirected passion. Sophrosyne – the Greek ideal of balance and reason – which is so desired yet so wanting in Euripides's queen, is utterly beyond the reach of Racine's character, even though she would prize a respite of mental peace. Indeed, it is not only Phaedra who suffers from affective imbalances in his play. Oenone is so crushed by her mistress's spite that she kills herself;

Theseus is so outraged by what his son has supposedly done that he prays for, and brings about, the hideous end that is suffered by Hippolytus at the hand of Neptune. In his "Preface" to *Phaedra* (1677), Racine allows that the guilt of his title character is ambiguous regarding her implication in, or absolution from, the events of which she is part – a status not uncommon among leading characters in tragedy, which tends to complicate the equally prevalent question of justice, human or divine:

> Phaedra is, in fact, neither wholly guilty nor wholly innocent. She is ensnared, through her destiny and through the wrath of the Gods, in an illegitimate passion by which she is the very first to be horrified. (3)

Racine's perspective here would seem to be accommodating, at least, toward his unfortunate heroine. He clearly sees her as victimized, with a fate that befalls her from without – "a divine punishment rather than a product of her own will" (3). He is appreciative of the horror she feels at her plight and of the resistance she puts up in the face of what cannot be helped.[17] And yet, Racine is finally unsympathetic. Indeed, he is sternly uncompromising with respect to his play's parsing of what is to be admired, forgiven, or deplored, with especial attention to the effects of love as sexual excess:

> The least faults are here severely punished. The mere thought of crime is seen with as much horror as the crime itself. Weaknesses begot by love are treated here as real weaknesses; the passions are here represented only to show all the disorder which they bring about; and vice is everywhere painted in colors which make one know and hate its deformity. (5)

It would be difficult to conceive of a more doctrinaire statement of Neoclassical aesthetics in connection with the depiction of character and genre, in this case a playwright's attitudes concerning the destructive power of emotion in the domain of tragedy. The delineation, and the opposition, of what constitute vice and virtue are, for Racine, so marked as to admit no ambiguity, no shading. Instead, there is a moral absolute that is without leniency, let alone escape, for the "ensnared" heroine.

That Racine's play features an individual agon between a hated passion and the imperative for restraint is obvious, and the fact that Phaedra cannot survive the contest, or the intensity of her dilemma, is without question. What is not so clear is the depth to which these opposing strains are situated within a character's personality, or set in relation to the social understandings of an era, or aligned with the particular biases of a dramatist's art or belief. In the chapter that follows, attention will be given again to the "real person" quandary, which, in short, pertains to how fully a dramatic character can, as a fiction, authentically represent the complexity of self as a unity among mind, body, and other factors of personal identity. From that standpoint, the naturalistic view allows for a totality, as well as an intricacy, of somatic, psychological, and experiential factors that comprise the individual. In this view, a coexistence of passion and reason need not be contradictory but can be assimilated instead into an approximation of the sum and variation that constitute a complete personality. This is not the case in *Phaedra*, and it is neither Racine's belief nor that of his epoch. Remarking on the playwright's dramaturgy as, in particular, an "art of plotting," Francis Fergusson speaks to a prioritization of logic, and the need to show "the tragic life of the soul as reasoning" (50, 53):

> Reason is the sole value: reason is always to be obeyed. From this both the selection, and the arrangements of the facts of the story, follow deductively. Such facts will be chosen as will best illustrate the eternal nature of the reasoning soul: i.e., its life as a conflict with passion. And they will be arranged in such a way as to demonstrate, again and again, the logical inevitability of its choices. So in his plot-making Racine (like one of his own heroes) seeks the cruelest constraints of passion in order to demonstrate to the mind of the audience that essence, that rational mode of action, which he politely assumes we share. (50–51)

The perspective here is self-evident, and it runs utterly contrary to the ambitions of naturalism with respect to the representation of a "real person" by way of lifelikeness.[18]

The purely aesthetic beauties of Racinian dramaturgy are, like his purposeful intensification of emotion in opposition to rationality, commonly recognized. The dramatist's unparalleled intuition of balance, proportion, and economy has long been exalted. Indeed, there is perhaps no more refined an orchestration of Neoclassical symmetries and balances than in *Phaedra*, and no finer articulation of the mechanisms of a cumulative fate, one that may belong to individual characters but that speaks also of a collective destiny, and one that is divine as well as personal. In Chapter 1, I emphasized the extent to which Greek characterization is tied by necessity to gods – a bond that applies directly, in Euripides's telling, to Phaedra and Aphrodite, or to Hippolytus and Artemis. In Racine's play, by contrast, the presence of Venus, and the relation of the goddess to this title character, is more ambiguous. In both cases, however, the conception of a power that overmasters the human is relevant to how the passions are shown and to what extent they can be resisted, or not. In a Neoclassical tragedy such as this one, the dramaturgy must, in effect, be obedient to

an aesthetic mandate but must also make a divine impression manifest, at
least to the extent that the power of a goddess can overwhelm a character
and dictate the action. Even if such a deity is understood only as metaphor, or as the projection of some shared human propensity, the effect on
a character's autonomy within a plot, and on the correspondingly fatalistic
progression, is profound. Turnell observes that "Venus is not something
external to man as she was for the Greeks, but a projection of his own passion which by this means becomes invested with superhuman, with irresistible force. Once Venus appears the issue is virtually decided" (*Classical*
200–201). It is early in the play (I, 3) when Phaedra, reluctant at first, at
last tells Oenone of her torment at the sight of Hippolytus and knew herself "possessed by Venus":[19]

> I stared, I blushed, I paled, beholding him;
> A sudden turmoil set my head aswim;
> My eyes no longer saw, my lips were dumb;
> My body burned, and yet was cold and numb. (23)

In either case, divine or metaphoric, there is a notable, in fact definitive,
authority of Venus over the presentation of character and event, and each
of these has powerful application in a tragedy such as *Phaedra*. Racine's
characters cannot elude the goddess, as divinity or as a stand-in for passion's force, nor can their creator avoid the artistic mandate – or, as one
schooled in a strict Jansenist tradition, the religious one. The artistic climate of seventeenth-century France was shaped by exacting beliefs and
guidelines. For theatre, the results of this authority pertained not only to
a dictating of an art's means of expressiveness but also to its effect upon
audiences: a sense of salutary usefulness within a social milieu, and with a
basis in reason.[20]

    The tragic genre itself, by guaranteeing an array of outcomes and des-
tinies for its characters, carries with it yet another aspect of conformity in
the Neoclassical context. Racine's dramaturgy is one of precision and of
principles that are esteemed as well as obeyed. Its purity owes in part to
the rigorousness but also the terseness of this obedience. Rarely is a play
so intricately wrought as *Phaedra* in its limning of what becomes a terrible
interconnectedness among the intentions of a few select characters, which
turns into a tragic progression almost from the outset. In combination
with the initial situation of Phaedra's attraction to Hippolytus, an intrinsically tragic momentum issues from just a few other causes. Oenone
means only to please her beloved mistress, but ends by betraying her with
Theseus; Hippolytus, by loving Aricia, inadvertently prompts the jealousy

that Phaedra would not feel were it not for the appearance of a competitor; Theseus, with the wrong information from Oenone and disdain for Aricia, dooms his son – and then tries, too late, to mend his hasty error:

> O bring me back my son, and let him clear
> His name! If he'll but speak, I now will hear.
> O Neptune, let your gifts not be conferred
> Too swiftly; let my prayers go unheard. (98)

But Hippolytus has no name to clear; he is innocent of the crime that will destroy everyone anyway. Throughout the relentless exposure of these intertwined relationships and events, the magisterial clarity and tautness of Racine's style is constant, despite the horror that arises from the purposeful or accidental instances of timing and the misreading of circumstances among the characters.

The question of interiority is especially provocative under these conditions, in certain ways belying the Neoclassical norm and making Racine's own tendency to dramatize ideas through characterization problematic. In the French seventeenth-century drama, comic or tragic, the typical pattern is for characters to be demonstrative of a prominent attitude, behavior, or point of view, rather than be reflective or introspective, although Phaedra is, in her anguish, forthcoming about her thoughts. Racinian characters tend to be performative, externally oriented, and declamatory, with passages of stichomythia rarer by comparison with lengthier speeches. For Phaedra, however, the issue is more complicated, owing partly to the volatility of her feelings but also to the way that her mentality is revealed by Racine. She is intensely aware of her emotive state and how it feels in all of its tempestuous variation and terror, and she is frighteningly adept at conveying her anguish. Is it her thinking process, then, that an audience is privy to, or simply her mood as presented, lived through, and described? Is her character "psychological" in the highly qualified way of her ancient predecessors, or in the manner of her own time? Bernard Weinberg theorizes in this regard that Racine connects the play's dramaturgy directly to his character's inner life, in a way that relates it to both a scenic and a thematic progression. For Weinberg, it is the "principle of 'interiority' or the 'intimacy' of the central action" that prompted Racine to place events of most importance "within the soul of his protagonist rather than in external episodes." In so doing, the playwright establishes an entirely unconventional progression, scenically portrayed but centered in his title character as she advances from "one state of soul to another state of soul" (256).

As a dramatic progress, then, that is internally felt but externally presented, the agon of passion and reason is situated by Racine chiefly within
the one character as she moves from a state in which escape is intensely
longed for to one in which it is achieved.[21] At her end point, or *telos*, the
calamity is complete and the results of her sinful yearnings have been
revealed utterly. Through this inexorable advancement, Phaedra is made
to experience an interior rending, or sparagmos, of the sort that I align,
in *After Dionysus*, with a divisiveness that is tragic, per se. In the case of
Phaedra, the alternating, and at times coincident, states of guilt and desire
are enough to ensure such an internal scission, but in the more inclusive
sense the rift also intrudes between passion and reason, with this master
antagonism playing itself out with increasing intensity within the single
character. More broadly, it is the ratio of emotive expression and rationality that takes hold as a broad substrate in the drama of this era, and in this
way cannot help but be manifested on the level of individual character.
Turnell does not exaggerate, in *The Classical Moment*, when he characterizes the "great problem" of the seventeenth century as "precisely the conflict of reason and passion" (14).[22]

What, then, is the authoritative power that brings about so fundamental, intense, and sustained a dramatic conflict at a given time? The
suppression of emotion, or at least a cautioning against unrestrained
feeling, can be seen as a societal as well as individual good; yet there is
also the larger and more inclusive strain – suggestive of a nearly cosmic,
or at least religious, imperative – and the vestiges of this are immanent
in *Phaedra*. Geoffrey Brereton points out, in this regard, that Racine's
characters are seen often as "dominated by a superior force against
which neither personal attempts at self-assertion or man-made (i.e.
social) codes of conduct are of any avail" (272). Also, of course, there
is the ancient Greek aesthetic, most notably Sophoclean, that underlies
classicism and exalts the moderate, the balanced, and the orderly, while
idealizing the rational in the face of immoderation. Thus, a gallery of
persuasive reasons exists for why theatre's attitude toward the volatile
nature of human feeling should, at once, be so definite and yet ambiguous with respect to censure. The nature of theatrical art itself – as a
public and, at times, highly influential forum – has at times added to
the need, not only for depictions that subordinate, query, or caution
against the passions, but also for rules that guarantee such portrayals, if
only because audiences (in full recognition of their own emotive states)
can be so available to persuasion through enactment.

Postscript: Eighteenth-Century "Character"

"Love" can be a passion, no doubt, and it is notoriously beyond reason. There is neither world enough nor time to look here into the vagaries of this versatile phenomenon – and that is not the point here anyway, except to note that the word and its connotations apply variously to dramatic characters, including figures such as Alceste, Mr. Dorimant, and Phaedra, and in the context of varying genres, comic or tragic or otherwise. Alceste loves Célimène and assumes that his love is returned (or he would not love her, he claims) – but he admires her beauty more than her personal qualities, and his feelings come across, even when from the heart, as more amusing or pathetic than touching. Mr. Dorimant loves to love, and seems to find within himself a degree of feeling for Harriet Woodville, but it appears unlikely that so fascinating a game as love (and a game it is in Restoration comedy) will be thrown over for a life of commitment, especially in the boondocks. In *The Misanthrope*, sexuality is all subtext; lovers admire and pursue each other but rarely touch and do not consummate. In *The Man of Mode*, adulterous sexual relations are a daily pastime, but physical desire is played out mostly for the sport. The physicality of Dorimant's affairs is less involving for him than the manner in which he arranges for them, and cuckolds are comical for the sex someone else is enjoying. In *Phaedra*, by contrast, the standpoint on love as an extreme state is so far from anything frivolous or ephemeral that Racine may as well be writing about a different species of the passions altogether. Phaedra is wrenched and torn within, and the mentality that she presents is one of agonizing duress. As if that were not enough, she suffers from overwhelming lustfulness, what Turnell describes as "a phenomenal sexual craving," a condition that can belong to no character of Molière's and to no rake of the Restoration (*Dramatist* 243).[23] Phaedra's "love," in other words, is tragic because it is pathological, solitary, ruinous, and unbearable; it is beyond hers or anyone's control.

Phaedra is a woman of regal stature and also of moral character, despite the blight of Venus. The quality of her passion, even in its destructiveness, is ennobling and her confrontation with it is sympathetic even while horrifying. Alceste is a splendidly theatrical personage and also an individual of estimable character: that is, he is honest, direct, moral, and a champion of truthfulness. By contrast, Mr. Dorimant is not a man of character – quite the opposite – yet he, like the others, is wonderfully successful as a theatrical persona. What, then, becomes of the relation of dramatic character to a representation of "character," upstanding and admirable or not, in and after the seventeenth century – and what is it, in particular, that will constitute a stage figure's virtuousness or cause admiration or emulation at a given time?

I do not mean to suggest that comedies of the high Restoration were negligent of such ethical scruples of the sort that can earn the appreciation of an audience. That would not be true, and dramatists including Etherege and Wycherley are, in fact, conscientious (if modestly so) in contrasting their libertines, poseurs, and liars with more truthful and less sexually compulsive sorts of folk. Bellinda, in *The Man of Mode*, is engagingly frank with Dorimant while Emilia is down to earth and a seemingly ideal match for Young Bellair. Alithea, in *The Country Wife*, demonstrates her integrity by standing by the foolish and foppish Sparkish even as she is courted brazenly by Harcourt, to whom she is clearly more attracted. Characters in Restoration comedy are, of course, not always so honorable, nor do they stand typically as models of such personal integrity. In the century that follows, however, the embodiment of a moral standpoint is more common, more overt, and more applauded – and less of a sidebar to the possibly more intriguing and pleasurable lives of the counterfeits. I call brief attention to this phenomenon, as it applies to the drama of the British eighteenth century in particular, simply as a means of underscoring the larger issue of authority over characterization in the theatre and the impact of such an influence upon dramaturgy.

The idea that a character in drama may serve as a role model emerges quite reasonably from a conviction that public enactments of the behaviors of others can have influence upon society and, as such, should have positive, helpful effects. Characters in plays ought to be appealing, in this view, not only so that an audience will like them and care about their fortunes, but also because such attractiveness can be the result, as well, of how such personages can stand for worthy examples of comportment, ethical choices, and good deeds performed. In Richard Steele's *The Conscious Lovers* (1722), the figure of Bevil Jr. is symptomatic, to say the least, of this tendency. He is profoundly solicitous with respect to the feelings of others, especially his admired father, Sir John Bevil, and dear friend, Charles Myrtle. As he inquires of his dad: "Did I ever disobey any command of yours, sir? Nay, any inclination that I saw you bent upon?" (334). Even as Bevil Jr. admires a young woman, Indiana, he is patient with his father's desire that he marry Lucinda, daughter of a wealthy family associate. Bevil Jr., in other words, is the embodiment of filial regard and of what constitutes noble and selfless behavior within a friendship. When Myrtle misunderstands his friend's intentions, believing that Bevil Jr. does have eyes for Lucinda, the object of his own attentions, a dual nearly ensues – and would, but for the fact that Bevil Jr. is able, through force of will, to rise above his anger. This scene of overcoming enmity is the one that Steele prized above all, as he notes in the play's "Preface," and it all but defines the moral sentimentalism of the day in a comedic context (McMillan 322).[24] In this regard, and in spite of some far-fetched convolutions of story, all turns out for the best, due in large measure to generosity on the part of the characters but also to Providence – a factor that, curiously, has a way of rewarding the steadfast and the good-hearted at propitious moments, with a power of making everything come out right for those who have meant well. Indeed, it is Providence in Steele's play that carries with it the weight of authority associated in other times with the will of gods, with Fortune, or with artistic or ethical mandates from without. It is the well-meaning, self-sacrificing, thoroughly honorable "character" of Bevil Jr. that, in this rarified air of what is Providential, appears to be tied directly to a benevolent, even a cosmic, destiny.

A similar point can be made with respect to George Lillo's *The London Merchant* (1731), although its hero, young George Barnwell, is neither so decent nor so fortunate as Bevil Jr. When poor Barnwell, utterly naive and lacking experience of any sort with women (including young Maria, who adores him), falls for the seductively scheming Millwood, his doom is promised – and is made certain when he embezzles and then murders his uncle at her bidding. And yet, virtue can still abide in one who comes to recognize its value, and who repents, even when execution draws near. "Thorowgood," in fact, is the name of George's generous employer, and it is he who forgives George and promises heaven and redemption in spite of the young man's crimes. John Gay, of course, turns the sentimentality of an age into a mastering irony in *The Beggar's Opera* (1728) by featuring an assemblage of folks who haven't a grain of uprightness among them but are nonetheless funny and charming. The Peachums are conniving, Polly and Lucy are beguilingly cutthroat, and Macheath is a polygamous, lying, whoring, highwayman – and also a thoroughly engaging good guy, the antihero as a leading man. Plays of the later century, especially in the hands of Richard Brinsley Sheridan and Oliver Goldsmith, will also mock or at least avoid the sentimental, but the value of an esteemed "character" – as defined at different times and by varying sources of authority, will survive and thrive in the melodramas of the nineteenth century and for a long time afterward.

CHAPTER 4

Scientific Character: The How and Why of Naturalism – and After

An irresistible current carries our society
toward the study of reality...

We are an age of method, of experimental science;
our primary need is for precise analysis.[1]

Èmile Zola's messianic treatise, "Naturalism in the Theatre" (1881), is a
plea for nothing less than a salvation of the art. For him, theatre was
handicapped utterly by traditions that were worn out, incongruous with
an age of scientific discovery, and lagging far behind the currents of modernism. The vestiges of Romanticism and of tragedy in their imitative
and dilute manifestations were especial targets of Zola's disdain, insofar
as they invariably featured (in his view) exaggerated, phony situations
with characters who postured and declaimed rather than speaking and
interacting as people who were genuine and recognizably resident in
the *now*.[2] Theatre had become histrionic for its own sake, Zola alleged,
and was out of touch with the vitality of an era that should find, in art,
reflections of its own energies and findings. Zola's call, in brief, was for
truthful representation in place of falsehood, and the summons that he
issued was for an unnamed writer of genius who could deliver the naturalistic goods. From where, Zola wondered, would the dramatist appear
who could "overthrow the accepted conventions and finally install the
real human drama in place of the ridiculous untruths that are on display
today" (351).

What avenues might lead, in the latter nineteenth century, toward a
newly conceived, more accurate representation of personhood through
dramatic character? From Zola's perspective, and with "truth" understood
by him as an achievable goal and reasonably objectified value, such a concept would be scientifically based and would emphasize specific markers,
including a precise attention to environment in particular, but also to the
"psychological and physiological study of the characters" that belonged

once to a tradition of tragedy but had been lost (366). With respect to the relation of a stage figure to his or her surroundings, Zola is unequivocal: "The environment must determine the character" (369). Moreover, a naturalistic drama must attend to the biological actuality upon which character should be based. Indeed, a fundamental part of Zola's complaint against the outworn or passé traditions he opposed is that they could never offer "the thorough analysis of an organism, never a character whose muscles and brain function as in nature" (363). Here, then, is a basic crux in the problem of representing the dramatic character as a "real person" – the relation of science or scientific knowledge – for Zola, the analysis of the "organism" itself – to the way in which a fictional theatrical figure is conceived. For him, authenticity of representation in the theatre is tied directly to dramatic character, as J. L. Stynan points out: "In all his dramatic criticism, Zola emphasized the importance of characterization as the best measure of a play's truthfulness" (9).

While it might seem reasonable, if not self-evident, to predicate character upon the most accurate and up-to-date information that is available with respect to the workings of the human mind and body, Zola's call was revolutionary if not entirely new. In the seventeenth century, certainly, neither Molière nor Etherege nor Wycherley would have considered such a project. Their characters owe more to genre, style, and social or political conditions than to scientific understandings, even of the early Enlightenment. The same might be said for Racine, except for the fact that his portrait of Phaedra is, to a significant degree, clinical. He does not set out to depict symptoms of pathology, as August Strindberg will in *Miss Julie* (1888), but he does so nonetheless, albeit in a nonscientific manner. In Molière's case, the closest the dramatist comes to science is through satirical portrayals of quack medicine, and the limning of Alceste has nothing whatever to do with biological or psychological facts, save perhaps for the character's spleen. Even as Etherege's dramaturgy in *The Man of Mode* is naturalistic in certain scenes, his characters, even when shown in intimate encounters, bear scant resemblance to the later prescriptions of naturalism. Whereas a prizing of environment is critical to the design of a play such as *Miss Julie*, Dorimant's lodgings or the home of Célimène or the palace of Theseus matter very little to the question of how one's surroundings might be understood as truthful or, certainly, as formative. This is not to say that locations are unimportant in these plays, when in fact they are manifestly so. What would Dorimant do, after all, without his menu of fashionable places to dine, attend theatre, and be seen? I mean, rather, that the surroundings in such plays are more pertinent, again, to genre and to style than to what forms an identity and contributes to making a person who he or she is.

Nonetheless, a scientific approach to characterization – or, to call this by a slightly different name, a science of dramatic character – has a lengthy history that predates the seventeenth century and has a basis, in fact, with Aristotle and the *Poetics*.[3] Strictly from a procedural standpoint, Aristotle's stipulations regarding character in drama entail both classification and systematizing, as if to define the genus and then the species, moving from a generality to a specific instance. His strategy, consistently, is to differentiate by example and particular case, maintaining a tone of objective analysis in doing so.[4] For instance, in the *Poetics* (XIII), a character's "change of fortune" is considered in relation to plot as, first, a generic issue and, second, one modified by hamartia as a component in tragedy and what is appropriate characterization and, third, a quality pertinent to particular families and, fourth, applicable to specific characters: Oedipus, Orestes, and others "who have done or suffered something terrible" (Fergusson 75–76). All of that said, the Aristotelian definition of character, as *ethos*, in relation but also subordination to *muthos* (plot), is one that came to be disputed, not only by a Romantic sensibility or a modern writer such as Tennessee Williams ("My characters make my play") but also by a naturalist like Strindberg (in *Miss Julie*, at least), who would no doubt advocate for a reversal of Aristotle's hierarchy. From this standpoint, what matters most is not the traits or ethical inclinations necessary for a character-agent's function vis-à-vis events, as the *Poetics* would prescribe, but rather the complex nature of the traits themselves in the context of a story.[5]

I once heard an acquaintance who is a neuroscientist refer in conversation to the "ingenuity of the experiment" as a key to successful discovery, a phrasing that neatly situates the imagination of the scientist in relation to a problem to be solved – or, perhaps, to the demonstration of a solution. There are playwrights also who, though not scientists, create works that might be regarded as ingenious experiments. Indeed, there are many dramatists who might qualify for that description, but the combination of originality and inventiveness with a truly scientific mind is a comparatively rare phenomenon. Strindberg is of this type, and so is that neo-Aristotelian, Bertolt Brecht. Although Brecht's subject matter was not often science-oriented (with the notable exception of *Galileo*), his theoretical writings, including segments of the "Short Organum for Theatre," reflect a consistent awareness of writing, and also directing, for "a theatre of the scientific age" (Brecht 186).[6] Brechtian theory is, of course, wholly and radically at odds with literary or theatrical naturalism, even with the latter's own claims to a scientific basis. In "The Street Scene," his illustrative model and analogy for Epic Theatre, Brecht alludes to a theatre that "will be largely breaking with the orthodox theatre's habit of basing the actions on the characters and having the former exempted from criticism by presenting them as an unavoidable consequence deriving by natural law from the characters who perform them" (*Brecht* 124). Clearly, the target here is naturalism, with its attention to formative environment and psychological factors. And yet, from the naturalist point of view of Zola or Strindberg, it is exactly such observation of "natural laws" with respect to dramatic character that is not only truthful but scientifically so and hence appropriate to an "age of science," albeit one that preceded Brecht's own era by several decades.

Strindberg, Science, and Dramatic Character

For Zola, the imperative was a post-Darwinian, scientifically based naturalism that could deliver, with detailed accuracy, the depiction of stage figures that would reflect actuality; that is, the experience of mentally and physically being in the world of the present day. His panacea for nineteenth-century theatrical excess and falsity was, in part, to end the traditions of depicting persons who "never existed" and to substitute the physiological for the metaphysical in the design of character (354, 367).[7] When he refers to the absence of "muscle" or "brain" of character, he is certainly not arguing that an understanding of anatomy, biology, or neuroscience is a prerequisite to the creation of fictional character. His point is that characters in drama should be representative of actual people and of a knowable reality, a "nature" with which a person is familiar through his or her own experience and observations. In the case of Strindberg, the ingenuity of his experiment in *Miss Julie* is due in part to how fully he responds to Zola's treatise (having failed to do so, at first, with *The Father*, 1887) and how thoroughly that response signifies a revision of how characters in drama were fashioned before this time.[8] Strindberg thought of himself, immodestly, as the deliverer whom Zola had called for – or, in Garner's phrasing, "the 'genius' of the theatre" who "extended Zola's naturalist prescriptions in what one might see as modernist directions" (74). It is no wonder that Zola's insistence on "precise analysis" and a newly conceived "study of reality" would find so apt a follower in Strindberg, whose passion for scientific analysis dates to his boyhood and to a medical apprenticeship in his late teens (Prideaux 45, 59).

In Strindberg's case, as in Zola's, the study of environment was an essential substrate in characterization. So, too, were factors of social class and economic status, gender, ancestry, and parentage – and, as for Zola, psychological as well as physiological factors. In the "Preface" to *Miss Julie*, a document devoted largely to theoretical issues having to do with the designing of dramatic character, Strindberg emphasizes the causes and effects that are anatomized in the play's action: Julie's upbringing (including the personalities and influences from each parent), aspects of her mental and physical states, the contrast of her nobility with Jean's servitude, and the particular time of day and year, including the atmosphere in which events transpire, the "festive mood of Midsummer Eve." Arguing that "the psychological process is what interests people most today," Strindberg places Miss Julie's psyche at center stage. Indeed, much of the drama is oriented toward the "how" and "why" of that mentality. In the "Preface," Strindberg refers to his title character as "modern," as "half-woman," and as a "man-hater," with evidence for such characterizations belonging, in the play, primarily to the reversals of gender brought about by a legacy of confused and confusing parents. With respect to the dramaturgy of characterization more generally, Strindberg makes the remarkable assertion that he has made his figures "characterless": to wit, he has abandoned the restrictions of typed or stock figures in favor of lifelike representations, people neither fixed nor finished, "vacillating, disintegrated, a blend of old and new" (Sprigge 63–65, 69). Indeed, Julie's self-knowledge, if it can be called that, includes the notion that she herself is without character or volition. As she wonders near the play's end:

> Who's fault is what's happened? My father's, my mother's, or my own? My own? I haven't anything that's my own. I haven't one single thought that I didn't get from my father, one emotion that didn't come from my mother... (112)

Does it follow, then, from the "Preface" and the play itself, that Miss Julie is a truthful representation, a figure who can be perceived as actual, as having an authentic existence that is recognizable through her many symptoms? And, do these symptoms (collectively, the how and why of her mental state and current situation) add up scientifically – psychologically, biologically – in a way that can reveal the complexity of her plight and basis for her likely suicide? Strindberg enumerates the reasons for Julie's "tragic fate" – but are these truly explanatory, and are the precepts of scientific naturalism actually up to the task of thorough analysis in so unusual a case? Strindberg's play contains many indices, or symptoms, with a scientific point of reference. Each of the major characters, Julie and Jean, relates the details of dreams replete with pre-Freudian symbolism, and their class and gender combat is given an avowedly Darwinian dimension, with comparative strengths, adaptability, and survival instincts very clearly at stake.[9]

In fact, *Miss Julie* is an anomaly in the context of Strindberg's complete works, certainly so among the expressionistic plays such as *The Ghost Sonata* or *The Dream Play*, and the relation of naturalistic principles to characterization is more profound here than elsewhere. Still, and despite the playwright's efforts toward a truthful and believable inquiry, *Miss Julie* is in many ways not only intensified in its presentation but nearly bizarre in its depictions. Even with the acknowledgment of the title character's failed relationships, lack of a sexual identity, parental betrayals, and psychological distress, hers is a strange portrait indeed. Her behaviors are erratic beyond the bounds of what Strindberg might call "vacillation." For someone so resolute concerning theatrical excess, the exaggerations here are marked. At the same time, though, and solely in connection to the playwright's intentions, the relation of dramatic character to scientific explication is almost clinical in texture: the placing of a subject for analysis within a set of specified (if less than controlled) conditions, and with demonstration of the results. For Strindberg, as Martin Lamm indicates, Julie was not only a character but also a "case" to be dramatized (212).

Just for the sake of comparison, there is a difference worth noting here between the scientific history and medical apprenticeship of Strindberg and the actual medical practice of Anton Chekhov, with associations in each instance with playwriting and with point of view. For Strindberg, the close-up exposure at an early age to a range of scientific studies was conducive to a drama that could be clinically analytic with respect to the underlying reasons for a character's behaviors and interrelations, with *Miss Julie* as the exemplary case. For Chekhov, whose plays share a naturalistic flavor but in ways very different from Strindberg's, the outcome is not so much analytic as it is pervasively ironic. The perspective of this practicing doctor results in theatrical portrayals of life as it is lived, very often with high contrast between what is hoped for on the part of characters and what is actual.[10]

In his "Preface," Strindberg aims for the reader (as opposed to audience) to know the terms of analysis concerning his title character's behavior and circumstances. Chekhov would be disinclined to do that in so formulaic a way. Even as he liked to converse and correspond extensively about his characters with others, as in letters or in discussions with members of the

Moscow Art Theatre including Konstantin Stanislavsky, the works themselves are not built upon such reasoning, scientific or otherwise, even as
they are exacting in their structures.[11] Instead, plays such as *Three Sisters* or
The Cherry Orchard often evince a lack of knowing or understanding – as,
in Olga's mystified plaint at play's end – "If we only knew!" – or Lyubov's
or Gaev's inability to listen to Lopakhin's good counsel on selling the family land before it is way too late. The everyday fabric of existence and of
time, as experienced by Chekhov's characters, comes across often as mysterious rather than as logical or, certainly, comprehensible. When, at the
end of *The Seagull*, Nina and Konstantin share a final encounter prior to
his suicide, there is no empirical sense of what factors have added up to
such an ending for either party, in spite of what the play has told us of
their hopes and plans and desires.

"Real" People

Modeling characters on real people, with reference to gestural or speech
mannerisms along with physical appearance or personality, goes back
to Plato if not to the beginnings of dramatic imitation.[12] On countless
occasions, narrative and dramatic characters have been fashioned with
an actual person as the inspiration or model for the likeness. Many playwrights have turned to their own families for life models, as in the case
of Eugene O'Neill's Tyrones or Tennessee Williams's Wingfields. Ibsen's
Hilda Wangel and Nora Helmer are based largely on Emily Bardach
and Laura Kieler, respectively, while Strindberg's Laura, in *The Father*,
is a reflection of the actress (and the playwright's wife) Siri Von Essen.
Kaufman and Hart's *The Man Who Came to Dinner* features a fictional
cast based on a host of real people including Harpo Marx, Alexander
Wolcott, Noel Coward, and Gertrude Lawrence. By and large, however,
actual persons are not a prerequisite for characterization. The basis for
realistic or naturalistic representation in theatre is the depiction of people and surroundings in ways that are sufficiently convincing to encourage a perception of authenticity. Indeed, the implications of this aesthetic
would be difficult to overstate, given its impact upon all components of
the art, from acting and directing to design areas and the relation of a theatrical event to the spectator.

Simply in regard to dramatic character, however, the realist idea presents an ongoing problem that may be described succinctly as one of correlation between what is understood of the human self and how such
understandings can be shown dramatically, in a limited time frame,

through a representation by writer and actor of personhood. In our discussion thus far, this factor has been characterized as the "real person" quandary or dichotomy, and, though not a conundrum, it is an art problem of considerable intricacy. In fact, the aesthetic representation of character turns especially problematic when disparities are evident between that which is imitated and the imitation itself – in other words, between the human subject, or self, and its artful depiction in drama or in literary narrative. Yet such disparities always exist, and are in fact innate, if only because characters are necessarily incomplete, in either theatre or narrative fiction, by comparison with living people. Moreover, the nature of selfhood as a model for character has, in itself, become more questionable, or ambiguous, in ontological as well as aesthetic contexts – and we shall look more closely at exactly that ambiguity, theatrically and scientifically, in subsequent chapters.

The rift, or disparity, between mimetic artistry and the object of imitation, can apply to any character (even Hamlet, as noted) but is especially marked with stage figures, for whom the circumstances of a life must be communicated with all necessary variety in the span of two or three hours only. Indeed, the built-in problem of realistic accuracy or congruency in characterization is underscored, once again, by specific differences that exist between the representation of character in the theatre by contrast with fictional narrative. In either instance, play or novel, an author with a realist intention may be exacting in the effort to convey verisimilitude. And yet, a basic question persists, perhaps more so for theorists than readers or spectators in a theatre, concerning the degree to which the artistic depiction delivers a "real" person to the eye or imagination or if such imitation is no more than a sleight of hand, a clever trick that dupes one into believing that he or she is confronted with persons like ourselves, when in fact the images that one perceives are prompted by nothing more than words on the page of a novel or in the script of a play.

A great deal has been written to tease out the complexities of this issue, but it remains a worthy discussion and one that is unlikely to be exhausted any time soon, especially as long as scientific discovery continues and differences abide between theatrical and narrative character depiction. These differences are, in fact, fortunate, especially since the relation of character and mimesis in narrative fiction, with its own corollaries regarding truthfulness, is called into question by the very existence of dramatic characters that are designed, in a realist context and others, for the faithful embodiment by actors on the stage. Indeed, any question of what is real or true or believable in the depiction of theatrical character must involve, of course, the actor and schools of acting that prize such qualities. It is no coincidence, in this regard, that Stanislavsky's principles concerning an actor's preparation for a role can align so congruently with the tenets of naturalism – and with a scientific, or at least analytic, approach to the art.

Stanislavsky's techniques, including affective memory and magic "If" along with given circumstances and circles of attention, share an emphasis on precise analysis and the prioritizing of believability and truth in performance. With reference to Zola's commentary on the "organism" of mind and body, it is the actor, in tandem with a character, who is instrumental in the showing of "muscle" and "brain," with physicality and agency manifested as components of the stage spectacle in combination with other aspects of characterization. When science is added to the equation, as when a theorist (such as Zola) lobbies for a scientific approach to dramatic storytelling, or when a playwright (such as Brecht or, more recently, Michael Frayn or Tom Stoppard) fashions the character of a scientist or conceives of a subject or even a dramaturgy that mirrors a scientific process, the depiction of people is tested not only by the contrast of theatrical versus narrative presentation but also by factors belonging to the sciences themselves.

It is curious, still, that critical and theoretical discussions of character have a way of freely intermixing examples from drama and narrative, at times giving scant notice to the contrasts between, say, an author's conception of a Don Quixote or a King Lear, when the differences among genres are so pronounced. From a strictly literary perspective, such a confluence might be unsurprising, given that in each instance, narrative fiction or drama, the clues to character depiction or reception reside in words on pages. But the theatrical factor undercuts this similarity in two important ways: first, the actor brings corporeal embodiment to a dramatic character, and second, the time allowed for stage representation necessitates an economy of presentation that markedly affects characterization.[13] Bereft of narrative description for the most part, dramatic characters are a distilled essence of speech and action, designed for a brief and yet total display. In this relation, the otherwise pertinent ingredient of reading, with all of its receptive and cognitive associations, is subordinated in favor of spectacle, spoken speech, and performed action.

Along such lines, the "real person" dichotomy is not only queried, but also challenged in the theatrical context. In "The Anatomy of Dramatic Character," Bert O. States develops "a characterological perspective on dramatic action: we can speak of action as *that which happens* in a play and we can speak of it as *to whom it happens*" (100). States's "anat-omy," with its own scientific basis, is predicated on the two key terms of Personality and Identity in addition to the base term, Character, itself. For States, Personality has a strongly external presentation. It is "the skin of Character, the 'place' of exchange between inside and outside" (92). There is emphasis here, clearly, on spectacle, on the outward appearance of a stage figure that is qualitatively different from the image of a literary char-acter that may exist only in the mind's eye of the reader or of a theatrical figure that is experienced through reading only. States proposes a connec-tion in this regard between his use of Personality and the Aristotelian idea of "*opsis* or spectacle, whereby the appearance and (I would add) behavior of the characters constitute the objects of our interest" (93). With respect to the "real person" quandary, States stresses the need to "worry the dis-tinction between our perceptions of character in life and a character in a play":

> The fundamental difference is that dramatic character unfolds in the closed field of an art object and a single action ... this much is self-evident, but it is the tension between a character's lifelikeness, or like-us-ness (greatly enhanced on stage by the person of the actor) and his perfection as a self-consistent entity that is doing *one thing* beneath all the things that he does – and moreover doing it in the invisible chan-nel of a precise future – this tension is the key to our fascination with dramatic character. (87)

Personality, apart from States's use of the word and his alignment of it with theatrical spectacle, is terminology with no small degree of slippage. There is, for instance, the way in which O. B. Hardison uses it, which in turn prompts a response from Seymour Chatman. "When we consider human actions," writes Hardison, "we think of them as the outcome of the character and intelligence – the 'personalities' – of the individuals who perform them." And yet, as he suggests (and his models here are dramatic rather than narrative characters): "Hamlet and Macbeth do not have 'per-sonalities' in the sense that living people do. Hamlet and Macbeth exist only as words on a printed page. They have no consciousness, and they do whatever the dramatist requires them to do. The feeling that they are living people whose personalities determine the actions they perform is an illu-sion" (122). Hardison's portrait is, clearly, of a character with considerably less "freedom" than the Hamlet of Harold Bloom or A.C. Bradley, and much more reductive. Directly countering Hardison's assertion, Chatman enters the "real person" fray with a consternated enthusiasm, grappling as he does so with the limitations of dramatic, or literary, lifelikeness:

> Of course Hamlet and Macbeth are not "living people," but that does not mean that as constructed imitations they are in any way limited to the words on the printed page. Of course their existence at the purely verbal level is relatively superficial. Why should we be any less inclined to search through and beyond the words of Shakespeare for insights into the construct "Hamlet" than through and beyond the words of Boswell for insights into the construction "Samuel Johnson"? (117–118)

For Chatman, "personality" is not so much an aspect of theatrical spectacle, as States would have it, as something that *we* give to the characters: "Characters do not have 'lives'; we endow them with 'personality' only to the extent that personality is a structure familiar to us in life and art" (138).

In *The Pleasure of the Play*, States proposes that "we perceive character on at least five levels… the individual, the dialogic, the thematic, the stylistic, and the mimetic" (132). James Phelan, in *Reading People, Reading Plots*, proposes three aspects of character as mimetic, thematic, and synthetic, with the third term standing for the "artificial" aspect of literary character (2–3).[14] To some extent, it is this "artificial" aspect that may complicate the "real person" contradiction, perhaps especially so if dramatic, along with literary, characters are taken into consideration. From either perspective, literary or dramatic, a naïve or at least facile reading of the problem is a possible danger, if only because characters – or at least their creators – go to such lengths to convince us of believable personages, what Phelan calls "creating the illusion of a plausible person" (11).

With all of that said, character can still be understood, aesthetically, from either theatrical or narrative standpoints, and in either case with real-world being and experience as points of reference. Porter Abbott raises a baseline question:

> How and where do characters exist? Do they exist in the real empirical world where people walk about and do things or do they exist the way many conceive stories to exist, as constructions that reside only in a mental realm – in the minds of writers as they write, of readers as they read, of audience-members as they watch, of people as they look at other people? (127)

The particular confluence that Abbott's question points up, a combination of writing, reading, watching, and real-world behavior, captures not only the layered quality but also the live aspect of the "real person" problem – the "live-ness," of course, being one of the quandary's signature qualities, and especially so with dramatic character. Joining up with Chatman (or Bloom, no doubt) one might resist Hardison's consignment of Macbeth and Hamlet to the page alone, since they are dramatic characters that were fashioned deliberately for stage life. And yet, as Abbott points out, "The words on the page describing Madame Bovary or transcribing her words do not refer to a character in what we call the real world, either past or present. There neither is nor was a real Madame Bovary, only marks on a page" (127).[15] And so it goes. The dialectic between text and reader, or play script and embodied character before spectators, will depend invariably upon the words and their reception – and with added twists having to do with the complexities of audience or reader psychology and with indeterminacies of language per se.

The Dramatic Character as Surrogate

The differences between characters that are created for performance or only for reading as a text are vast, and the questions that attend to this are large, too, in existential as well as aesthetic or cognitive ways. The characters that we come to know, in a theatre or in books or on film, accomplish a great deal on our behalf. It is not only that authors invent characters in order to tell a story, but that the figures they create become vehicles for our own experience as observers or as readers. Characters in drama and in fiction are made to look and be like us (a basic feature of the "real person" concern) and as such they represent us and, in effect, stand in for us. In doing so, they profoundly extend our own range of knowledge and awareness which that is necessarily constrained by the limitations of time and individual experience. Characters can, in short, be our experiential surrogates, just like we want them to be.[16] And, here again, a scientific relation to characterization can be pertinent. For this discussion, in fact, I am deliberately accentuating the dimensions of the "real person" question, in its relation to the contrasting genres of drama and narrative writing, in order to bring the scientific factor into yet a bolder relief.

In his "Anatomy," Bert States refers to a jealousy that we may harbor over the *completeness* that is enjoyed by dramatic characters in particular. Ontologically, he says, "we envy all dramatic characters, good and bad alike – not that we want to be in their shoes; we would simply like to *coincide* as they do. We would like to have the slack of indeterminate being taken up, to arrive at something, to *be* rather than to be forever becoming" (87–88). But our debt to dramatic characters (and of course to their authors) exceeds our jealousy. We are glad for their deeds, their thoughts, their interrelations that together become a completeness, which then contributes to our own. It would be a rare individual indeed who has lived the life of Hamlet, but how much would be lost to our lives without that character to let us in on his thoughts? Kenneth Burke, in his pragmatist way, viewed literature and drama as "equipment for living." In *The Philosophy of Literary Form*, he advocates a "sociological criticism of literature," turning literary (or dramatic) art to the practical purpose of application to actual life situations (293). In fact, and with reference once again to Burkean dramatism as described in *A Grammar of Motives*, one might extrapolate *drama*, or at least a dramatic metaphor, as equipment for living, with ratios among agent, act, agency, scene, and purpose having practical application to social relations and interactions as well as theatrical presentations (xv–xvi).[17]

At the same time, characters can always transcend the pragmatic and the utile. They are meant, through their stories, to take us elsewhere, which is often where we wish to go, providing yet another dependency between a character in fiction, his or her model in life, and the reader or spectator. Collectively, these fictions provide both a reflection of the roles we perform ourselves and those that we can only know about or understand from the distance between a text and our verbal imagination or between the stage and we as audience. A factor of need, and perhaps empowerment, applies to characters and the creators of characters as well. Bloom refers, in a related context, to "the particular sense of turning to the genius of others in order to redress a lack in oneself, or finding in genius a stimulus to one's own powers, whatever these may emerge as being" (*Genius* 5). Cumulatively, characters in both drama and narrative traverse a multitude of story lines so as to expand *our* experience, and fill in our world through the description or the enactment of theirs. "One truism about narrative," says Abbott, "is that it is a way we have of knowing ourselves. What are we, after all, if not characters?" (123). And this observation, of course, applies to the people of drama as much as to those of narrative or, for that matter, of life. If lifelikeness is a prerequisite for plausible characterization, so is like-*us*-ness, the credential to be our character surrogates in addition to players in the stories in which we participate. In this regard, it is the power of our investment in fictional characters, our involvement with their stories in relation to our own, that would, at least to some degree, mitigate against their consignment to "marks on a page." Another contrast is worth noting here, between a prescriptive model of character that is generated from authority, as in Neoclassical theory and theatre practice, and the figure who serves as a surrogate, by design or not, and thus offers a different sort of participation on the audience's part with dramatized models of behavior and experience.

Character and the Science Play

With respect, again, to the reification of fictional character – the "real person" illusion – one might look also at the scientific character as surrogate, not only historically but for a time such as now when science-oriented plays are especially popular. Fictional characters, on the stage or in books, carry out an extremely broad and varied range of activities in our stead – adventurous, romantic, intellectual, philosophic, investigatory, and so forth. But the character that stands in for scientific endeavor is invested with particular responsibilities, perhaps especially so when that figure is designed to embody not only a scientific pursuit but also the science itself, as, for instance, in Tom Stoppard's *Arcadia* (1993) or Michael Frayn's *Copenhagen* (1998). In *Arcadia*, briefly, the dramatic character with a scientific bent is young Thomasina Coverly who, with her remarkable curiosity and creative capacity, discovers a version of chaos or complexity theory and of the second law of thermodynamics. Thomasina is brave, relentless, and also charming in her quests to know, qualities that are magnified through her interactions with tutor Septimus Hodge in particular. Stoppard's dramaturgy, including the play's use of split time frames, is by now very familiar; still, I will give particular attention to the ideation of his characters, especially Thomasina and Septimus, in the following chapter. Suffice to say for now that the play embodies its scientific content through an emphasis on the contrasting eras and on the unfolding of patterns in nature as well as in events and among people.[18]

Copenhagen, by contrast, features the actual physicists Niels Bohr and Werner Heisenberg, and focuses on the unexplained meeting between the two in fall, 1941, with implications concerning the development of the atomic bomb. In this case, the issue of dramatic character in relation to the "real person" problem, and to a stage figure's surrogate function, has an added dimension in precisely the sense that Bohr and Heisenberg (and other physicists of the time) are not only historical figures but are also central players in events with wide-ranging global resonances. In effect, these characters, along with Bohr's wife Margrethe, allow an audience access into an intersection of occurrences at mid-century that have had inestimable consequences, not only because of the war's potential outcomes with respect to attaining atomic weaponry but due also to the ongoing results of these scientists' discoveries. In this sense at least, the surrogate experience – that is, the close-up view an audience or reader is afforded from Bohr's or Heisenberg's (or, perhaps especially, Margrethe's) perspective – is harrowing, particularly so given the later development of nuclear weapons that is known to us already.

Like *Arcadia*, *Copenhagen* embodies science in its dramaturgy, especially in scenes in which Bohr and Heisenberg enact, in the blocking, the behaviors of subatomic particles. In other words, the play's expository debates concerning complementarity and uncertainty are reflected not only by thematic and metaphoric attention to how quantum theories play out in the world and among these characters, but also by the actor's patterns of movement and speech in given scenes. Heisenberg, in one sequence, proposes the city of Copenhagen as analogous to an atom, with Bohr's wife Margrethe as the nucleus and Bohr himself as an electron. As Heisenberg speaks, it is easy to envision the actor's movements and interrelations on stage:

> He's here, he's there, he's everywhere and nowhere. Up in Faelled Park, down at Carlsberg. Passing City Hall, out by the harbour. I'm a photon. A quantum of light. I'm dispatched into the darkness to find Bohr. And I succeed, because I manage to collide with him… But what's happened? Look – he's been slowed down, he's been deflected! He's no longer doing exactly what he was so maddeningly doing when I walked into him. (69)

Through exactly this type of interrelation among dialogue, stage movement, and scientific reference, *Copenhagen* delivers successfully on what Kirsten Shepherd-Barr refers to as "an interdependence of form and content that often relies on performance to convey the science" (2).[19]

Both of these plays are widely produced and are the subject of extensive commentary. I mention them here briefly to accentuate the ways in which each one bears on the issue of scientific character and surrogacy, in addition to the "real person" factor that can be weighed in the context of science among others. A more recent play, Peter Parnell's *Q.E.D.*, offers an especially apt example of a dramatic character testing the limit of what constitutes the divide between aesthetic representation and the delivery of a "real" person. The featured character in *Q.E.D.* is named Richard Feynman, reflecting of course the renowned Caltech physicist and recipient of the Nobel Prize for discoveries in quantum electrodynamics. The play presents Feynman as a dramatic character in relation to a number of actual situations in the historical Feynman's life: his current research, earlier work on the Manhattan Project, the Challenger investigation, and hobbies that include painting, drumming, and performing in musical comedies on the Caltech stage. *Q.E.D.* provides a vivid and intimate portrayal, brought all the closer to audiences by the original performer, Alan Alda, an actor whose voice and mannerisms bring Feynman into a familiar and lively proximity. Heightening the immediacy of the life that is depicted is the fact that the physicist is faced with terminal cancer. His notorious, and often very funny, quirks of personality – Feynman as a "character" – are thus placed in juxtaposition with his illness and concurrent efforts to make scientific sense of what is happening to his body.

Thus, the figure of Feynman in *Q.E.D.* provides a particularly illustrative instance of the scientist as experiential surrogate. He is at work on a lecture titled "What We Know" – and, watching him, one is eager to understand what we *do* know scientifically, or glad perhaps that there is someone who knows or will someday know it. Feynman's innovative and unusual scientific methodology, together with his excitement at discovery, allows for a special access to his ingenuity. As he exclaims: "What I did was, I got inside the electron! I put myself *in* nature! As a darting photon. As a particle of light" (35). In such moments, Feynman becomes our representative, as other scientists in other plays can be – to wit, someone sharp enough to get the cosmos figured out on our behalf. The action is arranged so as to bring his confrontation with a deadly illness into direct collision with scientific insight and occasions of hilarity and passion. Toward the play's end, he is still in costume from that evening's campus performance of *South Pacific*, an outfit that includes, absurdly, a chieftain's feathered headdress. He ends up drumming and dancing in his office with a well-intentioned but slightly drunken female student in a sequence that leads Feynman, and the audience, to recognize that more life is still there, still possible for him, at least for a time.

In one sense, then, we meet a figure in *Q.E.D.* that remains a stage character in spite of the strong resemblance to a real person, Richard Feynman. Yet we also encounter a persona with a particular liveliness that, in itself, can provide a litmus test of the borderline between fictive representation and actuality, in this case within a scientific context. Feynman, like Einstein in a broader range of iterations in plays and films and stories, is *our* scientific genius, and in this way represents an audience's collective participation in discovery, in finding out "what we know." We suspend our disbelief, as it were, willing for the actor (as in the case of Mr. Alda) to become for us the late Dr. Feynman with his famous diagrams and infamous antics.

Even so, the antics and the diagrams, not to mention the headdress and the drumming – again, Richard Feynman as a "character" – are consciously theatrical as well as genuine signs of the life that was led by the actual Caltech professor. They help to make Feynman's actual history into a play, and indeed a spectacle. The man that we see on stage is in this respect a figure of theatre, and not of scientific life. *Q.E.D.* has a deliberately fashioned dramatic shape, an exacting order of events, and a number of telephone calls that by no means reflects how the physicist (or anyone) would truly organize a day. Moreover, the science that is talked about is, of necessity, diluted. In accord with the tendency of science-oriented plays, the subject matter must be kept within reach for a nonscientific audience. In this connection, the nature of the theatre itself, including the differences among audiences, cultural and geographical settings, dramatic structures, and time restraints, can be delimiting in the communication of science or even of scientific characters, especially if these are of a typed or stock variety.[20]

This can be the case, too, for a theatrical genre. In the ancestry of science-related drama, Christopher Marlowe's *Doctor Faustus*, referred to by Shepherd-Barr as the "ur-science play," is a case in point. In her words, "*Doctor Faustus's* central concern with the pursuit of knowledge and the use and abuse of that knowledge makes it the archetypal science play, and this concern only gets stronger as the issues of modern science become ever more ethically complex" (17–18). At the same time, *Doctor Faustus* is a species of genre; it is an Elizabethan tragedy, and one that belongs not only to its own epoch but also to a transhistoric lineage of tragic drama. Faustus may have an overarching scientific curiosity, and may epitomize the quest for knowledge and power at whatever cost, but he is also a tragic figure, one who is damned for his transgressive reach into the god-realm. But tragedy is not scientific. Tragedy is Dionysian. Tragic drama began with, and tends finally to confront, some variation of mystery, cosmic or immediate, rather than scientific or empirical problems and explanations. *Miss Julie*, too, is a tragedy, albeit of the modernist and naturalistic variety, and here again there is a factor of genre that belies the scientific intent. Miss Julie's fate may result directly, as Strindberg indicates in his "Preface," from the factors enumerated here in combination with her own psychological idiosyncrasies. But the tragic aspect does not arise from a scientific inquiry into character and situation. It emerges rather from the play's heightened intensities, consisting most notably of Julie's passion in the face of an impossible situation for which she herself, in her deliberate degradation, is largely responsible. To the degree that Julie's fate can be understood as tragic as opposed to scientific, or Dionysian rather than Darwinian, her character is rent by *sparagmos*, not corporeally but through a process of psychological and emotional scission.[21]

There are cases, in other words, in which the most basic conventions of theatre or the necessities of theatrical genre may alter or compromise the scientific content of a play or the depiction of scientific character. At the same time, though, correspondences and affinities among scientific and performative elements have provided for theatrical innovations and, on occasion, with an expanded sense of the stage capabilities of mimesis, as in *Copenhagen*. Yet here, too, limitations are encountered that would belie theatre's ability to fully convey scientific understandings, at least in their pure and possibly abstract forms. As an example I refer again to Niels Bohr, not the dramatic character but rather the actual Danish physicist who recognized an inability of language to capture the science of quantum phenomena. As Alan Lightman describes the problem:

> ... the work of Balmer and Planck, as interpreted by Bohr, suggests that the electron cannot occupy the space between orbits in any previously known way – otherwise it would radiate energy in a continuous manner. Somehow, it is possible for an electron to begin at one energy level, corresponding to one orbit, and suddenly reappear at another energy level and orbit. I have just now used the word "reappear." Bohr uses the word "pass." Some scientists use "jump." But, in fact, we have no adequate vocabulary to describe such phenomena because all of our vocabulary comes from our human experience of the world. And we humans have no experience, no intuition, no direct sensory connection with the atomic world of the quantum. In that world, our language fails us.
>
> Bohr himself was aware of these difficulties with language. In 1928, as quantum mechanics was being further developed, he wrote: "We find ourselves here on the very path taken by Einstein in adapting our modes of perception borrowed from the sensations to the gradually deepening knowledge of the laws of Nature. The hindrances met on this path originate above all in the fact that, so to say, every word in the language refers to our ordinary perception. (158–159)

How then is theatre, or narrative fiction for that matter, to mirror such a concept as "uncertainty," even within a sophisticated context such as that offered by *Copenhagen*, when there is no adequate language to transcend the ordinary and therefore limited perception of the phenomenon?

The question, admittedly, proposes an extreme standpoint. It is a perspective, however, that in its very extremity queries the limits of science plays and their characters when it comes to accurately portraying scientific processes or phenomena. And, by extension, it can also test the ratio of dramatic character to "real person" – that is, if the real is to be depicted in as thoroughgoing a way as is scientifically possible, at the limit of science's own understandings, at given times, of the human subject.[22] In a sense, too, it tests the capabilities of theatrical mimesis in depicting, if not the "real person" for whom a dramatic character stands, then a scientifically conceived reality in which that figure exists. To what extent, then, can scientific inquiry into human activity or behavior, or even nature at large, be imitated with accuracy through dramatic character and action?

Science and Characterization

With respect to plays on scientific subjects, or to theatrical characters who have a relation to the sciences, I have referred here to works having primarily to do with physics, which makes sense given that science's occupation with the nature of phenomena as well as the fact that several well-known plays have that association. Other sciences, with a more direct application to the components of the human mind, body, and self, might include biology, psychology, anatomy, and neuroscience, to name obvious candidates – each with a different sort of pertinence in a dramatic character's possible composition. Whereas Strindberg, for example, prioritized the emotional and physical states of Miss Julie in relation to psychological, biological, and evolutionary understandings of that time, the workings of mind and brain in particular were little known by comparison to standards of modern neuroscience or studies in cognition or consciousness.

What impact then, might advancing knowledge in the brain sciences have upon characterization? Ann Bogart's theatre piece, *Who Do You Think You Are?* (2008), explores interactive behavior – how people socialize and, especially, treat each other based on observed models – in direct relation to mirror neuron function. In narrative fiction, Richard Powers's *The Echo Maker* (2006) centers on events and relationships that proceed entirely from a severe brain injury. Following a rollover crash in his truck, Mark Schluter is left with Capras Syndrome, which takes away his ability to relate emotionally to those who were once close, including in particular his sister Karin. Karin, in her effort to find a cure for Mark's frightening condition, consults with neurologist Gerald Weber who, in his turn, is experiencing a slide into self-doubt and depression. In short, the story relies extensively on the mental condition of characters as experienced by them but also as they are diagnosed medically. Mark Schluter and Gerald Weber in particular are presented, in effect, through the lens of a brain condition, the one traumatic, the other situational. When Weber or Karin is seen by the reader as depressed, it is not because the author has said they are, but because Powers has shown the symptoms and causes from inside his people as well as from without. The pathology is, in effect, shown up close and personal.

On the other hand, perhaps there need not be so strict an obligation on the part of plays or novels or scientific characters to, in effect, *become* the science. Dramatic characters, whether scientific or not, are after all representative; they are fictional and not "real." Were they compelled to be more stringently and scientifically actual, we might encounter plays that, for instance, center directly on the biology of motor response or neuronal behavior, with character behaviors and relationships related directly, if not subordinated, to science itself. If a stage figure can be depicted through association with complementarity or the second law of thermodynamics, as in *Copenhagen* and *Arcadia*, respectively, why not through their synaptic chemistry? Dramatic characters could then have lines of dialogue such as Paul Churchland quoting his wife Patricia – both are professors of philosophy at UC San Diego, and each is involved with the neuroscience of the mind-body problem:

> Paul, don't speak to me, my serotonin levels have hit bottom, my brain is awash in glucocorticoids, my blood vessels are full of adrenaline, and if it weren't for my endogenous opiates I'd have driven the car into a tree on the way home. My dopamine levels need lifting. Pour me a Chardonnay, and I'll be down in a minute. (MacFarquhar 69)

Another extreme view, to be sure, especially if applied to a character instead of a "real" person. Yet, even if some balance is called for between knowledge in the sciences and a view of dramatic character as truly lifelike, attention might still be given, in that combination, to progress in scientific learning and how that can impact the creation of those fictive individuals who mirror us as we are – much like the case of Zola and his call for a naturalistic revolution that would suit the discoveries and the people of his own era.

CHAPTER 5

How Characters Think

The change is coming. I can sense it.
And I feel that it's coming closer.[1]

Characters in drama may think a great deal or not very much at all, and differences have been noted already between plays that emphasize and require thought on the part of the dramatis personae and those that do not. In very general terms, it is likely that a dramatic work that features outward show, such as the stylishly performative features of Restoration comedy, will give lesser priority to a character's rumination, introspection, or ideation per se than to, say, the display of appearances, mannerly behaviors, and badinage. With respect to genres other than the comedic, it is likely also that works that are dependent upon complications of plot and on suspense – the melodrama, "well-made" play, or mystery, for example – will emphasize the order of events over the complexities of inner being. Here, then, lies the familiar question of what is plot or character-driven. The issue is, of course, much more elaborate and subject to variables than such a generality would imply, and we attended earlier to how Greek tragedies, with their reliance on the mask as a stamp of character that is deliberately external, could be reflective also of the mental states and even thinking processes of the characters. A Neoclassical tragedy such as Racine's *Phaedra*, albeit with its reliance upon an increasingly tragic sequence of encounters and misreading of events, is designed in large part to provide an audience with a searing look into the title character's psychological state and emotional temper. In the case of *Hamlet*, it is the cognitive subplot, based as it is on the convention of the soliloquy, that allows Shakespeare's title character such opportunities for contemplation and self-revelation, thus offering audiences a finely wrought yet fragmented drama of internal experience – a superior character's interiority complex, as it were.

Indeed, the concept of interiority is often associated, as in *Hamlet*, with inward reflection or, more broadly, with consciousness itself, a quality that can be manifested positively in dramatic characters as attentiveness to experience, acuity of awareness or knowledge, or as a marked sensitivity to surroundings and the moods or actions of oneself and others. On the negative side, of course, there can be lesser gradations of these same qualities. And yet, the question of how characters think pertains to more than interiority by itself might suggest, especially when the term is meant to signify a totality of inner experience. Actually, and depending on the particular play or character, when the workings of a mind are dramatized together with actions planned or taken, wide-ranging modes of thought can be shown, including (to name just a few) reasoning, deduction, cognitive association, memory, intuition, or prescience – as in Master Solness's sensing, quoted earlier, of Hilda Wangel's imminent arrival as "youth" in *The Master Builder*. By way of specifying such varieties of mental activity, I classify them apart from modes of feeling and affect – in a way similar, perhaps, to the division of reason from passion that we have examined. Such a distinction can, of course, seem artificial as well as categorically useful, in that a character's thinking, much as a person's, will likely reveal itself in combinations of reason and cognition with the emotional. And, just as characters think and feel differently from one another, the types of thought that belong with different plays will be various in accord with imperatives of dramaturgy, including scenic structure, genre, use of language, and thematic content in addition to character traits themselves. *Miss Julie*, for example, is a noteworthy instance of how the drama of a character's state of mind can align directly with the precepts of a genre, such as the bias of naturalism toward the showing of formative environments and psychopathology, in this case with a notably tragic aspect. And, while Miss Julie's characterization may not be conceived as presentational on the playwright's part, she is consciously theatrical and self-dramatizing. She "acts out" an array of abuses and misconceptions and is unusually forthcoming about her neurotic fixations. On the face of it, at least, she would seem an apt subject for psychoanalytic critique. And yet, it is not Miss Julie's thinking that drives the story's action, it is her symptomology – or, in Strindberg's conception, her maladies and compulsions along with their histories as comprising a case for scientific demonstration. Indeed, Julie is probably right when she insists to Jean that she has no real thought of her own, but only parental influences.

The degree to which a character in drama is psychological or not, or available to inquiry by psychoanalytic means, is less important here than the aspect of thinking itself in relation to story structure and other dramaturgical factors. This is not to say that dramatic characters cannot be productively analyzed through their psychological makeup, which is by no means the case. On the contrary, they can be eminently available for such probing, on their own terms or as models for syndromes encountered in psychiatric research or practice, as in Sigmund Freud's reference to well-known stage figures as representative of "character types."[2] Countless psychoanalytic portraits of theatrical characters have been, or could be, assembled, and figures such as those included here already might be seen as particularly appropriate for such investigation, with Hamlet serving once again as prototype.[3] Is it truly possible, after all, to query the incestuous quality of his relationship to Gertrude, not to mention the relation to Ophelia or Claudius, without weighing such factors as archetypal, Oedipal, and unconscious aggressions and associations?

The linkage of psychoanalysis with drama has, by now, a familiarity that can border on the pat, with a history that dates at least to Freud and, later on, to psychodrama as a concept with a broad spectrum of usages and applications. Like Freud, Jacques Lacan used dramatic characters as signature points of reference, interpreting Antigone or Hamlet and, in the latter case, with "desire" as a master motive behind the Prince's actions (or lack of) and relationships, especially with Ophelia.[4] However, and despite such well-known associations of character and psychopathology, the concern of this chapter (with one exception) is not with that aspect of analysis per se, with its corresponding attention to diagnoses, motives, or subconscious impulses. The focus, rather, is on specific types or patterns of thought as demonstrated by stage characters and how these are represented dramatically. I am especially interested in cases where it is a character's thinking, and quite possibly a manner or style of thought, that propels the action of the play or narrative story.

The Character of Intellect

By way of illustration, I refer first to a literary character famous for the originality and acuity of his thought process: C. Auguste Dupin, the prototype for Sherlock Holmes and the focus of narrative attention in Edgar Allan Poe's "The Purloined Letter" (1844).[5] It is notable, in fact, that Dupin is not a dramatic character, even as much of Poe's story is dependent upon dialogue and scenic encounters. Its outlines are familiar, but suffice to say here that the stealing of a letter by Minister D –, with an intent of blackmail over a royal, has prompted the police, having failed to find the letter themselves, to consult M. Dupin. Dupin, in his turn, is able to match a quality of superior intellect with that of Minister D –, and thereby surmise his opponent's method of hiding the letter, in plain view, within his apartment. Dupin arranges for entry with Minister D – on the premises, recovers the letter through a diversionary ruse, and receives a reward from the flabbergasted police. This is the story in its basic movements, with these latter events proceeding directly from the unique keenness of Dupin's insights. The story is straightforward in the telling and extraordinarily complex, at the same time.[6]

What, then, is Dupin's intellectual process? As in the case of his later imitation, Sherlock Holmes, Dupin has a power of attention that is distinct from the norm. Rare, too, is his ability to observe and to arrive at conclusions through inference. He has a particular flair for combining the analytic with the creative or imaginative. The sophistication of Dupin's train of inference centers also on his ability to anticipate a basic fallibility in human perception and preconception, and to transcend it. He realizes immediately that Minister D –, also with full awareness of how searchers might expect the letter to be hidden, would "be driven, as a matter of course, to *simplicity*" (344). Thinking, in this instance, relates on the one hand to a cerebral match-up of the opponent figures, but is relevant also to how cognition, and perception generally, tend to operate, with emphasis on what is truly observed and not. Psychology, in this case at least, pertains as much to how phenomena are experienced or seen, and to shades of awareness, as to any of the characters' motives.

To say that Dupin's thinking drives the story forward is true enough, but to a larger extent the originality of his inferential method *is* the story. He hears what needs to know, develops a hypothesis, visits Minister D – 's apartments, secures the object in question, and leaves a clever facsimile in its place with an appropriate note for the finder.[7] In this relation, then, a character's way of thinking becomes a story's primary motivator and, thus, center of the reader's involvement.[8] Again, though, Dupin is not a dramatic character, despite Poe's emphasis on speech and scenic atmospheres. "The Purloined Letter" is more an exposition of Dupin's mind than a depiction of conflicts, complications, or even of actions taken. Whereas Sherlock Holmes would figure dramatically in plays and films as well as in Doyle's stories, Poe's fashioning of Dupin is much less available to theatrical portrayal. His inward process is the topic of interest, and what is seen or not in "The Purloined Letter" (a cerebral aspect in itself) emerges from what is received by a reader rather than observed by an audience.

The demonstration of a fictional character's intellect, whether in literary narrative or drama, is a particular challenge by comparison to the portrayal of known high intelligence. It is one sort of project, in other words, to depict the mind of a famed physicist and Nobel laureate such as Richard Feynman or Niels Bohr, another to dramatize, say, the brilliance of the fictional Thomasina Coverly, in *Arcadia*. In addition, the presentation of a mind by theatrical means is a very different prospect from such portrayal through narrative telling. In *Q.E.D.*, which is all but a one-person show, the inventive (and, many times, comically oriented) mind of Richard Feynman is given more or less continuous focus and celebration, and the audience is familiar with many of his points of reference, scientific and otherwise. With *Copenhagen*, the relation of the atomic bomb's development to the war and to the scientists involved in the Manhattan Project is also broadly known, and the credentials of Bohr and Heisenberg need no proof or substantiation.

Thomasina and *Arcadia*

Regarding the fictive Thomasina Coverly, however, Stoppard must demonstrate the quickness of her profoundly original and creative mind through what she thinks and says, primarily in scenes with Septimus Hodge, or through what is discovered about her later on by researchers in present time, and by Hannah Jarvis especially. Just as Dupin is aware of Minister D – 's status as both poet and mathematician, Stoppard dramatizes genius through combining, in Thomasina, the scientifically rigorous with the daringly imaginative. Just thirteen years old in 1809, she is irrepressibly curious and determined to solve problems that she is smart enough, in the first place, to recognize are there to be figured out. Her thinking is initiated through curiosity and wondering, moves from the conception of a problem's contours toward angles of approach, and arrives at theory, with hypotheses consistently refined along the way. "What a faint heart!" she chides Septimus, "We must work outward from the middle of the maze" (37). Thomasina *must* know. Knowledge, for her, is an imperative, whether the topic is thermodynamics, complexity, fractal geometry, or sex.

Indeed, Thomasina is driven to solutions, with unwavering confidence in her own deductive prowess and powers of ratiocination. And, she keeps on thinking for herself as well as demanding answers from others. The play begins with her coy question on a nonscientific subject – "Septimus, what is carnal embrace" (1) – but moves quickly to higher mathematics:

> If you could stop every atom in its position and direction, and if your mind could comprehend all the actions thus suspended, then if you were really, *really* good at algebra you could write the formula for all the future; and

although nobody can be so clever as to do it, the formula must exist just as if one could. (5)

Her reasoning, which combines a talent for inference with intuitive leaps, moves the action in *Arcadia* in several ways and with extensive reverberation in the story overall, affecting both time periods in the play. Her ready mind and inventive spirit so charm her tutor that, by the time she is sixteen going on seventeen, in 1812, she and Septimus are in love.[9] When she dies in the fire that he might have prevented were he not her teacher and also gallant, he pursues her theories mathematically to the point of madness, becoming known finally as the hermit of Sidley Park. Knowledge is a passion in this play, as both Septimus and Thomasina illustrate (as do those in the present day), and passion is by no means sequestered from reason. Instead, these two aspects of being are shown to be complementary and, in fact, mutually necessary, with neither one in need of modulation or correction, as in eras past.

Characters in *Arcadia's* contemporary setting – Hannah, Valentine Coverly, and Bernard Nightingale – cannot know what the audience sees directly of Thomasina and Septimus and, as a consequence, their thinking is often misguided or flat out wrong about what has taken place in the past. Here, too, the manner of a character's ideation determines the action – even if such thinking is wrong-headed – and is consequently central in Stoppard's dramaturgical design. To wit, the strategy is to depict persons in two different eras who have objects and artifacts (and tortoises) in common but only sporadic understanding of the relevant facts, and hardly any of the people or the relationships between them. Valentine can barely stand to admit to Hannah what he knows Thomasina has discovered; Bernard is mistakenly convinced, based on misinterpretation of evidence, that he has unearthed a literary scandal in connection with Lord Byron; and, as for Hannah, it takes time for her to realize that the student, not the tutor, was the genius of Sidley Park.

Stoppard's dramatic plan relates directly to his characters' thinking in precisely the sense that their thoughts in two time periods are consistently, if implicitly, compared through alternation in the scenic structure. Determinism, which makes up a goodly share of the playwright's focus in balance with free will and agency, is queried by Thomasina, puzzled over by others, and actualized tragically by Septimus. Stoppard is no naturalist, and yet the questions of how and why are very much under scrutiny in *Arcadia*, as is causation and related patterns in nature. Stoppard is, of course, famous for plays that put the cerebral at center stage, often with an ironic perspective, as a brainy comedy of manners. His *Travesties* (1978) features a character, Henry Carr, whose thinking is also determinate with respect to the play's structure and the telling of events – but it is the older Carr's vainglory, eccentricity, delusion, and faultiness of memory rather than any sort of intellect, let alone genius, that affect what is recalled and, consequently, the sequence of what the audience hears and is shown.[10]

Of Two Minds: *The Master Builder*

Thomasina Coverly and Septimus Hodge comprise, as it were, an ideational duet. Each character thinks independently, but in Stoppard's dramaturgy, and within *Arcadia*'s dramas of discovery, they are mutually dependent upon each other. Septimus is necessary for Thomasina's education and also the revelation of her insights – what she finds out and tells him for the audience to comprehend.[11] Plays do not often relate the story of a mind in isolation, and even *Q.E.D.*, with its focus on the lone figure of Richard Feynman, is peopled by all of those with whom he speaks by telephone, as well as his student Miriam Field. More often, a play that showcases thought is organized so as to exhibit a mind in action on a particular idea or strategy, and to this end there is frequently a secondary figure, one whose role it is to aid in dramatizing intellect or other mental capacities through interaction. Hamlet needs Horatio, and Poe supplies Dupin with the nameless but necessary friend who can relate his story, as in the case of Holmes and Watson. At a basic level, this arrangement is founded upon the convention of the confidant, which dates at least to Seneca – upon the imperative, that is, for a dramatic character to have a listener and, quite possibly, someone who will understand or empathize with what they are told. Philosopher John Searle may wonder, "… how do I know that other people have minds?" And further, "How do I know that you have a mind when the only mind that I have direct knowledge of is my own mind" (*Mind* 12, 13). Still we must assume that ours is not the only intelligence around – and, for that matter, if anyone among us can empathize with Searle's question, we might reasonably deduce that mind is a shared phenomenon. With respect to the character of the listener or dramatic counterpart, this figure can also be an embodied projection of inner conflict. Just as an individual with a dilemma can be of "two minds" (with that word's double "m" standing in niftily for its meaning) so too can a division of mind be sorted out into two characters. Or, there are cases where, as in *The Master Builder*, two characters are sufficiently codependent to be "consubstantial," to borrow Kenneth Burke's

term.[12] When Hilda arrives, as "youth," at Solness's door, she comes prepared not only to claim her Kingdom of Orangia but to know and assist
in his thinking – and she can, because hers is so available to, and reciprocal with, his.

Halvard Solness's mental state is, from the outset, placed by Ibsen at
the foreground. Solness is troubled, remorseful, and apprehensive of his
own powers and proclivities, and he is obviously in crisis with respect to
career and marriage as well as psychological well-being. In Ibsen's story,
like Poe's, it is not simply that a character's thinking is the primary motivator of plot; the working of Solness's mind *is* the story, as in the case of
Dupin or, for that matter, Feynman. Solness, too, is a unique figure, and
he is well aware of just how distant from the norm he is. He has a troll,
is prescient, believes that he can call upon his "will" for desired events to
occur, relies upon abstract "helpers and servers," and identifies with what
he calls "the impossible."[13] To demonstrate, and also to put these traits
and beliefs to a test, Ibsen situates the drama on a border, ambiguous
at times, between what is realistic and what can be construed as supersensory or metaphysical. I have written elsewhere and at length about
this character, so for the purpose here I will only stress the relation of
Solness's thought to that of Hilda Wangel and to Ibsen's manner of presenting their individual, as well as conjoined, psychic sensibilities – and
with emphasis on how these affect the order of events and also the play's
genre.[14]

To say that Halvard Solness possesses one of the most extraordinary minds among characters in modern drama is no exaggeration. The
uniqueness of his mental capabilities (and debilities) is apparent not only
by comparison with others in the play but also in a psychological field
that extends a range of effects markedly beyond the builder's individuality. If it is true, in other words, that Solness can inspire events through
an exercise of will or wishing, as he believes happened with his hiring of
Kaja Fosli, the impact of his mental powers extend well beyond the personal. The same is true for Solness's "luck," remarked upon by Aline and
Dr. Herdal as well as by Solness himself. The pattern of fortune in his life
is not simply happenstantial nor is it situated within himself only. There
is a pattern to his "famous luck" and, once again, too much of an impress
upon others for it to be a strictly individualized phenomenon.[15] Rolf
Fjelde observes that in Ibsen's later plays in particular, characters can be
viewed not only as individual figures in the storytelling but also as "aspects
of the mind, interacting components of the psyche" (*Ibsen* 781). Indeed,
the "two-mind" phenomenon can, albeit in rare instances, be broadened

into a multiplicity of roles that cumulatively expand the parameters of an otherwise localized mental life.[16]

This effect, of two minds or more comprising a portrayal of psyche, is rarely more vividly portrayed, if abstractly so, than in the duet of Solness and Hilda. Introducing his translation of *The Master Builder*, Fjelde counterpoises the play's "objective" and "subjective" aspects, and while I am not convinced that Solness represents an "objective psychological study of character in crisis," there is certainly an interplay, within this figure, between what is recognizably actual and what is dramatized as a linkage of mind with the metaphysical (781). Solness's power of intuition – sensing arrivals, anticipating occurrences, guessing at divine intentions – allows him a perspective through the veil, as it were. Even his guilt, which pertains mostly to a personal torment over the death of his sons and the consequences for Aline, seems to play out in some larger field of implication or exoneration, linking him to a pattern that transcends the play's past or present and leading finally into the argument with "Him" as the divine and controlling power. Yet this drama, concerned as it is finally with personhood in both immediate and supersensory contexts, would not be conceivable without the other, consubstantial mind – that of Hilda Wangel.

She, too, is attune to psychic realms outside the quotidian, and this, in essence, is what bonds her with Solness and enables the encounters in which he can, as it were, open his mind to her. Hilda's appearance at the Solness's door, ostensibly coincidental yet deliberately ironic on Ibsen's part, can be read also as a response by Hilda to the master builder's unspoken beckoning, despite his fear of threatening "youth." If Solness has in fact called for her, it is because he is in desperate need of a personal correlative: the imperative, first, is that Hilda understand him, and second, that she conjoin with him, that they become truly "consubstantial." Ibsen depicts Hilda as in tune with a different music, even as she can attend to Solness (and also Aline) with attentive directness.[17]

Hilda can, at once, be manifestly present in the immediate circumstances and not, as if listening and responding to conversation but also to an inner voice, simultaneously. Ibsen calls attention in his stage directions to Hilda's eyes, as they reflect the variations in her moods and as they watch and track Solness or turn inward to her own soundings. Or, her expression can be veiled, with a sense of "peering deep within herself" (847). There is a pivotal moment in the second act when she has "an inscrutable look in her eyes" following Solness's question:

> Don't you believe with me, Hilda, that there are certain special, chosen people who have a gift and power and capacity to *wish* something, *desire*

something, *will* something – so insistently and so – so inevitably – that at last it *has* to be theirs? Don't you believe that? (830)

He tells her of the need for "helpers and servers," which have to be summoned from inside: "But they never come by themselves. One has to call on them, incessantly – within oneself, I mean" (830), a reference perhaps to an earlier psychic signaling to her. The coparticipation is obvious as Solness tells her of the fire, the death of his children, "the crack in the chimney" that was not the fire's cause, and "the impossible," which she claims to know, too:

SOLNESS (*seriously*). Have you ever noticed, Hilda, how the impossible – how it seems to whisper and call to you?
HILDA (*reflecting*). The impossible? (Vivaciously.) Oh yes! *You* know it too? (826)

The "impossible," though known by both or mutually intuited, is also enigmatic, various, and at times ineffable, in spite of the shared recognition. The "impossible" is what cannot be done but must be accomplished – as, for example, an atonement by Solness for the death of the boys or for the loss of Aline's belief in his ability to build a true home. The "impossible" is delivering a Kingdom of Orangia to one's princess, exactly ten years following a promise to do so. The "impossible" is Solness attempting to recreate, despite his vertigo, the day at Lysanger when he was observed by the younger Hilda (so she says) as he climbed the spire of his church to hang the ceremonial wreathe – and she would, of course, share in this "impossible" glory, and hear once again a "singing in the air" (859). Yet the "impossible" is also what no person can do: to face up to "Him" and claim an equal power, as Solness says he did once and will do again.

SOLNESS. I'd never in my life been able to climb straight up to a great height. But that day I could.
HILDA (*jumping up*). Yes, yes, you could!
SOLNESS. And when I stood right up at the very top, hanging the wreathe, I said to Him: Hear me, Thou Almighty! From this day on, I'll be a free creator – free in my own realm, as you are in yours. I'll build no more churches for you. Only homes for human beings. (854)

The "impossible," finally, is what calls forth the tragedy: Solness's fall from the tower as a consequence of all that has come before and now brings about his final ascension. But Hilda had to prompt him, too; she was "consubstantial" not only in spirit or in mindset but in the actual terms of his fate. Without her urging to "do the impossible again," Solness would not be so rash as to climb once more to such a height (856). *The Master Builder* is authentically, even classically, tragic in its portrayal of a mortal in impossible relation to a god realm, but it is tragedy also in its portrait of an interactive mental process – the two minds that it takes to bring about such an ending for the one.

Two Minds in *Equus*

Peter Shaffer's *Equus* is no tragedy, but in common with *The Master Builder* it features the portrayal of two minds with interconnections that comprise the core drama. Martin Dysart is a psychologist with a specialty in disorders of young people. Alan Strang is his patient, and it is Dysart's job to discover why Strang has, in the stable where he works, blinded six horses with a metal spike. By looking at *Equus*, I depart somewhat from the bias of considering only the manner and the dramaturgy of how characters think, as isolated from psychological interpretation itself. And yet, this play's particular relation of patient to doctor, and the staging, as it were, of Alan's mentality, also bespeak a relation of mind, or two minds, to dramatic form.[18] The spectacle itself has a classical basis, with ancient referents, and recalls both the starkness of the Greek orchestra and the centrality of the chorus – in this instance, the stylized group of horses and the one, Nugget, that Alan rides in midnight ceremony and worships as a god. And the stage must be sufficiently open to ensure a scenic sequence that consists primarily of Dysart's sessions with Alan and that centers on the young man's memory – his recollection of the key events that are then reenacted.

The Dysart way of thinking is shown in two ways primarily: his professional, analytic approach to Alan's case and his own introspection, which takes the form of direct address to the audience, as if in soliloquy. His analytic technique is conversational and experiential, as he patiently encourages Alan to relate what has happened to him from a young age. By contrast, Alan's mode of thought is associational, a connecting of one image, experience, or impression to another, often with considerable distortion resulting from how his mind translates or comingles them, as the image of a horse's head with prominent, staring eyes taking the place, on a wall in Alan's bedroom, of a particularly agonizing view of Christ crucified. Together, the modes of thought that belong to these two characters comprise the basis of Shaffer's dramatic scheme. As Dysart goes steadily about the business of searching out Alan's most influential points of association, the audience sees them in a way that allows for its own assimilation and interpretation of the evidence. By the play's end, enough has been revealed of Alan's beliefs to allow for insight – a "why" – concerning the blindings, and enough has been shown of Dysart's doubts, including his dissociation from any sort of worship, let alone ecstasy or celebration, to reveal a man who now questions the "Normal" and is estranged from the modern world even while belonging to it.[19]

Although *Equus* is not tragic, it contains and portrays the Dionysian. Alan's midnight ritual, in which he rides the horse god naked while intoning and exulting in his ceremony, conjures the Greek *ekstasis* and *enthusiasmos* – the simultaneous separation from self and the infusion of a god's spirit. Although *Equus* does not resemble *The Bacchae* literally, its manner of invoking and embodying the god is ancient in its means. Though violent in the scene of blinding, the play is not untamed in the fashion of its ancestor or innately ruinous by comparison to the primal sparagmos and the death of Pentheus. It does, however, dramatize mystery conjoined with passion in a way that is religious in its essence if not its particulars.[20] Alan's associational thinking has, in this way, incorporated a translation of images and occurrences into a structured ceremony with a transcendent purpose. The audience is able to see, along with Dysart, the effect of Alan's upbringing by a devout mother and atheist father, the biblical stories she would tell, specific occasions such as riding the horse Trojan on the beach when Alan was little – all of which add up to a mentality as well as to a crime with its worshipful yet utterly mistaken basis. Dysart's inquiry centers not only on parental influences or patterns of learning and association on Alan's part, but also sexuality, which pertains to both the idolization of Equus and to Alan's failed lovemaking with Jill, as witnessed in the stable by the all-seeing horse god. With an instilled belief that God has eyes everywhere, Alan's mind cannot bear the contradiction of sexuality apart from worship, and the eyes of gods must be mutilated (44).

Through spectacle and ceremony, *Equus* evokes an ancient, ritualistic theatre, and in doing so delivers the truth of Alan's passion together with an authentic, if wrongful and brutally destructive, act of religiosity on his part. But the play also portrays Alan's confusion, and a mind that is not sufficiently trained or educated to make better sense of its influences. As William W. Demastes writes in *Staging Consciousness*, "Alan experiences guilty obsessions inherited from his upbringing, reflections of contemporary cultural dysfunctions, and he inserts them into his 'primitive' Equus religion" (135). Dysart, for his part, knew about sacrifice before knowing Alan. He has spent plenty of time already with his art books imagining glories of the past that can never be experienced, but his mind is altered nonetheless by his acquaintance with Alan. Hence, it is with a certain regret that Dysart goes about the "cure" of his young patient, depriving him thus of the ecstatic as well as the erroneously devout. *Equus* is conceived and constructed as a mystery, not only in the religious sense but also as a "whydunnit," with a scenic structure that guarantees the progression toward an adequate, if not complete, solution. From another angle, though, *Equus* is a play of two minds, a drama that arises directly from two interwoven modes of thought, with the one in supposed aid of the other. The fact that Dysart is, in his way, bereft at the play's end is due in part to a recognition that his thinking has not served him entirely well, despite his expertise in the thoughts of others.[21]

Collective Mentalities

By focusing so intently on the dyad of Strang and Dysart, *Equus* does not open itself truly to a larger field of mentality, even though each of these characters has other close relationships including the familial. The parental influences of Dora and Frank Strang are vital to Shaffer's portrait of Alan's early impressions and associations and of how they came about. But the Strangs are ancillary by comparison with Alan and Dysart, certainly insofar as the mental life of doctor and patient is linked directly to the play's core subject and to the succession of events. Alan's parents have had a formative impact on his psyche, to be sure, but they are not truly part of the play's broader mentality, in spite of that influence. The drama of actual collective mentality is, in fact, quite rare, and while we have looked here at States's theory of "world character" in *Hamlet*, that is by far the exceptional case. His proposition, that members of a dramatis personae are "made of each other," pertains more generally to factors of dramaturgy and play making than to a sharing of psychic components per se, although such aspects can pertain (*Hamlet* xx). And, the theory applies well beyond Shakespearean drama, and is in fact more inclusive than limited. States's view, again, is that the perception of individuality in theatrical characterization arises significantly from interrelationships and from the opportunities characters give one another for self-revelation and indeed, for becoming who they are. This is not to say that *Hamlet* cannot be looked at gainfully from a psychological perspective and even a collective one, but rather to observe that the mental context is not necessary, in itself, for such a standpoint on character relations. By contrast, we have seen that in Ibsen's late plays, including *The Master Builder*, the character field is very apt to be psychologically based, at times with reference to allegory or symbol, as in *When We Dead Awaken*, especially. The same is true of the major plays of Anton Chekhov, but in ways that are different from Ibsen and, of course, with the reflection of shared psychology through dissimilar dramatic structures.

In the case of Ibsen, it is clear that Halvard Solness and Hilda Wangel are two minds that are wedded centrally in the drama, and that the former's intellect and patterns of thought – guilt, prescience, and so on – include by necessity other figures such as Aline Solness especially but also Ragnar and Knut Brovik, and Kaja Fosli. Chekhov does not favor this type of construction, in which less prominent figures are used to enhance the psychological portrait around core characters. Rather, his tendency is to imbue an ensemble with a mentality that characterizes the group as well as individuals – albeit to greater or lesser degrees – and can include, along with the persons represented, what is atmospheric and even what is inanimate in the surroundings. One is accustomed to thinking of Chekhov, as it were, in terms of thought, and the panpsychic aspect of his plays has been recognized at least since Leonid Andreev described it in 1912.

The philosophical or intellectually deliberative qualities of Vershinin (*Three Sisters*) or Lopakhin (*The Cherry Orchard*) or Konstantin Treplev (*The Seagull*) have been evident, quite possibly, from their invention. These characters are remarkable, indeed, not only for their individual qualities but also in the distinction of each from a larger group. Vershinin's philosophizing, and his ruminations on the future of humanity, may entertain and endear him to Masha, but they are also idiosyncratic to the point of eccentricity and set him apart from the Prozorovs and members of his regiment alike. Lopakhin must struggle continually against the fixed and apparently immovable biases of Lyubov Andreyevna and Gayev, persisting nonetheless as the son of serfs to urge upon former masters the sale of their orchard and estate. Konstantin, convinced of the need for a daring and newly innovative theatre, is an outcast among many of his acquaintances, including his own mother, Irina Arkadina. Still, and concurrently, all of these highly singular figures, each with a pronounced attitude and style of thought, is part of a more inclusive and, in Chekhov's hands, even a universally situated mental landscape.

Here it will be useful to recall Andreev's descriptive vision, the spirit of which is not uncommon with respect to Chekhovian drama but is remarkable nonetheless for the time of its writing (just a few years after Chekhov's death in 1904) and for the rarified stage world that it conjures:

> Chekhov's specialty is that he was the most logical of panpsychologists. If in Tolstoy often only a man's body is *animated*, if Dostoevsky is exclusively

devoted to the soul itself, Chekhov *animated* everything that meets the eye: his landscape is no less psychological than his characters; his characters are no more psychological that the clouds, stones, chairs, drinking glasses and rooms. All the things in the visible and invisible world take part only as components of one vast soul; and if his stories are only chapters of one vast novel, his things are only thoughts and sensations scattered through space, a single soul in action and spectacle.

Chekhov's art, along these lines, is a "theatre of psychology" – and, adds Andreev, it is "the theater of that panpsychism whose purest representative in literature was Anton Chekhov." In such drama, not only people but "even things perform" – and "things are not so much things as the scattered thoughts and sensations of a single soul" (239–240). Panpsychism, the venerable notion that mind is a universal phenomenon and is shared, is applied in this case to that uncommon species of drama in which a collective mentality is linked to, and representative of, a play's entire world, including its atmospheres. Moreover, the collectivity itself is part of what lends Chekhov's plays an impression of consciousness as well as of thought, here again an extraordinary achievement in theatre by comparison with literary narrative. We will return to precisely that comparison, but suffice to say here that just as the problem of interiority must differ markedly between theatrical and narrative portrayals, so too does that of depicting consciousness, which is typically a much more elusive matter.

Interiority, for Chekhov, is a matter of profound fascination, even when his characters appear to be vacuous or callous or when their behaviors seem pointless or inane. Although we are not led to see deeply into Natasha in *Three Sisters*, we know what she is up to. Her devious craft and casual cruelties may be appalling, but the match-up of her narrow and determined mindset with the Prozorov sisters, and Olga in particular, is splendidly appropriate to Chekhov's drama of heartbreak, loss, and crushed values. With more complicated and less off-putting characters, of course, Chekhov is unequaled at eliciting the inner person, often by placing him or her in ironized relation to circumstances as well as to others. Here the Chekhovian cast is large indeed, but I will isolate Masha, also in *Three Sisters*, as one example among many. She is exemplary of a woman who cannot help but open up her thoughts, confessing finally her hopeless love for Vershinin – only to be left alone and devastated, stuck with her hapless husband Kulygin, when the regiment of soldiers, including her beloved "lovesick major," leaves their town. As so many have observed in one context or another, the final tableau of *Three Sisters* is a perfected moment, and Andreev himself calls attention to the playing of the band as if in counterpoint to the misery of those abandoned. Indeed, that sequence is for Andreev another instance of panpsychism, of that "single soul" in represented action, an instance when "all the protagonists of the play are thinking and feeling to the rhythm of the military march which, as if by chance, is being played in the street by the departing soldiers" (239–241).[22]

The idea of a group interiority, possibly counterintuitive, is pivotal nonetheless in Chekhov's dramaturgy, and here the playwright's evocation of his characters' inner lives, in combination as well as in relation to what surrounds them, is a matter of sophisticated dramaturgical portraiture indeed.[23] The scenic structure of Chekhov's works, as is commonly known, depends upon finely orchestrated interactions in a pattern that appears on the surface to be random or haphazard but is in truth exacting, with precise attention given to juxtaposition and ironic counterpoise. In this milieu, the characters behave symphonically, although they do not realize this, performing their tasks and delivering their arias in intricate movements. Their thoughts, singly or in combination, are brought forth to the tempo of this music. And, as the dramatist weaves all of this – thought, action, progression – into a perspective of time, such thinking, such interiority, becomes enveloping, total, and even cosmic in its purport.[24]

Familial Thoughts

Chekhov's drama is concerned often with family relations, as exemplified by the Prozorov sisters and brother, or Lyubov Andreyevna with her daughters and brother Gayev in *The Cherry Orchard*, or by Konstantin and his mother in *The Seagull*. Even when Chekhov's people are not blood-related, however, they can still share the familial aspect, especially with reference to what is shared or cumulative among them. This is true especially insofar as Chekhov's tendency is to populate his plays with characters that represent a full spectrum of years, from childhood to old age. More inclusively, though, the drama of family relations is an important subset of the collective mind in characterization, and it is not at all restricted to the Chekhovian vision. Family drama tends not to center on the "two mind" duet, if only because the dramatis personae are comprised typically of a larger field of interplay – involving of necessity parents, children, and siblings of various ages. And yet, even as the portrayal of families has been vital in the theatre for many centuries, ever since Greek tragedy and Aristotle's commentary regarding which houses are most appropriate for evoking the tragic feeling, the "family play" as a generic species is more common to recent times. While dramatists including Euripides, Shakespeare, Molière, Racine, Etherege, and countless others have put on stage groups of characters that share a blood relation, a conjoined mentality tends not to be the salient quality. There are exceptions, to be sure, and who would question the collective thinking among, say, the Capulets or the Montagues – or the Macbeths? Indeed, tragedy itself is built upon a history of internecine entanglements, rivalries, and vengeful retaliations, often with savage connections among related family mentalities as, again, in Webster's *The Duchess of Malfi*. Or, in a comedic vein, it would be difficult to miss the fact that Molière's Orgon, his mother Madame Pernelle, and daughter Mariane are not only related but bonded in their thinking, and perhaps appallingly so, as if being closed-minded or easily duped are traits that can be inherited, as in *Tartuffe*.

Even so, the drama of family interrelations, especially when expressed as a coparticipation of thought, is a mark of more recent drama, and one with a particularly American cast, one might say. Eugene O'Neill's *Long Day's Journey Into Night* is an epitome here, but a spectrum of American plays and playwrights are also representative, especially when the factor of memory is accentuated and called upon to conjure a family's past by way of vitalizing the present. Memory, of course, is imperative among modes of thought, for characters in drama or otherwise: in one sense, it is all that we have. For the playwright, all that is needed is a character who can recollect what the audience must know, at a given moment in the storytelling. Yet the dramaturgy of memory is quite a bit more versatile than such apparent simplicity might imply. In fact, entire dramatic structures can be built upon it, with a corresponding incorporation of a thematic basis, as in not only O'Neill's play but also in Tennessee Williams's *The Glass Menagerie*. Each of these plays has a unique dramatic structure and means of storytelling, and each is dependent upon the presentation of thought, especially memory, as depicted in concert with a mentality that is familial and collective among the characters, even as each one retains his or her own singular traits and individuality.

Because these canonical works are so broadly familiar, I will limit discussion here to what is especially pertinent in the relation of thought to dramaturgy and, in particular, to style of presentation. In brief, O'Neill's play uses the passage of one day only as the frame for his "four haunted Tyrones" to recall what has wounded them most, beginning with the marriage of Mary and James that brought unexpected sacrifices for her, the death of their baby Eugene and the blame for that on son Jamie, the difficulty of Edmund's birth and the corresponding onset of Mary's morphine addiction, and Edmund and James's recollections of all that they could and could not be. The very substance of the play is memory – but more specifically it is recollection accompanied by guilt, remorse, blame, and apology, in a recurring sequence.

The exquisiteness of O'Neill's dramatic pattern resides in the cumulative import of this reiterated cycle, which takes the place of dramatic event per se and propels the action forward even as it lays open the past. Hence, the manner in which the Tyrone family members think, and are aware of each other's thinking moment to moment, is crucial, and it must be choral and symbiotic even as it appears to be individualized. Or, put differently, the audience must sense the unspoken, unacknowledged agreement on the part of each Tyrone that he or she will always remember and, try as they might to the contrary, never forgive what they have done to one another – hence the cyclic progression. The voices are personal, but the core of O'Neill's vision is a familial chorus with each member knowing all too well the songs of the other. Memory, for the Tyrones, is a curse and also a destiny. They cannot forget the slights, hurts, or the disappointments, not to mention the tragedies of their shared past. From Mary's image of the girl she was before marriage to all that has resulted of that union, the Tyrone memory is both comprehensive and tragic. Indeed, it is one memory, expressed as a four-part fugue, and the telling of it, based as it is in the playwright's own family history, comprises the entirety of O'Neill's dramatic plan.

To situate the drama within the mind and memory of a single character is a different proposition from the purely familial, and one that may correspond also to the precise order and the tone with which a sequence of events is orchestrated. "The play is memory," Tom Wingfield tells us, and indeed all of *The Glass Menagerie* is built upon what Williams's narrator recalls of why his escape from mother Amanda and sister Laura became, for him, so necessary. "In memory everything seems to happen to music," Tom says, and the way in which he recalls events is nostalgic and elegiac, in spite of whatever rage or empathy he may have felt in some moment that is past. This, too, will affect the style of presentation as a connection, once again, of thought and dramaturgy. As Williams writes, "memory is seated predominantly in the heart." Or, from his "Production Notes" for the play:

> Being a "memory play," *The Glass Menagerie* can be presented with unusual freedom of convention. Because of its considerably delicate or tenuous material, atmospheric touches and subtleties of direction play a particularly important part. Expressionism and all other unconventional techniques in drama have only one valid aim, and that is a closer approach to truth. (xix)

The "truth" of Williams's story, or of Tom's, resides in Laura's fragility, her ethereal and broken loveliness, in their mother's well-intentioned but ruinous hopes and fantasies – and, significantly, in Amanda's own embellished memories of jonquils and gentleman callers. For Tom, the poetry that he relates as drama, as in the short story that preceded the play, is his memory of a "girl in glass."[25] Whether the particular scene is Laura's room, or the dinner table, or the parlor on the night of Jim O'Connor's visit, it is the memory of the one character that delivers and also colors all that transpires. What is collective and familial, the shared experiences of the three Wingfields, is contained also in what is singular and personal, as occurrences are related dramatically as a succession of recollections within the mind and sensibility of Tom only.

Memory, like a personal history, is something that we cede to characters in drama, whether it is germane to a particular play's telling or not. That is, since any person without a prohibitive impairment has memory and depends upon it for continuity and the sense of coherent experience and personality, we take it for granted that characters enjoy the same faculty. We are aware, too, that memory is subjective, and often less than accurate, in spite of the pride we may take in the acuity of our own powers of recollection. If Amanda Wingfield were to remember the same family dinners and arguments that Tom does, would her story be the same, or would Laura's? At the same time, though, most characters in drama are not in any particular need of a memory, and certainly not one that spans a lifetime. The focus here, however, is on cases where memory is essential in both characterization and dramaturgy – and to the linkage of both. One could infer, certainly, that memory is an imperative in *The Master Builder*, in that Halvard Solness is plagued by past events and that the veracity of Hilda's report of her experience at Lysanger is shown to be questionable even as it is vital to Ibsen's story. In *Equus*, Alan's memory is necessary so that he can recall what has happened to him for Dysart's understanding. In each case, memory is a requisite and, in *Equus*, is related directly to the structure of events. Alan's retrieval of his past is what turns into the scenic demonstration of what has formed his beliefs and, indeed, his religious fixations. In that case, the dramaturgy of two minds is wedded also to a past and to memory.

In Arthur Miller's *After the Fall*, the setting is one mind only, that of Quentin, a lawyer who, through recollection, is in the act of putting his own life on trial. Here the dramaturgy of remembrance has a direct correlative, not only in Miller's scenic structure but also in the psychological mechanics through which one is reminded of a past event – which in turn prompts the memory of another. In this arrangement, memory is, and is analogous to, the events that are depicted dramatically, in an order that is determined by what reminds Quentin of what – and, as a consequence, what his particular fixations are. His thinking, like Alan Strang's in this way only, is associational, but the points of association are not always clear. Something will remind Quentin of his mother, for instance, and he wonders why she has entered the mental picture on stage (111). His mind keeps returning, nonetheless, to certain topics, occurrences, and people, and so the play dwells thematically and purposefully upon exactly what is on Quentin's mind. And, once again, the mentality that is dramatized has both a familial and a collective aspect, as Quentin's memories are focused mostly on his closest relationships – with family members as well as, especially, his marriages to Louise and to Maggie and his friendships with Lou and Mickey. Miller's dramatis personae are alive inside Quentins's head, but his thought process, while necessarily subjective, is in no way nostalgic. There is no fiddle in the wings, as Tom Wingfield would say. His thoughts are typically inquisitive and analytic, and related directly to events in the world – the war, HUAC and McCarthy, the Holocaust, Party associations, instances of public and private morality – as well as to the personal choices that he has made for the better or worse.

Turning attention from the drama of one person's memory to a character's represented consciousness would seem to be a logical and straightforward step. The drama, or theatricality, of interiority is always a matter of turning the inside out, and the means of accomplishing this aim are numerous and varied. Hamlet has his soliloquies, Alan Strang his formative history, Quentin his self-evaluation and personal trial before a bench that has no judge. And, theatrical means of displaying interiority can at times be connected directly to a play's style in addition to its organizational principles. In Sophie Treadwell's *Machinal*, for example, the inner life of a Young Woman is revealed through expressionistic, often psychologically tortured, interior monologues, with the audience led to feel precisely the panic or claustrophobia or fear or revulsion that the character endures. "But, I can't go on like this, Ma – I don't know why – but I can't – it's like I'm all tight inside – sometimes I feel like I'm stifling! – You don't know – stifling" (193). The Young Woman's thinking is neither logical nor reasoned, but her emotions are vivid and, for her, real – and they come across on stage with an arresting and visceral immediacy.

Whereas I have focused deliberately in this chapter on thought as discrete from feeling, the more probable case, again, is that characters in drama, like ourselves, will experience these in unison.[26] In consideration not only of thinking per se but of consciousness and its means of presentation in the theatre, the intricacy of this combination must pertain. It need hardly be stressed that theatrical characters can be strongly emotive, or that affect is key to an audience's response to dramatic storytelling. What does Miss Julie feel, in given moments, toward Jean, or Solness for Hilda or Aline? What is the passion that Alan feels as he becomes one with his god in midnight worship? What is the felt quality of Quentin's remorse, or of Solness's? What are the levels and shadings of awareness that belong to these characters, and how do such variations of knowledge or insight or sense of being arise?

Consciousness

The problem of representing consciousness is different from the depiction of thought per se, and the issue is distinctly dissimilar with respect to theatrical art by comparison with narrative fiction. In this area, indeed, the means of both the portrayal and the reception of a character can be starkly contrasted, with the subject of imitation varying widely in accord with the genre. The revelation of consciousness is, in truth, among the sharpest of divides between dramatic and narrative characterization. In addition, and ironically, even though we are accustomed to graciously ceding consciousness to fictive characters, just as we do memory or a personal history, in this case are all but blind to the workings of the very attribute that we so generously grant. We may understand memory, or believe that we do, but we are flummoxed by consciousness – when we take the time to think about it, that is.

More often, we are pleased to take for granted what remains unsolved (in its more abstract dimensions, anyway) by science and is among the most profound enigmas that humans are aware of. As David Chalmers writes in *The Conscious Mind*: "Conscious experience is at once the most familiar thing in the world and the most mysterious. There is nothing we know about more directly than consciousness but it is far from clear how to reconcile it with everything else we know" (3).[27] As in the case of thought or thinking in general, however, dramatic characters are not necessarily in need of a portrayed consciousness. This is not to say that they need not be awake and alert to their respective worlds, but rather to observe that this particular and rarified variation of interiority, including perhaps the depiction of a mind's awareness, is not often probed and is frequently unnecessary in the drama. That said, the showing of consciousness theatrically by contrast with literary fiction is a formidable art problem that, in specific connection with how characters think, calls for a refined elaboration, and we shall do so here and in this book's remaining chapters.

Whereas literary narrative succeeds by various means in the delivery of this subjective and elusive phenomenon, theatre is constrained by certain key factors, including time and physicality – that is, on the stage, within a proscribed time frame, consciousness must be embodied, performed, and observed; it is not a reading experience. This variance, of course, goes to the heart of the difference between these arts, and for purposes here I will elide the fact that plays are as often read as seen, stressing instead that they are meant to be actualized in performance. Strictures of theatre, in this context anyway, might be seen as prohibitive, at least to the extent that a portrayal of consciousness, elsewhere a possibly vital component in characterization, may not be considered as a realizable, and certainly not a compulsory, goal for dramatic art.

That, however, is an extreme and exclusionary view, and in fact there are instances, unusual as they may be, in which theatre is capable of eliciting a capacious view into what is arguably the core of our mental activity, at least in its relation of mind to self and world. The question remains, however, of when, and why, the intent of a dramatist might take a play in this direction. It was observed earlier that consciousness relates positively to degrees of awareness, to knowledge and knowingness, and to alertness with regard to surroundings. While consciousness is individual, it necessarily includes an apprehension of other people, and of the fact that others possess this same trait. We have noted, too, the likely association within character, as in people, of the emotive and sensory together with the cognitive or intellectual. Antonio Damasio advances the case for a linkage of conscious awareness and knowledge with feeling – "Conscious states of mind are *felt*" (*Self* 168) – and has also emphasized the narrative affinities of human consciousness. In *Consciousness and the Novel*, David Lodge calls particular attention to Damasio's findings (and *The Feeling of What Happens*, in particular) to underscore how much of the "recent scientific work on consciousness has stressed its essentially narrative character," and refers also to Daniel Dennett's *Consciousness Explained* on the connection of self and mind with storytelling (14).[28] The reference of Damasio or Dennett is, of course, not to fictional characterization, except perhaps through illustrative example – but rather to the actual means through which the mind conceives and conveys a coherent awareness of itself and for itself, and of inner and outer realms, at once.

What, then, is the relation of a "feeling brain," as Damasio would have it, or of an arguably innate tendency on our parts toward story structuring, with regard to dramatic or narrative character and to states and understandings of consciousness?[29] A provisional response, at least, can be offered with reference to the brothers William and Henry James, singly and in combination. In *The Principles of Psychology* (1890), the former refers famously to the internal progression of a person's thinking as a "stream of consciousness," while the latter turned increasingly in his novels toward shadings of thought and to levels of his characters' internal awareness, often including their thinking, as reflector figures, about others with whom they interact.[30] The insights and findings of these two are, of course, familiar if not requisite touchstones in the project of defining and of representing consciousness – and there are points of contrast as well as intersection between them that are highly germane with respect to the translation of a scientific premise or inquiry to an aesthetic one. In particular, there is the difference between the psychologist's "stream of consciousness" that is suggestive of progression, sequence, and temporality by comparison with the novelist's idea of consciousness as a "chamber" – with one's sensibilities, in Michael Gorra's phrasing, "like a spider's web suspended within it, capturing everything that comes within reach of its filaments" (235).[31] The aspect of time, yet again, pertains in this instance, doing so in the specific sense of duration. That is, the portrayal of a process of thought, or of conscious being within a time sequence, is quite a different matter for a stage as opposed to literary character, even as each imitates the experience of actual, living awareness.

Henry James's image of a "chamber" is, it would seem, more concerned with what consciousness is rather than what it does; his image does not, in and of itself, imply a reference to time. In this scenario, Shakespeare (for example) is able, in effect, to stop time – or at least a play's stream of events – so that Hamlet can exist, in isolation, within the stilled time of a conscious mental chamber, as it were. But the soliloquy, especially when concerned chiefly with a character's interiority, is by far an exception in drama; and theatrical characters are generally not allowed such a luxury with respect to time, let alone a philosophy of being. By comparison with that particular stricture on the presentation of a conscious process in drama, and at the risk of anachronism, let us turn to what is perhaps Henry James's most famous characterization and to a well-known occasion of her self-awareness and manner of thought.

Isabel Archer is described in Chapter 6 of *The Portrait of a Lady* as "a young person of many theories; her imagination was remarkably active. It had been her fortune to possess a finer mind than most of the persons among whom her lot was cast; to have a larger perception of surrounding facts, and to care for knowledge that was tinged with the unfamiliar" (51). The balance of James's chapter is given to fully characterizing that mind – fully, that is, for her age and range of experience at this point early in the novel. Dramatic characters are not, and cannot be, like this. No such extended, authorial description of a mentality is possible in the actual embodiment and enactment of a stage figure. Much later in Isabel's story, after her unwise marriage has led to thinking of quite a different sort from when she was younger and more free in regard to self-determination, James devotes the entirety of chapter 42 to a lengthy rumination on Isabel's part as she sits alone through the night at Palazzo Roccanera, contemplating her situation with regard to her husband Gilbert Osmond among others until the fire has gone out and all the candles are burned down. Here, too, so sustained a focus on a character's mental process is almost exclusively the province of a literary rather than a theatrical imagination – although James's narrative style can, and often does, feature dramatic as well as scenic rendering.[32] Isabel's thoughts in real time would, after all, more than exceed the boundaries of duration for the stage. James's portrait is, of course, in large part exactly this, a picture of Isabel's mind over a span of time. In addition, his portrayal of her consciousness is significantly one of mental activity but also of states and gradations of awareness. Jamesian consciousness, as Gorra puts it, pertains to "how one knows what one knows," with *The Portrait of a Lady* itself being "a drama of the perceiving mind" (199, 311).

James's novel may not be drama in actuality, but in terms of knowledge or awareness at least, there are distinct similarities between what is possible in theatre or in literary narrative with respect to basic questions of representing consciousness. Isabel Archer is unaware of, or reluctant to confront, what everyone else realizes and tries to warn her about – to wit, Osmond will take away her freedom and reduce her to misery. The recognition of this comes to her in gradual increments of sensing and perceptiveness, intuition and observation. Dramatic characters, too, are available to consciousness of this variety, and the drama, as it were, of dawning and progressive awareness is by no means unfamiliar. Indeed, the message from the Ghost in *Hamlet* instigates this pattern, and Oedipus provides the ancient archetype for a variety of plot based centrally on what is known or not, and at what time. Consciousness, however, bespeaks more than knowledge or awareness. Gorra refers to James's artistry, especially in his later modernist novels, as a catching "of the human mind in the second-by-second act of perception" (300).[33] For Isabel Archer, certainly, thinking *is* the depicted action, even (or especially) as she sits alone in the darkened room, its own mental chamber, for all of chapter 42.

To know or not to know isn't the only question, however, and the depiction of awareness must be concerned also with what exactly is known and with what intensities and implications. The fascination of *Hamlet* is, in large part, concerned with the volatile effects of an expanding knowledge upon a particular sensitivity of mind. *King Lear*, too, is a tragedy built upon catastrophic realization, with both definition and destruction of the title character predicated on what is learned about himself and his daughters, and the utter starkness of what results. Tragedy, says I.A. Richards, is not "an indication that 'all's right with the world,' or that 'somewhere, somehow, there is Justice'; it is an indication that all is right here and now in the nervous system" (246) – and I know of no more succinct statement of tragedy's severity with respect to the solitary self, especially in its relation of mind and what is somatic in a moment of cataclysm.

Chekhov's characters in *The Cherry Orchard* arrive also at awareness, albeit slowly and with much resistance, thereby providing, in concert with Lopakhin's urgings to the contrary, a resonant center for the play's dramatic conflicts. Lyubov cannot bear to be truly conscious of her situation, and knowing too much, for Chekhov's people, is to live on a precipice: consciousness as an incipient ruin of the self. For Ibsen, too, consciousness can be associated intimately with tragedy, never more so than in *The Master Builder* and *When We Dead Awaken*, the latter being, in fact, what Brian Johnston calls a "tragedy of consciousness" (180). Each of these late plays is concerned predominantly with depicting the felt experience of a complex mind in confrontation, not only with surroundings or personal history or of oneself among others, but with a hyperconsciousness of a sort that can only precede a passage beyond the quotidian.[34] In spite of such particular and sophisticated variances, though, the portrayal of consciousness as mind and sensation as well as awareness, with a spectrum of implicit complexities, remains problematic in relation to dramatic character and to theatricality.

Aesthetic difficulties arise here fundamentally in the relation of character and audience by comparison with character and reader. The construction of a fictional consciousness is, in effect, a different project entirely for the dramatist and for the novelist – even, again, as the object of imitation remains the same for both. And, correspondingly, the translation or reception of a depicted consciousness varies immeasurably, based on the sensory experience of watching and hearing versus that of reading. In truth, the apprehension of characters theatrically, as visibly embodied personages, may allow for a more ready granting of qualities such as memory, personal history, or consciousness by contrast with the reader for whom such elements may require more detailed elaboration. By contrast, though, the act of reading facilitates a direct communication of one interiority to another, an intersection of minds that must in itself be psychological. Georges Poulet describes the phenomenon of reading a book as a transcending of the material object, the "falling away of the barriers between you and it. You are inside it; it is inside you; there is no longer either outside or inside." He, too, as reader and not as audience, is familiar with the ceding of traits, including that of consciousness itself:

> At the precise moment that I see, surging out of the object I hold open before me, a quantity of significations which my mind grasps, I realize that what I hold in my hands is no longer just an object, or even simply a living thing. I am aware of a rational being, of a consciousness; the consciousness of another, no different from the one I automatically assume in every human being I encounter, except that in this case the consciousness is open to me, welcomes me, lets me look deep inside itself, and even allows me, with unheard-of license, to think what it thinks and feel what it feels. (57)[35]

CHAPTER 6

Anti-Character

Can you tell me who you are?[1]

Luigi Pirandello's *Six Characters in Search of an Author* delivers nothing less than a seminal statement on the phenomenon of dramatic character. In doing so, it complicates, confounds, validates, but then finally refutes what has been considered thus far as the "real person" quandary, and accomplishes all of this as a concurrent, if paradoxical, discourse. In brief, this play in performance brings an audience into live proximity with other actual people who are actors rehearsing on a stage who, in their turn, attempt to make sense of the six fictional Characters who arrive at the theatre (also, of course, actors). The Characters demand that their own story be told – in part because, as The Father insists, their existence is more authentic than that of the Actors and Director (and, implicitly, of others, including the audience), whose reality is shown finally to be not only ephemeral but also illusory. Here, in Pirandello's most famed work, the very basis of the theatrical illusion – the tacit agreement between audience and stage artist concerning the "truth" of representation – is continually challenged if not negated by the array of prismatic angles on what is lived and what is acted. As noted already, Pirandello's vision of dramatic character and its creation (figures "born" to an author) can, for him, imply aesthetic autonomy along with being and lifelikeness, and a conception of characters who might, consequently, be free to pursue their own experiences along with completeness and authenticity. This standpoint on characterization, unusual as it may be, is evident in Pirandello's report of how his characters come to be, as tangible visitations upon his imagination – and also in his recollection of how these six in particular came into existence. What might happen, he speculated, if characters that have already been given life by some creator were denied participation in the very art that can make them actual?

> They are detached from me; live on their own; have acquired voice and movement; have by themselves – in this struggle for existence that they

have had to wage with me – become dramatic characters, characters that can move and talk on their own initiative; already see themselves as such; have learned to defend themselves against me; will even know how to defend themselves against others. And so let them go where dramatic characters do go to have life: on a stage. And let us see what will happen. ("Preface" 366)

And yet, stage characters cannot truly be so autonomous, in spite of any disengagement from an author and despite Pirandello's fancy (or Fantasy, as he names his impish spirit of inspiration) concerning their genesis. We have seen that not even Hamlet can manage the formidable transcendence of the lines and situations that he is given, no matter the vitality of his intellect.[2] For characters who are enacted in a theatre, in fact, the "real person" is an illusion of art, achieved as a collaborative synthesis of actor and role, embodiment and text. In the discussion thus far, the relation of a character's actuality to objective or scientific factors has been highlighted, including advancements in the knowledge of the human mind and body in relation to realistic or naturalistic prescriptions more generally. By comparison, attention has been given to authenticity in connection with characters who (as in Racine or Molière, say, or Shaw or Brecht) are associated more with ideas, behaviors, or points of view than with lifelikeness per se. In either case, problems of representation associated with the rendering of an actualized figure on the stage have been looked at primarily, so far, in the context of a model of personhood that is unified, cohesive, empirical, lifelike – hence the acceptance by a spectator as truthful.

Pirandello would scorn such a model, and his rejection of it is at the heart of *Six Characters*, with respect to the play's story and philosophy as well as to its modes of characterization. "Real person" implies for this dramatist not so much a quandary as a dichotomy, a concept that is internally self-contradictory, an oxymoron. Still, this contradiction, with its ontological as well as aesthetic implications, is vital to Pirandello's dramaturgy. For him, characters in drama must have a life and a voice of their own, whereas actual people are mutable and inherently vulnerable with respect to a coherence of identity and selfhood. Pirandello's creative facility is such that his stage characters can, and must, be imagined not only into their function within a play but into their own self-awareness. Because they live on a border of actuality and fiction, they are existentially torn, and, as in the case of Pirandello's six fictional selves, they are painfully conscious of their plight. Dr. Fileno, the central figure in the author's short story, "The Tragedy of Character," and an early model for The Father in *Six Characters*, is embittered over the treatment by his creator (not Pirandello), and is vociferous on the subject (99–101).[3] How could his author have done so masterful a job of giving him life and endowing him with ideas of brilliance and originality, then leave him to a dismal and ordinary fate? Would Pirandello, perhaps, be willing to stand in for the original author, and save Dr. Fileno's life, granting him the recognition and immortality he deserves? No, Pirandello is busy enough with his own characters, who are equally vocal concerning their own attitudes and demands. Such is the basis for the story, and for the existential fix in which the rebellious Fileno finds himself.

The Father, too, desires authenticity, if not immortality. He, also, is a character who knows that he is a writer's creation, and he is aware of a state of being and aesthetic relationship to the person who created him. The Father, however, is different from Dr. Fileno in a key respect: he is a dramatic character, a figure of the theatre, whereas Dr. Fileno was created first for someone's novel, in Pirandello's conception, and then borrowed for the short story. In short, The Father was designed for embodiment and performance, and Dr. Fileno was not. Consequently, The Father can engage in debate with the Director within the environs of a theatre and before an audience, thus complicating the dialectic of what is an actual or a fictive being, a subject with which The Father is expertly familiar. "Can you tell me who you are," he inquires of the Director, who is flummoxed by the apparent obviousness of the question: "What do you mean, who am I? – I'm me!" (247).

Here we encounter the unusual situation of a fictional character charging an ostensibly real person with not being real – and, in the bargain, claiming a greater authenticity for himself as a figure who does not experience alteration in the manner of the Director, for instance, or the other mortals on stage, their own status as characters in the play notwithstanding. The Father is stuck within his incomplete authorial design, and, moreover, is fixed in ways that he cannot bear, largely a consequence of the unintended meeting with The Stepdaughter at the establishment of Madame Pace. The Father suffers from an acute, polite, but excruciating self-awareness; his own "tragedy of character," in fact, pertains directly to the hyperconsciousness that is uniquely his, one that is not truly shared by any of the others, Actors or Characters. Save for Pirandello, for whom The Father speaks, there is no awareness comparable to his concerning the multiplicity of viewpoints that are presented by this play to its cast as well as the spectator. The Father's consciousness, then, is positioned exactly on borders that delineate the real, the fictive, and the illusory. His perspective, which must be that of a Character, includes of necessity the knowledge of what it means to be not only fictional but also imitative, with the imitation more actual, more enduring, than the life model.

What then becomes of mimesis in such a scenario, or of Aristotle's admonitions concerning what is "like," "consistent," or "appropriate?" What becomes of naturalistic tenets such as a plausible roundedness of character arising from factors of environment, parentage, formative events, psychological aspects, and so on? One might assume that The Father, as a dramatic character, should imitate personhood in a variety of convincing ways, and yet the very genesis and function of this figure, and his role as philosophical spokesperson in Pirandello's play, would belie such representation. He admits, in effect, to his own shortcomings as a fiction. Or, from another angle, if The Father were not a Character in this one play, and so keenly aware of the dimensions of his role, his status as a dramatic character could be more lifelike, and thus more authentic, at least by comparison with the mortal observers in the audience who do not share in his debilitating fixity. And yet, The Father's existential plight is this play's raison d'être. His particular, indeed unique, authenticity arises ironically in this very apposition of dramatic character and Character. He must exist in a perpetual state of relationship to, and comparison with, the Actors and Director, along with spectators in the audience. And he must, concurrently, bear the onus of the story and the scenes that he shares in present time and in the backstory with his fellow Characters, especially The Stepdaughter. Even though I have written elsewhere and at length about The Father, especially concerning the ironies that are part of his depiction, the intricacy of this figure as a stage persona, and the implications for a concept of dramaturgy and dramatic character more generally, merit further assessment in the context of a "real person" dialectic.[4]

Pirandello's centerpiece for *Six Characters*, The Scene, with its stagey reenactment of the encounter at Madame Pace's, is so definitive regarding the circumstances of The Father and The Stepdaughter that no other cast member, especially the Actors and Director, can help being diminished by their own association with the fictive – that is, with imitation rather than actuality. Whereas the Actors are, by profession, necessarily versatile (or multiple, in Pirandello's vision) the Characters are denied such alterability to the point that only a single mask (as remorse, for The Father) is conceivable. Or, to put this a bit differently, the Pirandellian mask belongs in the philosophical sense more to the Actors, and to those who observe them in the audience, than to the Characters who are in this instance imitated. This is ironic, given that Pirandello, in his stage directions, recommends a particular sort of masked appearance for the Characters (214–215). As I have noted in a related context: "The business of the Actors is to mirror the human models upon whom character is based; the Characters, in turn, are the mirrors of the action that was invented, but left incomplete, by their original author. The Pirandellian mask, in this situation, is more than an alterable face of character or personage before the observant world; it is the representation of an extreme, indeed ultimate, variation and indeterminacy, Dionysian in both its spirit and versatility" (*Irony* 114). A substantial effect of this variation is to fragment the conception of self and personhood, both real and fictive, and indeed to guarantee a range of uncertainties and vulnerabilities in their definition along with depiction.

Moreover, Pirandello's alterations, paradoxes, and multiple stand-points are wedded to a factor of opposition that pervades the action, not simply as dramatic conflict but as a fundamental behavior, a law of existence as well as of art. This, notably, is also the matrix of contradiction that informs the designing of his characters. As Anne Paolucci observes, Pirandello "has perceived the opposite in life, and perceived the opposite of the opposite myriadfold. And it is out of the depths of mirrored opposites that he brings up his dramatis personae out of his *sentimento del contraria*, the feeling of the opposite" (324–325). The Father, from this perspective, is the play's embodied emblem of contradiction: a fiction who can bear witness to actuality, and do so with greater authority than the "real persons" with whom he converses and before whom he performs. The logic of The Father's ontology, moreover, brings with it an inborn self-nullification, not only because of his own fixity and incompleteness but also because of what his characterization implies for others, both fictive and actual. The "feeling of the opposite" can only signify, in such a case, states of existence that are questionable and images of selfhood that are built upon equations of contradiction, leading only to self-cancellation.[5] A concept of "anti-" character, from such a perspective, emerges directly from principles of active opposition, inversion, or negation, as these relate not only to stage portrayals per se but also to such unstable or indefinite models of personhood as are represented. With reference to such instability, the "anti" can refer also, and perhaps even more basically, to that which is false, not actual, what is perturbed by artistic intrusion itself into the ostensibly real.

Character, Portrait, Model

From one angle, certainly, dramatic character is a very different phenomenon from portraiture in paint, especially if the latter is defined in the historically traditional sense of a still, pictorial depiction of personhood with a bias toward representational accuracy. Portraiture, along such conventional lines at least, is typically posed, staid, designed to confront the viewer not only with lifelikeness and personality but often with the accoutrements or indicia of social position, class, or cultural values. A dramatic character, by contrast, is dependent upon the actor's physical embodiment coupled with action: doing deeds, interrelating, often with an arc of activity and, most likely, conflict in the play that is being performed. Portraiture is, from this standpoint anyway, the representation of a body at rest, whereas character in drama depicts the body in motion. And yet, in spite of such contrasts, the similarities between dramatic character and portraiture are multiple. A portrait is, normally, a type of characterization – and, moreover, a portrait traditionally has a name, that of the real person who is portrayed. Even as a painted portrait may be stilled, an effect of motion and a complexity of interrelation with others (including the viewer) is common if not standard. As Lawrence Gowing observes, in connection with a portrait by Louis Tocque in the Louvre, "Portraiture is nothing if not a social art" (488).[6] Indeed, it is in the context of such resemblances between the two arts that the playwright and the painter can be faced similarly with aesthetic problems that are attendant, and perhaps innate, to the captured image of actuality. Literary works that aspire to a pictorial or descriptive portrait of a singular character or set of characters – as, again, Henry James's *The Portrait of a Lady* or James Joyce's *Portrait of the Artist as a Young Man* – can perhaps narrow the gap between literary and painterly portrayal, particularly in the case of a writer such as James with his bias toward a scenic, dramatic, and pictorial narrative. Taken a step further, Tennessee Williams's short story, "Portrait of a Girl in Glass," as the prototype for *The Glass Menagerie* and the figure of Laura in particular, brings literary portraiture up close to dramatic character.

Together with such differences between portraiture and characterization, there are oppositions between the strictly representational and the abstract, in the context of an artistic limning of persons, that apply to stage figures as well as to portraits – and, in either case, the demarcation is often more subjective than precise. The border between abstraction and fidelity with respect to lifelikeness can be as blurred as it is exacting. In the case of classical or traditional portraiture (with reference to

Ingres, say, or David or Reynolds or Gainsborough) the effort is toward an elaborate faithfulness required of depicting a patron or client whose image is custom-designed to please and possibly exalt. And yet, John Singer Sargent, another master of the commissioned oil portrait and, frequently, of the depiction of class and station and privilege, can deal in equal measure with layers of abstraction along with exactitude, depending upon the subject, especially when it comes to the picturing of mood or psyche together with physical features and comportment.[7] In either case, however, the representational or the abstracted, shades of mutability are encountered in the cause of lifelikeness. In this relation, at least, the phenomena of portraiture and of dramatic character – each art involved as it is with the portrayal of personhood with a viewing audience in mind – are subject to an "anti," in this instance an intrinsic range of disconnections or incongruities that belie the potential completeness and faithfulness of the mimesis.

Pirandello's fame is not as a painter, and his play is not, ostensibly, a portrait of The Father. Nor is The Stepdaughter a model in any conventional sense, despite her versatile status at the establishment of Madame Pace. And yet, as is typical with this dramatist, the opposite view is worth assessing. From one vantage point, at least, *Six Characters* might be understood as presenting a finely wrought, if incomplete, portrait of its central figure in crisis, while The Father's primary antagonist (or, in truth, any of the six Characters) may be imagined as a model in the sense of a quintessence or epitome – in The Stepdaughter's case, an exemplary case of betrayal and outrage at the horror of an unintended, if mutually shared, circumstance. The Father's mask of remorse becomes, in this view, a model, or replica, of regret that is stuck in its place and cannot be removed. From this perspective also, the prismatic layers of illusion and truthfulness are complicated further by artistic vagaries that must attend to portraiture or to modeling as a means for portrayal – even when the subject is a theatrical character that is depicted dimensionally instead of a real person who is represented through painting. With attention to what he calls the "authority of the likeness," Richard Brilliant situates portraiture in a consistent relation of subject, painter, and viewer, an "oscillation between art object and human subject" (7), and a baseline question that he poses is not so different from The Father's to The Director ("Can you tell me who you are?"):

> Conflicting views on the nature of personal identity have confounded the
> very concept of the portrait as a significant genre of representation because

they affect the answer to a basic question presented by art works of this kind: "Who is the who that is being represented?" (13)

Who is the who, indeed? – and how does that "who" wish to be represented, and before whom? Portraiture, in common with dramatic character, offers a likeness, an impression of identity, a name – a *who* – but one with varying degrees of falsity and misrepresentation that are coincident with fidelity or lifelikeness.

The Father struggles to be represented fairly, but his aspiration is doomed if only because so many standpoints on such representation are possible. His portrait, if aligned with any one discipline of painting, is stylistically "cubist," to borrow Wylie Sypher's term for Pirandello's art (69).[8] The Father could not, certainly, be shown by any traditional (let alone classical) means of portraiture, if only because of the multiple and concurrent angles that comprise his depiction. It is an irony, perhaps, that his "cubist" portrait cannot be restricted to the frontal, as the traditional painted portrait must be of necessity, even as the actor who stands in for him must direct his face toward an audience of observers. There is a potential sense, indeed, that The Father can be no more than a figuration of theatre, a construct of characterization and performance coupled with the shifting truths of his apprehension by viewers.

In actuality, though, The Father may well be perceived as the plaintive, regretful, defiant, philosophical figure that he is rather than as an artifice – even in the light of the multiplicities of being and the fictive aspect that is built into his authored self. In this, his dramatized portrait before an audience shares another propensity that a painting has with respect to the viewer. As Brilliant observes: "There is great difficulty in thinking about pictures, even portraits by great artists, as art and not thinking about them primarily as something else, the person represented" (23). Whereas Pirandello's theatre foregrounds the illusory aspect of personhood, portraiture is very often designed to convince a viewer of an artistic illusion's reality. Pirandello's own portrait of The Father, which is theatrical rather than painterly, nonetheless combines these two modes of observation: The Father is, after all, both illusory and true, at once.

To complicate the question further, there is a long-standing tradition of representing, through portraiture, an actor in a particular role, thus adding to the layering that already exists – and, of necessity, making a viewer's experience of what is actual yet more intricate. That is, just as portraiture necessarily presents a challenge to one's perception, through art, of a real person, that challenge is redoubled when the subject is an actor and when the actor's role is also depicted.[9] With respect to painting, Brilliant notes "the common assumption, perhaps most strongly engendered by portraits, that there is some substratum of mimetic representation underlying the purported resemblance between the original and the work of art, especially because the sign function of the portraits is so strong that it seems to be some form of substitution for the original" (40). The reference here is to the force of portraiture's persuasive effects, a proclivity that is shared also by embodied theatrical performance. A theatre audience, in common with the viewer of portraits, is well aware and also unaware of the art, in this case the acting process that often depends for effectiveness, especially in a realistic context, upon disguising its own means and thereby presenting a believable image of personhood.

Even so, there is the necessary, underlying falseness, the "anti-" that is built into the mimesis itself, in theatre as well as in portraiture. The audience for theatre, like the viewer of painting, gives in to art's legerdemain and in this way participates in the knowing of ostensibly real persons. With respect to an ontological relation of person to portrait, Brilliant underscores the problem of "likeness" and of "faithfulness," saying that each has its limits, "despite the claim that portraits make such specific reference to particular persons that they affirm their existence" (40). The same might be said of dramatic characterization, in that theatre both affirms and questions the existence of The Father – as an extreme case that proves the rule – even as he himself insists on a personal truth despite his status as a fiction. A portrait has an extraordinary power to reify, as Brilliant would have it, but the live, theatrical dimensionality of an embodied character can be particularly seductive with respect to actuality – even with the "anti," the caveat made necessary by the inherent limitations of "likeness."

For Pirandello in *Six Characters*, the mask of the stage persona is both versatile, in the sense of a changing face of mutable selfhood, and fixed, as in the unalterable distillations of his title figures. The Characters, especially The Father and The Stepdaughter, are each reduced to a simulacrum of emotive (or, in The Father's case, philosophical) response to their shared situation. The mask becomes, in this way, a model of being. While The Father defends the truth of his existence, he must still be a replica, a reproduction. Modeling, as what Wendy Steiner calls "the relation between a reality and its representation," becomes in this way highly germane to dramatic characterization from the Pirandellian standpoint – and it, like portraiture, is subject also to intrinsic intrusions of the "anti," or what by its nature must be unfaithful. A model can be an artist's subject;

the model can embody what is imitated or copied; and the act of modeling itself can stand for what intrudes between representation and the object of imitation.

While Steiner's inquiry in *The Real Real Thing* centers on an array of contemporary variations on (and implications of) modeling, and of posing as a standing in for the real as against the virtual, there are innate connections with the ontology and to the dramaturgy of theatrical characterization. "The model is a figure of ontological paradox," she writes, "real and at the same time artificial" (5). Whereas an oil portrait will often provide the image of a real person with a name, a "who," the model can be nameless, and simply be substituted – as an image, a persona, an example, something to be emulated. And yet, like the portrait and also like a theatrical character, the model must be paired with an observer, with audience. A theatrical character is typically designed, of course, to model a self, reflecting a person's appearances, behaviors, and actions. However, it is precisely the modeling function that undermines the project of embodying the actual, perhaps especially so at a time in which the virtual – a term with its own alignments with the Pirandellian – has come to signify so many variations on what can be perceived as authentic. Steiner offers that "models straddle an ontological divide. And it is for this reason that they are ubiquitous in the arts today, for their doubleness allows them to symbolize the growing permeation of the virtual into everyday reality" (12). Dramatic character, too, is "double" in a related sense: the necessary union and concurrent separation of actor and role, coupled with the fundamental theatrical illusion that asks for belief in the face of obvious and deliberate artifice. Although we, as audience in a theatre today, may not worry these aesthetic doubles as we might the virtual, or bring the paradoxes of Pirandellian characterization to each and every stage figure that we meet, the "doubleness" must abide nonetheless, for character as for model or portrait.[10] A model will pose for a picture; a person may pose for a portrait; an actor must pose as a character – but in each of these cases, the pose itself is a source of the false.[11]

The "Anti-" for Ionesco and Beckett

Pirandello's standpoint on character in drama, unique as it is, stands for only one departure among many from the "real person" model of theatrical representation – from the paradigm, that is, which is so persistent with respect to realistic or naturalistic depiction especially. When Eugene Ionesco chose "An Anti-Play" as his subtitle for *The Bald Soprano*, he was, in effect, finding a name for a drama that is based on a negative, or inverted perspective on conventional dramaturgy, an inversion that includes the delineation of dramatic character together with story logic, locale, and (especially) employment of language in aid of intelligible communication among persons. Ionesco's characters – Mr. and Mrs. Smith, Mr. and Mrs. Martin, Mary, and the Fire Chief – lack any sort of coherent background or personal history (except, possibly, through some preposterous ancestral relation to "Bobby Watson"). Indeed, they are products of illogic and are nearly bereft of traits altogether, with the possible exceptions of gender and what it takes to be "English" within the playwright's parody of identity and discourse, not to mention what may constitute cause and effect or serve as a recognizable location. Ionesco's characters are, in this play at least, more generic than individualized. Also, they are types, representative more often of a theatrical style than of personhood. Defiant of individuation, they end up, as Ionesco says, "interchangeable: Martin can change places with Smith and vice versa, no one would notice the difference" (*Notes* 180). Indeed, the play ends with the Martins reiterating the conversation between the Smiths that began the action in the first place. They are "anti" characters that become, within Ionesco's satiric reflection of theatrical genres and with behaviors that are clichéd to the point of inanity, caricatures of character.[12]

As a result of these inversions, the Pirandellian principle of the opposite (*sentimento del contraria*) is analogized in *The Bald Soprano*, once more in relation to a self-cancellation that pertains to the delineation of character. For Pirandello, an effect of opposition is to multiply standpoints and states of being so that, in effect, the definition of personhood becomes confounding if not impossible. With Ionesco, the action contains a negative momentum – in part because of interchanges among characters and correlations that make less and less sense – that results not in a prismatic fragmentation of the self, as for Pirandello, but as a nihilistic progression toward a final and pervasive "anti" that includes the persons that are represented.[13] Ionesco's world in *The Bald Soprano* is, in other words, a realm not only of contradiction or opposition but of nothingness brought about by nonmeaning, and vacuity in characterization becomes the principal signature of all that is absent.

There is a diary entry from 1951, not long after the initial production of *The Bald Soprano*, in which Ionesco underscores the full scope of the "anti" through repetitive reference: "Anti-thematic, anti-ideological, anti-social-realist, anti-philosophical, anti-boulevard psychology, anti-bourgeois, the rediscovery of a new free theatre" (*Notes* 181). Such a vision is dependent necessarily upon what has preceded it – for there to be an "anti," in other words, there must be something in place already to refute or negate, including a standpoint on personhood and use of language along with ideology. In this relation, the characterization of, say, Mr. Smith or Mrs. Martin depends in part upon an ironized relation to an ancestry of other dramatic characters, especially of the naturalistic sort – that is, figures with qualities of personality or behavior that are built upon formative influences and believable environments. Of course, in Ionesco's vision, the Smiths and the Martins have no need of such background, and the action is not at all dependent upon such qualities.[14] The play aims instead for a progressive disintegration of personhood and identity and a devaluation of language that deprives the characters of the ability to make sense of their existence.

One is reminded, of course, that such utter absence of verisimilitude, taken together with such radical departures from conventional cause and effect, logic, and other, more traditional features of dramatic structure, are hallmarks of absurdism and have long since become conventional in their own right.[15] The stability of dramatic characterization, especially as a reflection of actuality, has over the past many decades been questioned repeatedly – both aesthetically, as an interrogation into limitations of theatrical mimesis and of dramatic form, and as a challenge to the continuity of selfhood per se as a model for character. We shall turn presently to that very issue, but it will be advantageous, first, to gauge the depth and persistence of an "anti" factor as applied especially to the legacy of Samuel Beckett and to the theatrical depiction of consciousness as a negative proposition.

Reliance upon the inverse is a typical if not definitive behavior in Beckett's works. In *Happy Days*, for instance, a vividly negative image, quite literally a reversed positive, is central to the play's philosophic ontology as well as to the circumstances of the two characters and the mise en scène. Beckett's works, including novels as well as plays, offer a range of fictive persons with likenesses that transcend the differences of form and genre, sharing as they often do the impression of a life stripped of ornament in which awareness itself can be a curse. Colm Toibin points to Beckett's deep interest in "states of nonbeing, nonconsciousness, and nonlanguage," in which a concept of the inverse applies to being itself and the potentials (generally diminished) for understanding experience or even thought. Beckett, writes Toibin, "loved the tension in *cogito ergo sum* and took a dim view of the connecting word, the *ergo* in the equation. Cogitating was the nightmare from which his characters were trying to awake" ("Sam" 24–25). Such a status may be true of Beckett's novelistic characters, in situations of extremity and duress as they often are, but they are certainly true also of Winnie in *Happy Days*, for whom existence itself is a tortuous daily undertaking, despite the cheer that she can summon frequently in the face of it.

Winnie's situation is one of extreme displacement. She survives in what is, in effect, an "anti-" realm that is the inverse of a recognizable past world, a presumably more conducive relation of humanity to earthly surroundings and to a natural order that has since gone cosmically as well as locally awry. Or, as Daniel Alpaugh puts it, Beckett's tactic in *Happy Days* is one of "negative definition. Beckett presents his vision of modernity not by showing us what life is but rather by showing us what it is not" (Caputi 586). Location, here, is not the preposterously "English" home of the Smiths (or Martins), where there is nothing outside the walls except for someone who may or may not be there when the doorbell rings. In *Happy Days*, even though Winnie's environs are abstracted, symbolic, and barren, they are also immediate, vivid, and dangerous: "Expanse of scorched grass rising to a low mound," is how Beckett begins his description of the setting. And then, "Imbedded up to above her waist in exact centre of mound, Winnie" (Caputi 403). In the second act, she is buried to the neck, and the future is clear. Despite the disappearance into the earth that awaits her, though, Winnie does not dwell on her predicament, giving her steady attention instead to the minutiae that constitute the substance of, and justification for, a happy day. By contrast with the Smiths and Martins, Winnie is adept and versatile with language; indeed, she is learned, articulate, and adroit with literary references in spite of her observation to Willie that "words fail." They may, indeed, but they also signify, and in modestly reliable ways, even though signification may refer to an order of existence that is gone, or to a context of being without apparent shape or meaning.[16]

Yet words for Winnie are not only necessary but also imperative. Reduced as she is in mobility, she must define her existence verbally and in specific relation to her belongings, meager as they are, and she does so with elaborate exactitude and even, at times, finesse. The dramaturgy of this characterization demands an intricate orchestration of detail, especially since Beckett's script calls for cadences of specified gestures in concert with Winnie's speech. In fact, Winnie is not only a character but also a performer, complete with an act, a routine, and the props that go with them. She sustains her spirit – and, in fact, her cheery mood – through performative actions, as minute as they often are, together with a her prattle of narration, reflection, and discourse with herself as well as Willie.[17]

As a dramatic character, then, Winnie embodies a demonstrative self-reflexivity that is especially ironic given that she is temperamentally histrionic but is stuck in circumstances of greatly inhibited opportunity for spectacle or conventional theatricality, not to mention movement.[18] There is a key distinction here, however, in the use of the term "character" in relation to Winnie and to what she represents – to wit, a person in extremis, yet a person who is, in her way, just like us. It is a distinction, in fact, that sharpens the import of what she endures and by extension, stands for. In *Just Play*, Ruby Cohn argues on behalf of the variety, as against similarity, that distinguishes Beckett's stage figures, emphasizing the fact that the playwright himself referred to his creations as "my people" (13). Not that such a conflation of invented character and personhood is uncommon; indeed, such a unity is to a large extent the whole point, and we are inquiring extensively here into exactly that aesthetic codependency. Nonetheless, Porter Abbott takes up this very distinction in his parsing of Beckett and the postmodern, with *Happy Days* seen as a possible fulcrum point in Beckett's dramaturgy of characterization over time – to wit, as a play on the cusp of the playwright's "abandonment of character" in favor of a later "theatrical austerity." And yet, Abbott argues emphatically on behalf of Beckett's "people" *as* characters, as creations that are "as fully and legitimately Beckett's as anything he has created" and that in this way run counter to a postmodern discourse that would question, diminish, or disqualify such a status. For Abbott, indeed, it is especially ironic that, "our leading exponent of the disintegration of the self should have produced some of our most memorable characters" (43–44).

If Winnie could not be seen as standing for "people," her circumstances would be nowhere near so dire, nor would her progressive burial be as horrifying as it is broadly representative. As Pozzo, another of Beckett's creations, cries famously: "They give birth astride of a grave, the light gleams an instant and then it's night once more." Yet it is Winnie, more so than anyone in *Waiting for Godot*, who turns the starkness of that verbal image, condensed as it is, into a tersely embodied stage experience and spectacle. At the very same time, though, Beckett's dramaturgy in *Happy Days* – which in itself is a signature of how much is achieved in this minimal yet embracing play – includes a cosmic as well as a localized and reduced perspective, and does both at the same time. The invented location is, here, a site of disruption that is vast yet also immediate and personalized. In *Back to Beckett*, Cohn describes the scene as "at once heaven, hell, and scorched earth" (180), while Andrew Kennedy alludes to Winnie's "cosmic environment" and to the "cruel cosmos" over which she has no control or even influence (80).

There is certainly an immediate sense in which Winnie's steady business with her props keeps her rigorously in touch with daily routines. Yet, at the same time she inhabits a world where time has lost its application, and where some nameless calamity of possibly astronomical scale has qualified every expectation except, perhaps, another day of survival. Richard Gilman points to the paradox (with its own cosmic implication) that while Winnie exists "*in* time," she also lives "without past or future" – without points of empirical reference of the sort that would guarantee context, continuity, and perhaps even reassurance (*Making* 261). Significantly, Gilman also calls into question the idea of character itself (he is writing this in 1972). With reference to Beckett's later works, including *Happy Days*, Gilman describes the action collectively as "irreducible human responses to the actuality of being alive: to the grip of time, the illusion of freedom, the coercion by what has been." With respect to the "characters" who are enduring such circumstances, though, Gilman wonders parenthetically, "if we can still use that conventional term" (*Making* 258).

And yet, how can, or could, we not? Even in so stringent and dire an environment, Winnie, along with Beckett's larger cast of people, are assuredly dramatic characters, just as they are figures whom the playwright names as "people." Winnie, moreover, is one such figure – and explicitly a woman – whose humanity is not only emblematic but is also felt empathetically, despite (or because of) the bizarre nature of her situation. Cohn, who consciously identifies herself in *Back to Beckett* with Winnie as a woman, calls *Happy Days* "the quintessential drama of modern humanity" (192). The image of Winnie must finally be one of stoicism and courage, even if her pluck is seen as a darkly ironic whistling in the dark. Yet, more importantly, there is affirmation of Winnie's ability to value what exists, on however small a scale, and to appreciate what can be construed as a mercy even in the face of cataclysm and while all is so obviously being taken away.[19] What Beckett is dramatizing through the experience of one member of his collective "people" is a supremely human response to a flatly negative idea, to an "anti" that is an inverse of all that would nurture, sustain, and validate a human cause under what are now bygone and forever disappeared conditions.

Character, Consciousness, Self

Winnie's state of wakefulness, in the glare of Beckett's "blazing light" and in the course of what is now a "day" in the new normality of an eerily cosmic yet brutally terrestrial landscape, is one in which she is, in her way, hyperaware of her perceptions, of Willie, of memory, and use of objects. Her consciousness, in other words, is shown to be alert and vigilant, despite the strictures on physical movement. Winnie is reflective, hearing herself as she listens for Willie, making decisions – including one to set aside the revolver that she keeps along with her toothbrush, parasol, and other paraphernalia. We are party to her thoughts, as if invited into an extended soliloquy. Winnie is manifestly alive, perhaps especially and even extravagantly so because of the very rigors with which she must live. At the same time, we recall that for Chekhov's people (if he were to use the same term as Beckett), consciousness can be equated with incipient heartbreak if not ruin, when perceived as the end of a way of life and possibly of self-definition. To become aware, or begin to, as Lyubov Ranevskaya must in *The Cherry Orchard* or the Prozorov women do in *Three Sisters*, is to recognize and then to admit what may prove to be one's own spiritual destruction, or at least an end to what has been a more or less stable state of identity. Consciousness, simply as knowledge or awareness, is from this angle threatening or forbidding, a variation perhaps on Winnie's citing of Ophelia's "woe" at what she has seen, and sees now (*Hamlet* III, 1). With respect to Winnie's sustaining comforts, and to the severity of her difficulties, Kennedy writes: "Her world of thoughts and talk is a source of inexhaustible consolation for Winnie, even though consciousness (for a person suffering in isolation) might be the source of torment, and talk (for someone aware of the possibility that there is nobody 'out there' to listen) might intensify the threat of existential emptiness" (83).

Is Winnie better off conscious or not – and to what degree? If the comparison to Chekhovian drama is warranted, as in the case of Lyubov, say, or Masha in *Three Sisters*, then a heightened awareness will correlate only with increased dread. Even as Winnie's plight is considerably more acute than what Chekhov's characters (and, for that matter, most others in drama) will confront, what is shown of the despair that can result of an ending is, in *Three Sisters* or *The Cherry Orchard*, more personally manifest for them than for her. Winnie's effort, after all, is to manage her day, not assess or explore her situation in its totality, which would imply facing her death. To be alive, to exist, is in Beckett's vision and for his people a bane, the inverse of blessing, a baseline "anti" that is the absolute negative of productive being and of knowing. The burden of consciousness, in this view, is that to be aware is to understand inconsequence and recognize nonmeaning. Consciousness does not imply transcendence but must, for Winnie, be earthbound and mortal – as in the case of we mortal, nonfictive beings as well. It is physical and biological, a "qualitative, subjective, first-person process going on in the nervous system," as philosopher John Searle describes it. It is, too, "a part of the ordinary physical world and is not something over and above it" (*Mind* 87, 88). Must consciousness, then, be yet another reflection of an "anti" in characterization, along with being itself? For Beckett, the answer would have to be yes, in spite of the relative tenacity, cheer, or jocularity of his people, and apart from any determination on their part to press on without significance or solace. To be conscious, in Beckett's world, is to know and suffer the awareness of nonbeing. A final breath is drawn, and so ends the conscious self.

And yet, the mystery of consciousness persists. In this sense, perhaps paradoxically, the phenomenon implies not only gradations of awareness but at the same time signifies what is not, and perhaps cannot, be known. When considered as a mind-body problem – a linkage of brain and mind with a feeling of identity and a coherent sensing of the physical and mental self – consciousness is unexplained by science (if this is, after all, a scientific as against philosophic problem per se).[20] Indeed, there are those who, like Colin McGinn, do not believe that consciousness is solvable, that it is beyond the grasp of human intellect. Might the "hard" questions of consciousness, in David Chalmer's well-known usage, thus be passed by, for purposes here, as lacking any particular or innate connection to character in drama?[21] Undoubtedly so, in the sense that such characters are representations of persons not unlike ourselves who go right on about their daily behaviors and endeavors without explanation of an attribute that is shared by everyone. But, at the same time, assuredly not, in the sense that consciousness is correlated so directly to that of self, and that selfhood is arguably the primary subject for mimesis in character representation, the fundamental component that differentiates one stage figure or person from another, one set of beliefs or values from another, one conviction of individuality from another, on the stage as in life.

Beckett's theatre, and his fiction, too, may indeed reflect a "disintegration of the self," as Porter Abbott would say. But what if the self, as being or as concept, were more broadly vulnerable to an "anti" – in this case, to an impossible if not a precisely negative conception? And then, as a consequence, under what circumstances might "real person" be read again, as for Pirandello, as an oxymoron? For Damasio, "Consciousness is a state of mind with a self process added to it" (*Self* 167). Yet, what precisely is that "process" or that "self?" For Searle, the question of consciousness pertains to a principal feature of experience, "what one might call a 'sense of self.' One way to put this is to say that there is definitely something that it feels like to be me" (*Mind* 205).

The sense of a "me" and of a "myself" are properties that belong to persons and also to fictional characters in both drama and in narrative story telling. The consistent feeling of what belongs to one individual as against another is at the core of what differentiates our own experience of being from that of others with whom we exist and interact – and a play's dramatis personae are, with unusual exceptions, comprised of just such differentiations. In spite of States's theory that characters are made up of one another, they are also individualized – and, indeed, they are typically presented in drama in terms of oppositions to one another, despite their necessary coparticipation in a larger dramatic conception. But again, how to approach a definition of self that amounts to a center of being, for a person or a fictive model of personhood, even if it is a core that contains these variations and oppositions? The range of inquiry and of disagreement on this basic question is vast, even given the shared investment of cognitive scientists, neurologists, and philosophers of mind in addition to novelists and playwrights. Searle, for example, is at odds with Damasio's conceptions of both self and consciousness. Summarizing what Damasio proposes in *Self Comes to Mind* as the outcome of interaction among three key terms (mind, brain, self), Searle concludes: "When we put this all together we get the following result: conscious minds begin when the self comes to mind, when brains add a process involving a person's sense of self to the mind mix" (51). And the logic produces a question: "The self is introduced to explain consciousness, but if it is to explain consciousness we cannot assume that the self is already conscious. How did it get to be conscious?" In short, a circular reasoning must result from "assuming consciousness to explain consciousness" ("Mystery" 51).[22] In fact, the delineation of mind, self, or consciousness from brain tend, as a rule, to be of crucial importance and disputatious, at once.

From the standpoint of theatrical characterization, there are significant implications in these uncertainties that pertain once again to differences between dramatic and narrative character, the abilities of either to reflect actual persons, and the capabilities of theatre by contrast with literary fiction especially. In this relation so far, we have looked at the "cognitive subplot" in *Hamlet* and, in further elaboration of how characters think, the drama of consciousness for Henry James's Isabel Archer by contrast with characters in plays. As noted, the aesthetic portrayal of consciousness is among the most rigorous points of differentiation between the literary and theatrical arts – and a similar rigor might extend to the depiction of self and selfhood. In more recent fiction, including but not limited to the so-called neuronovel, considerable attention is given to the concept of consciousness, including not only its nature and process but also its potentials for embodiment or portrayal by artistic means.[23] There is a difference, in this recent deliberateness, from the Jamesian or Joycean technique, in that fictional characters today can be more conscious of their own consciousness, as it were, including its uncertainties; they are aware of it *as* a point of interest and educated concerning what has been learned about it.

Richard Powers's *The Echo Maker* and *Thinks....*, by David Lodge, are exemplary in this regard. In each, there are characters who are knowledgeable about brain science and whose actions and perceptions are tied closely to this awareness. As we have seen, the figure of Gerald Weber in Powers's narrative is a neurologist and a writer of books for a general public on the brain, especially in relation to cognitive disorders. When he experiences an onset and gradual deepening of depression, his mental state corresponds accordingly with his perception of, and participation in, events – which, in turn, affects the reader's sense of them. In one scene, as Weber delivers a public lecture, the reader is drawn to his shaky self-awareness along with what he is saying, with the two in ironic counterpoise: "We think we access our own states; everything in neurology tells us we do not" (363). Here, then, is a mind that is actively part of the novel's narrative strategies (and one that is brought to bear on the medical treatment of another, mentally damaged character) and that is subject to variations that alter the perception and tone of events as experienced by the reader. In Lodge's book, Helen Reed is a teacher and writer of fiction who is contrasted, vocationally and ideologically (and, as it happens, romantically) with Ralph Messenger, the director of an institute for cognition and consciousness studies. Both she and Messenger are attuned to their own states of consciousness and, again, to its centrality as a subject – as seen from literary or scientific standpoints, respectively. Helen is baffled by the fact that scientists see consciousness as a "problem" that has to be "solved": "This was news to me, and not particularly welcome. I've always assumed, I suppose, that consciousness was the province of the arts, especially literature, and most especially the novel." For her, the challenge of consciousness is, "how to *represent* it, especially in different selves from one's own" (61). The "problem" is not about the fundamental yet enigmatic nature of consciousness as a variation of the mind-body question, but is rather an issue of how conscious states can be revealed artistically. And, as we have seen, this is a problem with differing implications for the playwright as opposed to the novelist. The tendency of theatre is to emphasize a showing of emotive states, typically nuanced or heightened and linked to a dramaturgy of conflict and to what is at issue among characters, as opposed to their states of consciousness per se. King Lear, after all, may lose equilibrium and his grip on conscious, interior states, but what the audience sees is fury and imprecation.

This is not to say that theatre is ill-equipped for portraying consciousness (we have seen otherwise), but rather to underscore basic differences between dramatic and narrative art. In either case, literary fiction or drama, the elusiveness of this intangible concept itself – whether understood as consciousness or as the self with its frames and degrees of awareness – is intrinsically problematic and, in the parlance of this chapter, can be noteworthy as a component of the "anti" in characterization. While this elusiveness can imply more intricacy and perhaps difficulty for the dramatist than for the novelist, in that a revelation of conscious states is accomplished by the writer and received by such different means for a theatre audience than for a reader, a feature remains that effectively correlates interiority with dramatic action. Even as the dramatist may not be as equipped as the novelist to "go behind" a character, in James's usage of the phrase, the theatre is demonstrably adept at enacting the drama, if not exactly the phenomenon, of selfhood.[24] Countless plays, from *Antigone* to *Hamlet*, from *A Doll House* to *After the Fall* and in many eras and geographies, are fundamentally stories of self-discovery, self-confrontation, or authentication – or even of defeat in the face of obstacles to that awareness.

There is an important corollary here, however, that goes to the heart of the difference between dramatizing or presenting character through narrative description. Whereas a literary narrative of interiority can take its time, the theatrical revelation of a character's reflective mind – or, indeed of consciousness – is delimited, at least by the factor of duration, as we have seen. Thus, another of the primary differences between dramatic and literary character is that the former shows or demonstrates within a convention of performance time, whereas the latter tells or is described, and with the factor of duration less stringent. Still, there is a significant qualification here that pertains to the contrast between showing by theatrical means – visually or by enacted demonstration – as against describing through narrative focalization. In *The Echo Maker*, Powers doubles the voice of an omniscient narrator with the first-person thinking and observational processes of Gerald Weber to include "the character's own self-narrating voice," with a result that "what seems like 'telling' is in fact 'showing' by a different means."[25] As a narrative description of consciousness, then, the technique of showing through a given character's eyes, as it were, can be understood as another acute point of contrast with theatrical portrayal, with the soliloquy or other means of spoken thought as perhaps the closest approximation for a dramatic character.

Yet again, though, what is the nature and the substance of the self that can be so much at issue and for which so much can be at stake in the drama? V.S. Ramachandran is confident, on the one hand, with respect to a definition of the self – but from another angle is attentive to what may be an unsolvable mystery. "What exactly is meant by the 'self,'" he asks, and responds with five components: continuity (with a continuous sense of past, present, and future), unity and coherence, embodiment or ownership, agency or free will, and reflection or self-awareness.[26] Concurrently, though, there is the "problem of self," which is unexplained and persistent and which may yet require "a radical shift in perspective." As Ramachandran confesses, "I have no clue what the solution to the problem of self is, what the shift is perspective might be" (*Tour* 96–98). This very antagonism, between assurance of definition and a persistence of enigma or even impossibility, has long since turned into a signature quality of this inquiry, scientific and philosophic both, into both consciousness and the self. With respect to fiction or to drama, the very attributes of personhood that Ramachandran enumerates can belong to fictive characterizations as well, perhaps especially so with respect to an actor's approach to a stage role. Values such as unity and continuity of experience, embodiment and self-awareness, and even free will or autonomy of choice and action can be understood as vital to both the conception and the presentation of invented selves in the theatre. Yet still, the impossible aspect continues, the enigmas endure, and the "anti" ensures that absences of understanding will intrude, barring new discoveries, upon the project of selfhood and, correspondingly, its theatrical imitations.

Although his primary reference is to literary and not to dramatic character, J. Hillis Miller attends directly, in *Ariadne's Thread*, to the problem of self and its representation, a problem that verges again on an aesthetic conundrum. Miller's perspective is distinctly postmodernist, and his deconstruction of figurative signs, cultural or ontological, applies to the actuality of personhood and of being as well as to the literary imitation of such. He decries the viewpoint that would equate one's apprehension of fictive characters with "real people" and not as constructs of language (29). To experience fictional characters as if they are real, or not to understand that "unitary selfhood" is an "ideological construct" is to fall victim to an "illusion of selfhood," in novels or in life (31). Miller asks:

> Does this mean that the "self" is a fiction? Does the self not exist as an independent, substantial, extralinguistic entity, either in real life or in fiction? It depends on what one means by "exist," though there is no doubt some dubiety about the existence of an entity that cannot be straightforwardly sensed and named, as a table or a leaf apparently can. Whatever can only be named in figure may be only a figure, a phantasmal effect of the displacements and exchanges of language. On the other hand, such a thing may exist, but in a realm inaccessible to direct seeing and naming.

For Miller, then, "the 'self' is one of the most important and problematic of such strange entities generated by speech acts" (32–33). His postulate is that even in the context of a reader's usual and casual suspension of disbelief with respect to storytelling – that is, of apprehending fictional characters as real while knowing full well they are not – there is a suspicion that such an acceptance of illusion applies to real selves along with fictional ones. As Miller phrases this, "All men and women living within a culture and accepting a certain notion of character have an uneasy feeling that their belief in character, even their belief in their own character, maybe be confidence in an illusion" (98).[27] Such a theory, of course, strikes at the heart of the mimetic agreement between writer and reader, artist and observer, playwright and audience. It goes to the core of the question of the reality of the self that is being imitated as well as to the imitation itself. So it is unsurprising that Miller condemns the "mirror theory" of fiction with reference to what he names as the "fiercely maintained yet manifestly absurd theory of mimetic representation" (99).

The successful creation, performance, and reception of dramatic character is, however, dependent upon exactly that means of representation, just as it has been ever since Aristotle based a theory of playmaking upon it. In addition, the most commonly practiced and effective means of performing stories in a theatre is to do so through mimetic impersonation: the actor imitates a person, whether or not that person is granted or is in need of a "consciousness" or a "self" or a "mind," and that fictive person interacts meaningfully with other fictional creations, with such meaning ensuing largely from an audience's willingness to accept the stand-ins for a reality and a concept of personhood that are not in themselves illusory. I should emphasize once more, in this regard, that my focus here is on characterization and its vulnerabilities in text-based drama, and not with an "anti" that questions the basis or validity of mimetic representation per se or that deviates on principle from text-based theatre. We shall entertain those very questions in the following chapter.

Even in light of mysteries and contradictions, is there not possibly a different sort of contract between playwright and audience, or novelist and reader, that can still affirm exactly what the deconstructionist or even the neurologist might question? One that does not argue the point that a self may be neither definitive nor fixed, yet still affirms its existence and the vital necessity for its depiction in drama? As Bert States declares in his response to Miller: "I have no wish to conflate real and literary character, but it is my belief that mimesis is capable of rendering, in graphemes and phonemes, in paint and in language, the qualities that are observable in human character; otherwise, there would be little point in reading fiction or making art" ("Mimesis" 459). How to go forward, then, with a qualified validation of mimetic artistry in the theatre and in particular relation to dramatic character, even in light of an "anti" and with a persistence of that obviously complicated, embracing, fascinating question by The Father: "Can you tell me who you are?"

CHAPTER 7

Dramatic Character Today

My characters tell me so much and no more,
with reference to their experience, their aspirations,
their motives, their history.[1]

Harold Pinter's dramaturgy of mysterious motives and ambiguous histories, at one time puzzling if not astounding, turned into a touchstone for contemporary characterization in drama – that is, of the fictional embodiment of real world dreads, tensions, and uncertainties, together with corresponding schisms and silences in relation to expressiveness and comprehension. Along these lines, states of estrangement or misunderstanding became more normative, not as a Brechtian distancing or alienation but as theatrical characterization that stands for a personalized anxiety in the face of discomfiting contingencies and threats to existence, individually and collectively. The strikingly theatrical yet unfamiliar quality of Pinteresque unease in its original iterations, vague and amorphous as it could be, came to reflect a more publicly shared, if privately experienced, disquiet with respect to unknown or unknowable circumstances. In specific relation to dramatic character, such a combination of ambiguity with lack of explanation or articulation bespeaks a stage persona that may be realistically fashioned but is naturalistically incomplete. A figure such as Lenny in Pinter's *The Homecoming*, living as he does in a recognizable North London home amid family kinships, reveals few of the symptoms of Zola's or Strindberg's naturalism with respect to psychology, formative environment, economics, or even parentage, the overbearing presence of Max, Lenny's father, notwithstanding. Rather, Lenny is a mystery – and so, for that matter, are his brothers Teddy and Joey, Teddy's wife Ruth, Max and brother, Sam – which is to say, the play's entire cast. "Eh, listen, I wonder if you can advise me," says Lenny to Ruth, upon meeting her in the late evening. "I've been having a bit of a rough time with this clock. The tick's been keeping me up" (32) – but Lenny doesn't need

Ruth's advice; this is just another of his gambits, along with his tales of a beating under a bridge or the use of an iron mangle, the intentions of which go undeclared save for the tacit message on how he is accustomed to treating women.

"*The Homecoming* changed my life," recalls John Lahr in "Demolition Man," his memoir of the play's personal impact. Lahr recalls that Pinter's "spectacular combination of mystery and rigor had taught me something new about life, about language, about the nature of dramatic storytelling. Pinter had taken the narration out of theatre: *The Homecoming* offered no explanations, no theory, no truths, no through line, no certainties of any kind" (54). In effect, Pinter had invented an arresting new dramaturgy for the portrayal of characters in situations, based not on inversion of rules or expectations or an "anti," but rather on a belief that behaviors are considerably less readable and much more inscrutable, more buried, than traditional dialectics of logic or cause and effect or even psychology could possibly fathom. As Lahr notes, Pinter's dramatic scheme relies mainly upon radical departures from trustworthy codes in conversation, and on a panpsychic coparticipation of objects in space with speech, silence, and gesture. "Before the play," he writes, "I thought words were just vessels of meaning; after it, I saw them as weapons of defense. Before, I thought theatre was about the spoken; after, I understood the eloquence of the unspoken. The position of a chair, the length of a pause, the choice of a gesture, I realized, could convey volumes" (54).

Pinter's style and strategies would not, perhaps, have been so jarring, disjunctive, or affecting were it not for the fundamentally altered view of personality, motive, and social discourse that his plays can offer. As in *The Homecoming*, the characters may tend in their behaviors to foil any expectation of conventional social grace, comforting or familiar context, or sexual decorum – and may also, in their contrariness, deliver a conflicted, enigmatic reflection of human selfhood as solitary, unforthcoming, wary among others, and beset from outside. This, however, is far from a detriment when it comes to our engagement with their activities. It is, rather, a basis for their fascination. For Ruth in *The Homecoming*, mysteriousness is not only a signal trait but is also a source of power and allure. None of the other characters, her husband Teddy included, can make sense of her appeal, motives, or moods – not to mention her past. The spectator, meanwhile, is given nothing to bank on concerning her background, reasons for being with Teddy, or rationale for staying in the household with his brothers and father – or, as seems less likely, for being kept by Lenny as a prostitute on Greek

Street with her own flat and a personal maid. With respect to a theory of traits and its attendant dramaturgy, such a quality of mystery is, in itself, eminently workable – in spite of naturalistic or scientific approaches that would value the delineation of character with definitive points of reference and details of personal history. Whereas I have referred to a "roundedness" of dramatic character, especially in realistic depiction and in situations where the illusion of a full portrait is a virtue, what is missing or incomplete in this instance becomes paramount in precisely the sense that it rings true to experience and is dramatically effective in the bargain. Suspense, here, relates both to plot as an expectation of what will happen next, and to character as the engendering of a potent curiosity about motive or personality but with stern limits on the amount of evidence that is provided. In either case, the result is dramatic, with "drama" built into the characterization as well as the dramatic structure.

Character, Mystery, and Drama

Ten years prior to the London premiere of *The Homecoming, Cat on a Hot Tin Roof* opened in New York.[2] Soon after, Tennessee Williams responded to a review by Walter Kerr in the *New York Herald Tribune*, aiming to refute that critic's charge of "evasion" with respect to Williams's characters and to the figure of Brick Pollitt in particular. Countering that charge, which pertained especially to the depiction (or lack of the same) of Brick's sexual preference, Williams claimed that "mystery" is not only an asset in a play's characterizations but is in fact a requirement if human experience is to be reflected truthfully. As Williams wrote then, in relation to audiences who would see his play in New York:

> Every moment of human existence is alive with uncertainty. You may call it ambiguity, you may even call it evasion. I want them to leave the Morosco as they do leave it each night, feeling that they have met with a vividly allusive, as well as disturbingly elusive, fragment of human experience, one that not only points at truth but at the mysteries of it, much as they will leave this world when they leave it, still wondering somewhat about what happened to them, and for what reason or purpose. (*Where I Live* 73–74)

By way of connecting the depiction of character directly to the lives of people in the world, Williams argues that, "Some mystery should be left in the revelation of character in a play, just as a great deal of mystery is always left in the revelation of character in life, even in one's own character to himself" (*Live* 72).[3]

Clearly, Williams's theory of mystery and Pinter's evocation of it are not the same or even closely related phenomena. The enigmatic in Pinter's work pertains to an existential incompleteness and lack of contour that is not precisely what Williams is after with an approach to dramatic character that is "allusive" as against categorical. Moreover, Williams's defense is of a particular mystery – Brick Pollitt's sexuality in connection with his wife Maggie and deceased friend Skipper – even as the playwright believes also in a more pervasive fallibility in one's understanding of others or even of oneself. In truth, Williams is much more concerned in *Cat on a Hot Tin Roof* with not pinning Brick down than he is with Maggie (the Cat), Big Daddy, or any other character in the play. Maggie, in fact, could scarcely be less mysterious – an attribute that relates directly to the complexities of "real person" characterization. In Margaret Pollitt, Williams invented a character of astonishing vivacity as well as true-to-life desire, arch canniness, and irrepressible verve. She bristles with a crafty intellect and perceptiveness along with a sleek sensuality – so much so that the playwright had no compunctions about centering his first act on her lengthy but energetically animated speeches to her unresponsive husband. When she cries out to him, "Maggie the Cat is – *alive*! *I am alive, alive*!" – the audience has no doubt whatsoever of that claim's veracity (45–46).[4] In the hands of an actress, and with respect again to the "real person" duality, Maggie the Cat on a stage is the epitome of a vital, even indomitable, spirit and of blood and sinew lifelikeness.

Yet still, a quality of mystery is prized in drama and, as Pinter or Williams might agree, it is a factor that connects one's perception of, and interest in, dramatic characters directly to what is unknown or not yet understood. In addition, the enigmatic in characterization can intersect in the theatre with a complex dramaturgy of what is undefined or even unreadable, embracing dramatic structure and use of language along with the depiction of characters per se. What is left unsaid is potentially suspenseful, by intention or not, as any dramatist knows. Again, however, there is a contemporary sense of mystery that, when connected not only to plot but also to a fundamental basis in ontological uncertainty, has become more usual if not normative. Or, from a slightly different angle, there may be too much doubt or apprehension or uneasiness in the air by now for characters in drama not to be marked correspondingly and significantly, in one way or another, by unseen variables.

This includes, of course, the conundrum of self-comprehension itself. With reference once more to what the character of neurologist Gerald Weber observes in *The Echo Maker*: "We think we access our own states;

everything in neurology tells us we do not" (363). And, in a seeming paradox, even as more is understood scientifically, psychologically, or sociologically about the constitution of personhood or the individual in social discourse, less certainty with respect to a theatrical reflection of modern character can be a likely result. Characters have become, in other words, much more available to open-ended questions of motive, intention, and behavior than to psychological or otherwise scientific explanations.

That said, however, the need for a correlation between conventional suspense and dramatic character has been challenged, and so, indeed, has the factor of "drama" itself in theatrical performance and as embodied in characters. It is worth looking more closely, therefore, at what might otherwise be taken for granted in dramatic storytelling, in particular relation to the nature of drama itself. Suspense, of course, has a long ancestry in the theatre, and Sophocles certainly knew what to keep Oedipus from finding out for two hours. For an audience, suspense evokes and then sustains or heightens attention. This involvement can, of course, assume many forms, such as investment in a character's well-being, curiosity about what may result from plans made or actions taken, a fascination with aspects of personality in relation to those actions, or an absorption in conflicts with others or with personal dilemmas. What is the tension within characters or among them? Who knows what, or does not, at given moments? These are long-standing markers of an onlooker's interest in stage figures, even as they are subjective and variable with respect to the dramatic situation and the particular viewer.

This is a dramaturgy, again, that has been remarkably durable, not to say indestructible. Ibsen, a master of the technique, employed it often to invite the spectator's apprehension concerning, for example, the developing complexities and corresponding threats to Nora Helmer or Hedda Gabler in their respective personal and marital dilemmas. The melodramatic plot, as wrought by Ibsen or a dramatist of lesser inspiration, is thus a feature of genre but also of character as the personification of that which must elicit and then hold attention. Melodrama, in other words, may be predicated on suspense, but even though it is primarily a formula for structuring a dramatic plot, it is also prescriptive with respect to character types and traits that will engender the desired response. Both *A Doll House* and *Hedda Gabler* are, after all, ideological melodramas in which each of the imperiled heroines embodies a set of principles in addition to living with a rotten marriage.

The question remains, though, of how or if "drama" – as against theatre – can exist without such expectant contingencies, and under what circumstances. Brecht, of course, would reject the idea of empathetic suspense outright, and especially in relation to character. He famously (and unsuccessfully) endeavored to lessen if not eliminate an audience's sympathy for Mother Courage, while at the same time writing a death scene for her daughter that is shocking in its affective power. Even ideological suspense is a transgression of Brechtian theory, since the point is not to engage an audience with the finding or the future of an idea, which is likely embodied in characterization anyway (as in *Galileo*), but rather to encourage the discovery, on the audience's part, of a new perspective through demonstration. Suspense, like empathy, belongs to the "theatre of illusion," which through its magic hypnotizes the spectator into believing in what is false. As Martin Esslin emphasizes, Brecht would also deplore "identification," as standing in the way of the Epic Theatre's intention to bring a gestus into the starkest relief (*Brecht* 125). Imitation, like empathy and suspense, is also fake. The spectator must not be entranced, must not confuse a "now" that is presented in the theatre with a historically distanced analogy that is designed to apply to, and alter, the now. The actor must demonstrate an action rather than become a character. This is the theatre of gest over mimesis – or, as the playwright himself says, the "gestic principle takes over, as it were, from the principle of imitation" (*Brecht* 86). This key distinction stands among the signature contrasts in modern acting theory, separating utterly the gestic, instructive, or parenthetical idea of the relation of actor to character from that of the naturalistic school in particular. "The actor does not allow himself," writes Brecht, "to become completely transformed on the stage into the character he is portraying. He is not Lear, Harpagon, Schweik; he shows them" (*Brecht* 137).

The "Death" of Character and Drama

To what degree, then, are theatrical representation and storytelling dependent upon conventional understandings of mimesis, suspense, and empathy, and to what extent are these necessary to the engagement of an audience with dramatic character? How much is a spectator's involvement dependent upon a ratio of characterization pattern to plot or to the variety of suspense that arises from mystery, even if the interest that is evoked is in something other than a melodramatic action or narrative of discovery? Or, more simply, how might expectations regarding character in drama have changed as a result of departures, including the Brechtian, from such paradigms? In "The Death of Character" (1985), an essay that Elinor Fuchs included some years later in her book by the same name, it is argued that even as character once assumed precedence over plot, it was replaced itself in a new hierarchy that emerged in a postmodern context. Fuchs's claim is that, "just as Character once supplanted Action, so Character in turn is being eclipsed" (171). Illustrating the notion that, "of course, character has been dying for a hundred years" (171), she points to Strindberg who, in his "Preface" to *Miss Julie*, refers to his people as "characterless." Fuchs does not seem to recognize, however, that what Strindberg means to say is that they are not types, not that they are lacking in traits and qualities of character (in fact, the opposite is true, as observed). With respect to Pirandello, Fuchs proposes a difference between his philosophy and dramaturgy and the postmodern, asserting that works of the latter sort "no longer worry the question of illusion and reality. The question has disappeared with the new perception that all fixed reality is a fiction" (174–175). Without worrying the considerable intricacy of that distinction herself, Fuchs proceeds with a fundamental question: "If we are approaching the end of character on the postmodern stage, what is replacing it?" (175).

In her book (*The Death of Character*, 1996), Fuchs revisits the premises of the essay, but with similar conclusions – to wit, that an alternative, postmodern theatre revealed ways in which dramatic character had been subordinated to other components of dramaturgy.[5] Alluding to a supposed "waning of interest in character moving through narrative," she attributes this phenomenon, among other factors, to a "dispersed idea of self" and to "an explosion of doubt about ontological grounding" (12, 14). Her reference is not so much to dramatic character in relation to complexities of selfhood and its representation as investigated in the preceding chapter, but rather to ways in which other aspects of dramaturgy have drawn attention away from the primacy of characterization. She underscores the "emergence of dramaturgical and performance strategies that deliberately undermined the illusion of autonomous character," to Brechtian dramaturgy as "a direct challenge to psychological acting techniques and their essentialist appeals to a transcendent human nature," and to a "theatricalism" that emerged in the past century as "a favored dramatic mode to express the relative and multiple nature of self-identity" (31–33). In the earlier essay, Fuchs answers her own question of what can replace character on the postmodern stage: "Perhaps a flux of Aristotle's six elements, with Character and Action no longer holding dominion over Music, Diction, Thought, and Spectacle" (176). In the book, by contrast, she offers an alternative ancestry of dramatic character in the twentieth century, which leads "not through the highway of Ibsen's social drama and Zola's naturalism to the dominant realistic tradition, but through the mysteries of the symbolists to the fallen religious world of *Waiting for Godot*."

Actually, Fuchs situates this shift not with the advent of the postmodern but earlier: "The decline of interest in the psychological depth and substantiality of character toward the end of the nineteenth century made room for the emergence of dramaturgies that were not character-generated" (49). In truth, however, and even with the acknowledgment of significant trends that evolved over decades toward an emergence of performative, theatricalist, or postmodern techniques and methodologies associated with an alternative theatre, recent history reflects a persistence rather than a diminishment of reliance upon ancestral models of dramatic character – and, indeed, of conventional formulas for suspense. The realist tradition continues strong, albeit in versatile ways that can accommodate wide variation, and remains effective in the representation of persons and personalities, as well as their interrelations in dramatic terms. If that is so, then how might these vastly differing assertions – a sustained versus a declined investment in dramatic character – be reconciled, if at all?

Michael Vanden Heuvel speaks to exactly this question, and to a climate in which more conventional, text-based ("literary") drama has coexisted, if uneasily, with alternative theatre. What underlies the latter's argument with the former is, to be admittedly reductive, a skepticism concerning the efficacy of theatre's more traditional means of reflecting the world of its time – in this case, our own. In this regard, Vanden Heuvel underscores the "notion that orthodox realism and traditional naturalism by themselves lack the necessary structural, linguistic, and ideological flexibility to voice accurately contemporary society's sense of chaos, uncertainty, and alienation – are unable, that is, to 'accommodate the mess,' in Beckett's phrase – and are impotent to privilege the contemporary urge for process, dispersal, deferment, and play." Yet, still:

> But because textual drama (especially realism) retains certain alluring features – an open but generally verifiable system of semiotic codes (linguistic, symbolic, etc.) narrative structures with which the audience can be comfortable, psychologically developed characters who engage the spectator's active sympathies, and a cumulative method of knowledge acquisition (as opposed to a discontinuous and therefore disquieting one) – the form is thought not to have lost altogether its attraction and usefulness. (15–16)

Here, then, is today's crux: a polarization of long-established and newer methods of theatrical portrayal when it comes to engaging the world of the now in all of its violent atonality, self-reflexive irony, and array of lively divergences from prior norms. Realism is challenged for precisely the mimetic qualities that a realist artist would affirm, yet realistic portrayal goes on apace in theatre as well as on film and television, and actor training still references the Stanislavski system's prioritizing of truth and belief with respect to character.[6] Under such circumstances, the fact that diametrically opposed aesthetics and ideologies can coexist is remarkable in itself – and the implications of this tension for dramaturgy and for characterization in theatre are considerable, to say the least.

In *Postdramatic Theatre*, Hans-Thies Lehmann looks, as Fuchs does, at recent gravitations toward a prominence of theatrical spectacle over character, with "visual dramaturgy" replacing one that is "regulated by the text" (93). Most arresting, though, is Lehmann's severance of character from drama, and of drama from theatre. Recalling Pirandello's conviction that a dramatic character must have his or her drama, it is perhaps difficult to conceive of such a lack. Is it not the province of stage characters, after all, to be conflicted, to grapple with dilemmas, to provoke or battle one another, to have much that can be gained or lost, and to win our interest in direct relation to such stakes? Lehmann refutes that idea, and claims rather that the stage is mistakenly conceived as a "theatre of dramas," and that it is misguided to categorize "imitation" together with a connection of "'action'/'plot'" that is taken for granted. "Dramatic theatre," offers Lehmann, "is subordinated to the primacy of the text" (21).[7] His argument, though wide-ranging and inclusive, is concisely summed up: "Everything indicates that the reasons why dramatic action was formerly central to theatre no longer apply: the main idea no longer being a narrative, fabulating description of the world by means of mimesis; the formulation of an intellectually important collision of objectives; the process of dramatic action as the image of the dialectics of human experience; the entertainment value of 'suspense' where one situation prepares for and leads to a new and changed situation" (69).

What, then, is left? And, where does (dramatic) character fit with so thorough a departure from action, imitation, the primacy of objectives, and the progressive alteration of a fraught situation through character relations, conflicts, and behaviors in a story? Moreover, to discredit mimesis is, implicitly, to disarm poetic metaphor and metonymy as these belong to theatrical or literary works and presentations. Indeed, doing so devalues the theatrical illusion itself, which is dependent not only upon mimesis but also on the willingness of an audience to buy into the artful pretense upon which theatre depends. In short, the vision is not Dionysian; ceremony may be present, but the god of character and of the mask is not. And yet, the postdramatic idea persists on its own terms, as in Joseph Danan's perspective, which is closely related to Fuchs's as well as Lehmann's. For Danan, the impact of performance art has "shaken mimesis, the bedrock of western theatre from Aristotle onwards" (3–4); the emphasis of an alternative trend is on the actor, event, and the performance in real time, not the dramatic character and not the representation of an invented action or fictional story. Indeed, Danan questions the very basis and veracity of characterization: "What's to be done with characters when we don't believe in character anymore and we want to see a performer accomplishing a series of actions that refer only to themselves, without mimesis?" (8). The argument, of necessity, is for an alternate dramaturgy with respect to what has been regarded historically as fundamental, especially regarding plot, character, and their interrelation. In Danan's view, conventional stories are "too obvious," traditional dramatic structures are "too robust" (he notes the disappearance of the word "plot" from the discourse among dramaturgs and writers on contemporary theatre) and characters have "too much characterization" (13). In common with Fuchs, he notes a decline in the prominence of dramatic character generally, referring to "the weakening of character in the course of the twentieth century" and naming such decline as "a major symptom of the critique of mimesis" (13). Many playwrights would, no doubt, take issue with such an assertion. Again, however, the fundamental disagreement here is not only with the long tradition of text-based theatre and drama, but also with the aesthetics of representation itself – the artistic situation in which one thing stands for another with the aim of being accepted by a viewer as the latter (or, in the context here, an actor standing for a character).

In truth, what Lehmann aspires for most for a postdramatic theatre is a "real" that can correspond to a contemporary and "desperately psyched up sense of life" (118). He advocates for ceremony, and for a theatre that can accomplish its ends without resorting to imitative techniques that can only "fabulate." Even so, it is precisely a "theatre of drama," in its many guises and iterations, that continues still to offer the principle and most commonly practiced means of situating human figures, complete with names, identities, ideas, and problems, within a context of circumstance and action that must earn, because of curiosity or fascination or mystery, an audience's attention. In spite of the obviously stimulating capabilities of a thought/spectacle ratio for theatrical performance, it is difficult to bypass or override the dynamic of character/plot (or vice versa) as an established and significant point of access for the observer, especially with respect to characterization that is situated within a story structure. The self, as object of imitation or participant in dramatic action, may be elusive or even indefinable for all manner of reasons – ontological, linguistic, psychological, scientific – yet its complex subjectivity, along with its volatile availability for change, still comprises no small part of the allure of drama as well as theatre, and of the two in combination.

Character, Self, Agency

I have referred already to the profound identity that can develop in theatre between the depicted personality of a character and the spectator – a contentious idea, as we see. In fact, this is a relationship of considerable nuance and interdependency, despite the more straightforward aspects of spectatorship per se, and it has gained in complexity as well as immediacy. We have looked already at the phenomenon of the surrogate as it applies to the relationship of dramatic character and audience or of character and reader, noting that fictive personages, theatrical or literary, can deliver experiences that we might not otherwise have, stand in for us and broaden our range of knowledge, and even embody an extension of our own life history.[8] As an elaboration of this idea, the identification of an observer or reader with an invented character can extend to an actual adoption of that figure's fictional traits and qualities as one's own, sometimes in order to compensate for – as, perhaps, in the desire for a surrogate – shortcomings or gaps in experience, knowledge, or self-image. In *Who Am I This Time?*, Jay Martin proposes the "fictive personality" as a psychological phenomenon that, in his view, became increasingly common during the twentieth century. His reference is to "real people who find their identities in literature," and to the ways in which "normal personalities are defined by and normal identities realized though fictions" (12).

While theatrical and literary works are available to this syndrome, film and television in particular are contributory to what is by now a profusion of fictive characters that are presented by dramatic means. As Martin notes, "modern culture has become increasingly differentiated from traditional societies by the enormous enlargement of fictions through the fiction-producing qualities of the media" (13).[9] And, adding to the "fictive" is the "virtual," which has come to signify both a perpetual and perceptual "as if" with respect to who we are and what we do. With reference once again to Wendy Steiner's *The Real Real Thing*, the virtual intrudes "doubleness" into the space between what is actual and what is modeled (12). Characters who are "literally" virtual may be more common in film than in theatre, and the virtual as a stand-in for actuality may belong more to the internet or to the computerized film techniques than to the stage, but such a status contributes nonetheless to a perception that our lives are shadowed by an "other" that can be a fictive version or revision of our own selves and endeavors.

Given such an array of replicas, substitutions, and ambiguities with respect to identity, how can dramatic character, if understood primarily as an imitative substitute for personhood, maintain its veracity and stability? Or, to frame the question somewhat differently, why and by what means does dramatic character continue as a reliable center for dramatic storytelling, even with the concepts of "self" or "drama" or "mimesis" under challenge? With reference to plays by Caryl Churchill and Suzan-Lori Parks, Elin Diamond has referred to certain basic tenets of characterization as something past and passé. Such plays are, "as it were, post-identity, with characters in quasi-mimetic settings yet nearly devoid of identity markers – the (illusion of) interiority audiences once expected of theatre characters" ("Identity" 66). And yet, since a concept of self is often the basis for identity, and by extension for characterization, to what extent is a consistency or trustworthiness of selfhood still a requisite for particular theatrical genres, in both contemporary and historical settings?

We have noted that a quality of agency can be understood as one of the fundamental markers of selfhood, and it is also one of the basic attributes of dramatic character. Both Ramachandran and Damasio identify agency as an intrinsic component in one's sense of self. For the former, it is "what we call free will, being in charge of our own actions and destinies" (97); for the latter, a feeling that "actions being carried out by my body are commanded by my mind" (196–197). For Searle, it is the capacity for "acting on reasons," which is notably different from "having something happen to one causally" (*Mind* 203–204). We looked earlier at the question of free will in relation to theatrical characterization, and the degree to which an illusion of autonomy can be conveyed, albeit within the constraints of story and text. Even for Hamlet, who can appear so self-aware of his status as a character in a play that he threatens to transcend and usurp the work that bears his name, we see that possibilities for actual free will in characterization are severely restricted.

That said, though, the illusion of freedom, and of choice, remain indispensable factors in characterization. An audience must be able to believe that a character can make decisions with regard to his or her future. Moreover, the phenomenon of agency itself can be understood as intrinsic to the framing of dramatic action and, thus, to the delineation of stage figures. We have considered Kenneth Burke's dramatism as a pentad of "motives," including the ratios among the five key terms. One such ratio would be "agent/agency," or the way in which a motive or action is carried out by one to whom it has importance. Another could be expressed as "agency/purpose," signifying the correspondence between performed action and a goal. Burke's theory is sociologically based, but his terms are derived from drama and apply to the actions of depicted persons, including their intentions and strategies. Within the terms of the pentad, then, agency is necessarily embodied toward a purpose, and a drama is enacted through deeds ("act") with particular backgrounds and locations ("scene").[10] When Burke's terminology is compared to, or combined with, agency as an attribute of selfhood, the result is a dependency of dramatic action upon a motivated exercise of will on the part of a character, a formulation that implies, in turn, a narrative of action carried out by represented persons – essentially an Aristotelian formula with a concept of "self" substituted for agent.

Here I do not seriously question the idea that theatrical art can be based solely or in large part on performative aspects that underscore a relation of thought (idea) and spectacle (visual dramaturgy), or that advance a conception of self as a construction of a culture or of political hegemony, the bias of a given epoch, or something that is by nature indeterminate. Rather, I argue for the current as well as ancestral status of dramatic character as a viable reflection of what may be termed selfhood in relation to mind, thought, personified ideas and feelings, actions contemplated and embodied, and as a key point of identification for a spectator. I believe also that the factor of agency is critical in this regard, particularly as it pertains to freedom of action or choice on the part of a character, or at least the appearance of the same – what might be termed a dramaturgy of autonomous choosing and decision making. In this relation, indeed, there is a significant further connection of self with character when it comes to powers of determination versus determinism. If, on the one hand, it is theorized that persons are bereft of actual volition, given that one has little or no control over the physics of neuronal firings that prompt an essentially mechanized and determined behavior, then a person is very much like a character in a play – a figure whose progress and outcome, despite appearances, are assured. Or, by contrast, if it is believed that a person is in charge of his or her own thoughts and actions, and thus responsible for the same, then the possibilities for deliberative choice on the part of dramatic characters – or, again, the appearance of such – are greatly enhanced by such a model of cognitive self-awareness.

In *Who's in Charge?*, Michael S. Gazzaniga confronts this very issue, the implications of a deterministic model versus one of autonomous choice. His focus is on a human problem that is universal and yet worthy of Hamlet for its existential layering and ontological intricacies. In brief, Gazzaniga's aim is to show that, even in the face of scientific evidence, we are still the captains of our personal ships. But in order to reach that conclusion, he argues also for a mind that oversees brain – that is, for behaviors that are chosen, not dictated by purely physical, neuronal processes. His theory is simply expressed, that "all of the spectacular advances of science still leave us an unshakeable fact. *We are personally responsible agents and are to be held accountable for our actions, even though we live in a determined universe*" (2, italics original). Gazzaniga allows that the "physiochemical brain does enable the mind in some way we don't understand and in so doing, it follows the physical laws of the universe just like other matter." The view of many in neuroscience, indeed, is that "because our brains follow the laws of the physical world, we all, in essence, are zombies, with no volition. The common assumption among scientists is that we know who and what we are only after the fact of nervous system action" (3).

Gazzaniga's position, by contrast, is that "the mind, which is somehow generated by the physical processes of the brain, constrains the brain," and that this, in effect, is what delivers volition back to us. His idea is not at odds with the science, but is consistent with an "emergent mind" that is not synonymous with brain and is able to constrain or govern certain of its processes. For Gazzaniga, the issue could scarcely be more critical:

> How the mind relates to brain, with its implications for personal responsibility, no matter who addresses it, keeps grabbing our attention. The importance of the answer to this question, which is central for understanding what we humans are experiencing as sentient, forward-looking, and meaning-seeking animals cannot be overstated. (5)

We have seen that the relation of mind (or self, or consciousness) to brain remains open to inquiry from a number of standpoints, including the philosophical as well as biological. Searle, for example, distinguishes "psychological freedom" from the neurobiology that is its substrate and that is deterministic. He believes, too, that "the conviction of our own freedom is inescapable. We cannot act except under the presupposition of freedom" (158, 164).[11] Here, yet again, a phenomenon that connects directly to conceptions of consciousness and selfhood can be seen as related also to dramatic character, in terms of the model of personhood that is being imitated and the extent to which that person is capable of free choice in terms of beliefs, motives, and actions taken deliberately toward a purpose. This is fundamental in drama, and it is situated within the province of characterization as a depiction of mind together with the physical, emotional, and behavioral self.

Character, Self, Spectacle

My ambition here is not to question Aristotle's hierarchy of dramatic elements or any subsequent reshuffling of same, especially on the plot/character ratio or the primacy of any one component over another. Obviously, there are plays in which a supremacy of spectacle, or of language, or of music is essential. There are those, too, in which a particular combination of characterization and dramatic structure along with spectacle produces a total effect that will belie the question of hierarchy entirely. In Caryl Churchill's *Cloud 9*, for example, what is shown as a reversed image of gender and race is essential to an ironized portrait of how characters are seen (literally) and what the play has on its mind. One need only observe the figure of Betty as played by a man in the first act and a woman in the second, or Joshua as a black man played by a white actor, or Victoria represented by a doll – to appreciate Churchill's satirically Brechtian gestus of appearances, sexuality, gender identity, and politics. In that case, the way that character appears is at first paramount, in the setting of the nineteenth century, but then turns from ironic spectacle to heightened levels of consciousness that are discovered among the characters a hundred or so years later, especially with respect to gender and its signifiers. Gender, indeed, is for Churchill an "ideology" – to wit, an image of self that is an outcome of cultural biases and tendencies, particularly so in that it arises from a dominant belief system rather than sexual identity per se. "When gender is 'alienated' or foregrounded," writes Elin Diamond, "the spectator is able to see what s/he can't see: a sign system *as* a sign system" (*Unmaking* 47). In *Cloud 9*, writes Diamond, "sexual identity in the hallowed institution of the Victorian family is not 'natural' but is constituted by prevailing gender codes" ("Refusing" 277). Churchill's play delivers, of course, an extremely sardonic relation of character and spectacle, especially in the first act. It opens with a musical sequence in which Clive introduces his "family" one by one, beginning with Betty:

> "I am a father to the natives here,/And father to my family so dear."
> (He presents Betty. She is played by a man.)
> "My wife is all I dreamt a wife should be,/And everything she is she owes to me."

And Betty responds:

> "I live for Clive./The whole aim of my life/Is to be what he looks for in a wife./I am a man's creation as you see,/And what men want is what I want to be." (3–4)

Yet Clive has no character to speak of. He is a type, a cliché, an epitome of colonization and racism, with a sexual appetite that is at once voracious and indiscriminate. Character accrues, however, as the play moves into the second act, and is learned rather than imposed. A relation of thought and spectacle is underscored from the start in *Cloud 9*, with the characters defined at first by ironic reversals and later on by the discovery of more authentic identities and relationships, familial and otherwise. And yet, while Churchill's marriage of character with performative spectacle is marked in *Cloud 9*, the linkage itself is by no means unique. American plays as disparate as Wendy Wasserstein's *The Heidi Chronicles*, Luis Valdez's *Zoot Suit*, and Tony Kushner's *Angels in America* are exemplary also of a character's relationships, concerns, and crises reflected directly through visual imagery, sound, and music. For this study, I am focusing exclusively on plays rather than musical theatre, but the centrality of dance, song, and orchestral elements can be definitive with respect to the dramaturgy of characterization as well as the structure of a musical.

Dramatic Character and Genre, Revisited

The idea that certain types of dramatic characters are aligned with particular genre categories has a lengthy ancestry, as we have seen. Indeed, this linkage extends to beginnings of theatre and corresponding developments in the direction of comic and tragic drama. In the English Renaissance, Hamlet's debt is to a popular tradition of revenge tragedy along with his own promptings of conscience and the singular exigencies and oddities of Shakespeare's plot. An alliance, or interdependence, of character and genre has tended, historically, to be usual if not intrinsic in dramatic composition. Theatrical genres have a way of being capacious and restrictive at once, so there can be room, as in Hamlet's case, for a character's individuality within the broader contours of an artistic style. Of course, the concept of genre itself has been queried often, and traditional categories have been challenged over time – as, in the eighteenth century, when Richard Steele extols the value of sentiment as evoking, in a comedy, "a joy too exquisite for laughter," or when George Lillo recommends that tragedy admit the common person into its fold.[12] There are, naturally,

many plays that are notably innovative, even singular, that do not conform to any established style or format, sometimes (but not always) as
an early iteration of what may become more normative. Still, and while
the structural or stylistic dynamics of, say, a melodrama, farce, comedy of
manners, or conventional family play may be ironized or presented satirically at times, they have been markedly consistent in terms of their defining capabilities – due in large part to the long-standing popularity of these
venerable and versatile types of drama.

When artistic categorization itself is questioned, it is sometimes in relation to how a genre might be perceived as falsely exclusive or out of touch
with the spirit of an era. To what degree can "tragedy" achieve immediacy or find a social application except in a historic as against contemporary sense?[13] Is "comedy" too embracing a term for what might be farcical,
bawdy, sentimental, satirical, absurd, romantic, dark, or tragicomic? And
yet, even with such inclusive considerations taken into account, the relationship of dramatic character to genre remains profoundly intimate,
especially to the extent that the qualities of the former can be dictated
by the rigors of the latter – or, conversely, the degree to which varieties
of character behavior are essential to the style of a particular sort of storytelling and theatre experience. Bearing strongly on this relation, too,
is a factor of necessity; to wit, the performance of a dramatic character
is vital to the constancy of forms that may be historical in their origin
but continue nonetheless and are essential parts of theatre's ancestry, very
often with a present-day appeal and resonance. Farce, after all, began in
the ancient world, but its frenetic pace and manic characterizations can
feel absolutely appropriate to the energies and absurdities of differing eras
including our own.

Tom Stoppard's *Travesties* provides an illustrative, if ironic, case in point
regarding the natural rapport between dramatic character and theatrical genre, especially when juxtaposed with Oscar Wilde's *The Importance
of Being Earnest*, which is nested into its action. In Stoppard's farce,
Wilde's comedy of manners – with its famously stylish and epigrammatic
phrasing – is borrowed not only for its wit and exuberance but also for the
purpose of confounding the borders between real and fictional personages,
thus producing, in effect, an arch and anarchic commentary on characterization itself. *Travesties* centers on four real, historical personages: James
Joyce, Lenin, Tristan Tzara, and the less famous Henry Carr, all of whom
happened to be in Zurich in 1917, with two of them, Carr and Joyce,
actually involved in a production of Wilde's play. Stoppard's cast includes
"Cecily" and "Gwendolen," who are not Wilde's infamous consumers of

tea and cucumber sandwiches but mirror and fondly satirize them anyway. The action is seen through the engaging, amusing, and utterly unreliable filter of the aging Carr's memory, with his self-aggrandizing recollections placing himself usually at center stage, even as political, artistic, and literary history is taking shape around him.

Yet Carr is considerably more than a figure of comical senescence; rather, he appears doubly as "a shabby old man" and younger, as "his youthful elegant self" (viii). Moreover, he is self-dramatizing, particularly when it comes to remembering himself in relation to the famous and to his role in *The Importance of Being Earnest*. Carr, then, is a metatheatrical character, embodying the methods and language of theatre, existing in one play while talking about another, recalling or misremembering events in relation to a historical Henry Carr. The play, too, is metatheatre, with a debt not only to manners as a comedic style but also in direct connection to what is arguably the genre's most renowned and exemplary work. Stoppard is an admirer and an imitator of Wilde, so much so that he provides *Travesties* with a butler, called Bennett, who stands in for the figures of Lane and Merriman in *The Importance of Being Earnest* (a similar character, Jellaby, brings in letters in *Arcadia*). Stoppard, in obvious appreciation of his literary ancestor, has Carr mentioning the production of Wilde's play:

CECILY: *Earnest*??
CARR: No – the other one.
CECILY: What do you mean by *Earnest*?
CARR: *The Importance of being Earnest*, by Oscar Wilde.
CECILY: Wilde?
CARR: You know him? (49)

Earlier, Joyce has remarked to Carr, describing the character of Jack Worthing (the other one) and hoping to interest him in the role: "He says things like, I may occasionally be a little overdressed but I make up for it by being immensely over-educated. That gives you a general idea of him" (33). In sequences such as these (and *Travesties* is built upon several) Stoppard is, in effect, riffing on dramatic character types along with the borders among genres and having a tremendously good time with stage figures who can, in effect, cross boundaries between plays while swapping traits and speech mannerisms among themselves.

Nevertheless, and just as George Etherege needs a Mr. Dorimant to phrase truewit ennui to perfection – "But the devil's in't, there has been such a calm in my affairs of late, I have not had the pleasure of making a woman so much as break her fan, to be sullen, or forswear herself, these three days" (18) – Wilde (or Stoppard) must be able to fashion a character who can balance a line, bring intellect and wittiness to an observation (or a non sequitur), carry on a courtship, confuse identities, and savor a canapé – that is, one who can speak and embody (or satirize) comedy of manners to perfection. The fact that there is an ancestral lineage from Etherege and Wycherley to Wilde, Coward, and Stoppard is due in part to characters who, from Dorimant or Horner to Lady Bracknell or Cecily Cardew (or Carruthers), can stand for and sustain the pleasures of a theatrical genre type. In this regard, Henry Carr remains a stage figure bound to a style, even in the context of Stoppard's mix of historical and fictional persons, and with the dramatist's blending of satire with manners. The play's metatheatricality is, in other words, capacious enough to admit stylistic variations while observing the prescriptions of more than one genre type.

I do not mean to imply, though, that such typologies are definitive, either sternly demarked with formulaic guidelines or inhibitive with respect to characterization. That sort of rigorousness, seen in connection with Neoclassical rules and stipulations in particular, may not be authoritative outside of the contextual circumstances of a given social or historical setting. In fact, dramatic genres can be understood also as flexible and adaptable, as, for example, when a combination of metatheatricality with a genre type becomes a means of expanding theatrical capabilities. *Travesties* combines farce with satire and comedy of manners, historical coincidences with literary references; it delivers the performative Henry Carr along with his remembered others, even while conjuring Wilde and that playwright's most famous play. Here, then, a blending of categorical yet disparate elements results in a play of arresting vibrancy in which genre and character types are varied but at the same time coparticipatory.

Not long after the premiere of *Travesties* in London (1974), Luis Valdez's *Zoot Suit* opened in Los Angeles (1978) and introduced El Pachuco – himself a metatheatrical central figure who is involved in historic events and provides the play's narrative voice.[14] He serves also as alter ego to the play's ostensible main character, Henry Reyna. El Pachuco is the play's emcee and impresario, yet he can also participate in the action – or put a stop to events with a snap of his fingers.[15] He links the two historical occurrences that were source material for Valdez – the Sleepy Lagoon Murder case and the Zoot Suit Riots of 1940s Los Angeles – yet he maintains a distinctly contemporary and street-smart attitude toward those same histories and to the racist attitudes of the society in which the play takes place. El Pachuco is, in effect, a flamboyant tour de force of theatrical characterization. Strutting and defiant, he smoothly yet edgily merges the play's levels of personal, global, and familial dramas, even while defying such apparent unities through Valdez's use, in the staging, of Brechtian gestus and estrangement.[16] The play is far from subtle in its politics or its scorn for the Hearst-dominated media or the racially opinionated courts that landed Henry Reyna and his *batos* in San Quentin, some of them with life sentences for a murder they had nothing to do with. Instead, and much like Valdez's earlier *actos* performed by El Teatro Campesino, the play is spare and confrontational in terms of its political savvy and socially activist strategies, even in the context of its flamboyant theatricality.

Dramatic Character and Family, Revisited

Yet *Zoot Suit* is, at its heart, also a play of familial relations, and is illustrative in this way of another long-established genre, the American variation of the family play. Even as Henry Reyna belongs and is loyal to the members of his gang and fellow arrestees, and though he comes over time to esteem and trust both Alice Bloomfield, head of the Sleepy Lagoon Defense Committee, and George Shearer, his court-appointed attorney (both of whom are white), Henry is shown to be close with each member of his immediate family – Enrique and Dolores, his parents, together with brother Rudy and sister Lupe. Henry's family grounds him as a continuing source of learned values and earned allegiances. They allow an audience, in short, to witness and appreciate where Henry comes from. Moreover, the Reynas are recognizably typical, with the parents admonishing the kids on, say, the shortness of Lupe's skirt or the cut of Henry's "drapes," the attire that gives the play its title. The ending of *Zoot Suit* is open-ended, and the audience is left to speculate about various possible outcomes for Henry's life after prison – in effect, one is asked for a prediction regarding the "character" of his character. The final image of the play, though, is of Henry opting not to defy his father and, instead, joining all of his family – Enrique, Dolores, Lupe, Rudy – in a shared embrace. *Zoot Suit* may be Brechtian in its style, performative and presentational and with a theatricalist swagger, but it relies also upon familial bonds that are depicted as realistically deep and reliably constant. While Valdez's strategy is to assemble a portrait of racism, prejudice, and betrayal of Henry by media and the courts – and by his country – and to demonstrate a range of responses and consequences, the impact of this portrayal is felt most strongly against the contextual and necessary foundation of Henry Reyna's family.[17]

Racism informs August Wilson's *Fences*, too, although in this case the drama of family relations centers on that which intrudes between a father, Troy Maxson, and son Cory – and also on Troy's marriage to Rose, including the consequences of an affair with Alberta and the birth of a child outside of his marriage. In many ways, certainly, *Fences* is an utterly conventional family drama. It is structured in two acts with a total of nine scenes, and the play's setting is the realistically presented front yard and entrance area of the Maxson house, in 1957. While Troy was once a baseball player of uncommon talent, as a black man he could not play in the American major leagues. Now son Cory wants to pursue a football career, but Troy cannot see or trust that the times and attitudes might have changed enough so that his son could have a chance that he, Troy, was never allowed. Because of this past experience, Troy is adamant in his convictions, and even though he wants to do the best by his son, he cannot see that he himself stands in the way of Cory's possible success. Troy betrays, in this way at least, a kinship to Arthur Miller's Eddie Carbone who, in *A View from the Bridge*, cannot perceive, let alone admit, that he has romantic feelings for his niece, Catherine. In both cases, Troy's and Eddie's, there is blindness to a factor that turns causally into each play's core antagonism.

Indeed, the conflict between Troy and Cory builds toward a confrontation that comes at the end of *Fences* and is very nearly brutal in its outcome, as father and son narrowly avoid violently injuring one another – ironically, with each threatening the other with Troy's baseball bat. Cory swings twice at Troy, who keeps coming after him:

> TROY: You're gonna have to kill me! You wanna draw that bat back on me. You're gonna have to kill me.

Wilson describes the action that ensues, with Cory backed up against a tree and Troy advancing toward him: "Cory and Troy struggle over the bat. The struggle is fierce and fully engaged. Troy ultimately is the stronger, and takes the bat from Cory and stands over him ready to swing. He stops himself" (82).

The "fully engaged" power of this scene results in part from its rapid and vivid escalation toward potential violence. Yet, the forcefulness of this interaction comes mostly from the enormity of what Troy has at stake and from how the audience has been led, over the full course of the play's action, to understand those stakes. Much is learned about Troy's past, including the violent and formative incidents that took place with his own father, a time in prison, his attitude on race in connection with

professional sports, his current job as a garbage collector, and how he conceives of a personal battle with "Death." As he says to Rose, "I ain't making up nothing. I'm telling you the facts of what happened. I wrestled
with Death for three days and three nights and I'm standing here to tell
you about it" (17). The drama of familial relations has been investigated
here so far in relation to how characters think and, in particular, to how
stage figures who are related by blood can participate in ways of thinking
that transcend any one individual and become collective – with O'Neill's
Tyrones as an exemplary case of a "collective mind" in characterization.
The family setting can also be marked by an intensity of emotional expressiveness that belongs especially to those who share a depth of background
and have a history of experience in common, along with whatever rivalries
or loyalties pertain in the current circumstances of a play. Such is the case
in *Fences*, where Troy's passionate attitudes are shown as vital to all that
transpires – not only for himself but also for those around him.

The ability of a dramatic character to embody states of emotion that
arise from an interplay of background and long-standing relationships,
familial or otherwise – or that, in related fashion, reveal what has been
formative with regard to present attitudes or beliefs – can be essential to
particular types of stage figures and their stories. These are factors, too,
that frequently pertain in "real person" characterization of a sort that is
designed to impart a depth (or, again, roundedness) of experience that,
in turn, can have a significant impact upon a play's current relationships
and interactions.[18] In *The Heidi Chronicles* (1989), Wendy Wasserstein
attends to exactly this formulation, to what has, over a span of time, contributed to making her title character the woman that she becomes. The
play depicts Heidi Holland in her present circumstances, as an art historian disillusioned by what has became of past ideals and beliefs, but
most of the action (spanning twenty-four years, from Heidi at age sixteen
to forty) is concerned with showing what has been formative, publicly
and privately – with regard to her profession, points of view on events in
the world, romantic relations and friendships, and especially her feminist
and humanist convictions. Feeling abandoned by those who shared those
beliefs, Heidi has, in effect, lost not only sisterhood but also a sense of
family connection. By the time she reaches a point of feeling "stranded,"
the audience knows precisely what has led her to this conclusion (232).[19]

With this sort of focus on the playwright's part, the representation of
character in drama turns to more than a replication of personhood or
self – and to more even than the "real person" illusion would imply per
se. Here, the dramaturgy of characterization delivers not only a person

but also a life, complete with what has formed that life, and is able to do so, remarkably, within the time constraints of theatrical presentation. There is a relevant passage in Bernhard Schlink's novel, *The Reader*, that speaks tellingly to this connection of a character to what has, in effect, comprised its formation. The passage appears very near the end of the book and connects the experiences and realizations of the story's narrator, Michael Berg, to ways in which events and memories have intersected for him, thus shaping his current attitudes and feelings. He thinks back on his long relationship with Hannah Schmitz, which began as a sexual affair in his middle teens, continued through his adult discovery of her illiteracy and prior involvement with Nazi death camps, and ended with her suicide. Now he recalls that, "All of this happened ten years ago. In the first few years after Hanna's death, I was tormented by the old questions of whether I had denied and betrayed her, whether I owed her something, whether I was guilty for having loved her. Sometimes I asked myself if I was responsible for her death." Berg lets the reader know how he has tried to write his story and Hannah's many times, and how he has debated its possibly happy or sad – or, regardless, simply true – aspects, and then he concludes:

> At any rate, that's what I think when I just happen to think about it. But if something hurts me, the hurts I suffered back then come back to me, and when I feel guilty, the feelings of guilt return; if I yearn for something today, or feel homesick, I feel the yearnings and homesickness from back then. The tectonic layers of our lives rest so tightly one on top of the other that we always come up against earlier events in later ones, not as matter that has been fully formed and pushed aside, but absolutely present and alive. I understand this. Nevertheless, I sometimes find it hard to bear. Maybe I did write our story to be free of it, even if I never can be. (216–218)

Although Berg's recollection is told through fictional narrative, he speaks to a natural human situation and tendency that is absolutely within the domain of dramatic character also. In either play or novel, the "tectonic layers" must be shown or recounted so that an audience or a reader will appreciate their interplay and impact. And yet, Berg's remembrance is suggestive – albeit not by intention – not only of a similarity but also of a profound difference between characterization in drama and in literature. A dramatic character, more so perhaps than a comparable figure in fictional narrative, has the particular ability to have one's formative past be vividly "present and alive," if only because of the brief duration coupled with the immediacy of theatrical performance. The layers of a life, in their tight and ready juxtapositions, can in this way be embodied through the actor in real time as opposed to a conveyed imagery in the mind of a reader.

Heidi Holland exemplifies this capability, and so, in a different fashion, does Troy Maxson. In both cases, the dramatist shows us the past and present life of a figure who has been shaped significantly by events, by personal choices and relationships, and by changes of attitude that have come to be essential in the context of a play's current circumstances and tensions. In Heidi's situation especially, a self is shown to be fluid and available to change over a twenty-four-year span of time, as opposed to fixed or empirically defined at any given moment. In this respect, anyway, the dramatic approach of Wasserstein or Wilson differs markedly from a play such as *Angels in America: Millennium Approaches*, where Tony Kushner's focus is sustained on the immediate and interrelated crises among the characters rather than on what in the past has brought Louis or Prior or Hannah or Joe to his or her own emergency. Of course, *Angels in America* is exemplary also of metatheatricality and ironic referentiality with respect to character and culture on many levels, as in the opening scene of Act III that depicts a frightened Prior Walter facing one and then another ghost of other (prior) Priors. As the scene concludes, Prior attempts to sing away his terror with a snippet of Eliza Doolittle's song from *My Fair Lady*: "All I want is a room somewhere, far away from the cold night air" (85–89) – as in the case of *Travesties*, the knowing quotation of one play by another.

Theatre artists have endeavored in many ways and over many decades to find a viable synchronicity in the portrayal of character, depiction of action, use of language, and means of dramatic structuring. Artists have looked for congruity, too, between the figuration of people and events with what Lehmann calls the "desperately psyched up sense of life" – or its equivalent in terms of the particular zeitgeist, mood, or pace of an age. The problem is formidable, perhaps particularly so in the relation of realistic depiction and causally based dramaturgy to the very sorts of contingencies, uncertainties, and vagaries of selfhood and experience that are in discussion here. Is it possible, then, for the situations of contemporary persons in the world, with all of that world's fits and tempos and variations of consistency or illogic, to be reflected through a cohesive representation of character and a causal dramatic structure? The question bears strongly on what numerous playwrights – from Buchner or Wedekind to Pirandello, Brecht, Ionesco, or Pinter among many others – have confronted with respect to artistic unity or lack of same, or the problem of depicting (or not) life as it is lived or as it is imagined – to state this problematic challenge at its simplest. Here again, the question of genre type can pertain, in that a genre can enforce or be at odds with conjuring a lifelikeness, an "air of reality," as Henry James might say, in relation not only to a given play or place in time but also to the feeling of being alive within that time.[20]

In this respect, Jon Robin Baitz's play, *Other Desert Cities*, provides a final case in point, especially so in that it is a conventional, contemporary, realistic drama in the setting of an American family home, with a traditional, two-act structure. In spite of these familiar associations, though, it succeeds in capturing the tensions, fears, and uncertainties of its day, and does so largely through characterization – including how the characters think, perform, feel, speak, and interrelate. It is ironic, perhaps, that *Angels in America* and *Other Desert Cities* have something in common in the figure of Ronald Reagan, who appears in neither play yet haunts both of them. Kushner's play, of course, is situated in the midst of the AIDS crisis during Reagan's presidential administration, while the parent figures in Baitz's play, Lyman and Polly Wyeth, have been friends of Ron and Nancy and belong to a Republican social circle that includes Washington D.C. and Hollywood along with Palm Springs, where the Wyeths now live. In addition, Lyman is a former movie actor with a specialty in Westerns – and, perhaps in further irony, in the playing of death scenes. Polly is a brainy, no-nonsense socialite who, one can presume, was perfectly comfortable with Nancy or with Betsy Bloomingdale at places like Sunnylands, the Walter Annenberg estate, and Republican gathering place, which is presumably not far from the fictive Wyeth's Palm Springs home.

Thus, both of these plays are situated in relation to contemporary American politics, albeit in the 1980s versus the early 2000s. Each play, too, contains an opposition of political voices – in the case of *Other Desert Cities*, it belongs primarily to the unseen character of Henry, one of the Wyeth's two sons who was radicalized and participated years before in a bombing that left a man dead. The Wyeth's daughter, Brooke, crushed by what she assumes was Henry's subsequent suicide, has set out to publish a memoir of her family, with the blame placed squarely on Lyman and Polly. Suffice to say that, in a stunning turnabout, the situation turns out to be not at all what Brooke believed it to be. Henry is still alive, and while Lyman and Polly don't know his whereabouts, they admit having abetted his escape from law enforcement to Canada. In terms of structural dramaturgy, a play could hardly bring about a more perfected Aristotelian unity of reversal and recognition than this one does at the end, as truths are told and Brooke is made to realize all that she has had wrong for so many years.

Other Desert Cities takes place at Christmas, 2004 (with a coda in March 2010) and the attacks of September 11, 2001, are in very recent memory. "*They flew planes into buildings!*" exclaims the Wyeth's son Trip, who produces a wry television show, "Jury of Your Peers" (7–8). In ways that edgily reflect how American politics, news media, film and television have intersected to the point of becoming symbiotic, Baitz brings Hollywood – film and television, but also a long-standing social establishment – into what is a familial as well as a political setting. The tone that results is nervously agitated, in its own way "psyched up," and is in this way transcendent of the conventionally realistic setting and scenic structure. Indeed, these are characters who create, inhabit, and respond to a *now* that is charged with their intelligence, hyperawareness, and, within this family enclave, a shared wavelength that is frenetic in its combinations of dreads and allegiances and betrayals. In short, the preoccupations, behaviors, reactions, and language used by the Wyeths reflect a knowingness that contains within it the anxieties of their time, and so does Baitz's dramaturgy, albeit realistically and in the well-known contexts and rituals of generational family drama. The play not only references film and television but also incorporates the tones and idioms of media, thereby expanding the terrain of a standardized theatrical form. For this reason among others, the relation of dramatic character to genre type is, in the case of *Other Desert Cities*, productive of a play that can, on several levels, surmount its own ancestry and dramaturgical traditions. In this case, the dramaturgy of "real person" characterization, and of realism more generally, is shown to be adaptive as well as contemporary – and ironically so, in that Baitz's play calls upon and quotes the very dramatic media that have been competitive with theatre over decades and, in doing so, encouraged new theatrical forms. Even the convention of the living room setting is updated, here with a sleek and modernistic contour.[21]

The characters in *Other Desert Cities* behave archly, theatrically, and often spitefully with one another – along the lines, for instance, of Noel Coward's people in *Private Lives* or *Hay Fever*. There is a Wyeth family "show" that asks for a very different sort of coparticipation among its members than, say, the Tyrones with their choral thinking and remembering. As self-consciously demonstrative as the Wyeths can be, however, they do not acknowledge the theatre audience. The fourth wall is firmly in place, and there is no transgression. The play is highly aware, in other words, of its own species of entertainment – a drama that references other dramatic media – but the Wyeth family members, while performative by nature, do not engage conversationally or otherwise with the spectator. Or, from a slightly different perspective, they do not admit that they are dramatic characters. There is a caveat, however, in that Polly and Lyman have each and every day been playing a role socially and before the family – that of ignorance of their son's fate. Acting for them is a way of life, and especially so for Lyman, the former movie actor, who says near the play's end that, "acting, you know, it's easy for me. It's easy" (62). The Wyeth parents, in other words, are realistic, strictly representational characters who are also very adept at putting on the mask. The difference here is significant, in that a presentational stage figure's admission of being fictional (El Pachuco, for example, or even The Father) may detract from one's perception of their actuality – but, at the same time, they may equate themselves with we, the members of an audience, and in doing so accentuate their own qualities of personhood. Apart from the Pirandellian aspects of this duality per se, and in spite of the possibly counterintuitive aspect, the deliberate identification of a dramatic character with "us" in the audience can serve at times as yet another means of establishing the perception of "real person" in characterization.[22]

Dramatic Character: A Legacy

The project of reconciling a "real person" model for the representation of dramatic (or literary) character with uncertainties (scientific or otherwise) and with innumerable subjectivities with respect to being can be understood as formidable but not confounding or, certainly, defeating. The concept of selfhood as object of interest can be shown – scientifically, ontologically, existentially, aesthetically – to be elusive and possibly indeterminate but by no means discredited in relation to theatrical characterization as mimesis, the fashioning of a self-replica for the artistic purpose of playmaking. From the standpoint of a philosophy of mind, Searle admits that, yes, "we must postulate a self" and one that is based upon "notions of rationality, free choice decision making, and reasons for action" (*Mind* 201), criteria that apply also to character traits, motives, and behaviors in drama. Indeed, the very elusiveness of selfhood (or, for that matter, its construction artistically or psychologically) has itself been a basis for modernist and postmodernist literary and theatrical art – and, consequently, for models of character portrayal. Consciousness as a "hard" problem may be unsolved scientifically but is extensively explored theatrically in relation to a dramatic character's experience, perceptiveness, and awareness.

Characters that are depicted by dramatic means are by now ubiquitous. The apprehension of fictive characters takes place now across a vast interplay of drama, literary narrative, film and television storytelling and internet representations of persons, at times actual and at times virtual. Even as innovations in performance and alternative theatre have delivered an arresting array of variations on, and departures from, text-based drama, and while the concept of "drama" has itself been reevaluated, dramatic character continues to be situated prominently within a lengthy heritage (among the longest of artistic lineages) as well as a present-day confluence of mediated and live depictions. Moreover, that ancestry – which is today's and tomorrow's artistic inheritance – is based not exclusively but primarily upon characters who are fashioned by dramatists to reflect human thoughts, feelings, and experiences through the imitative portrayal of deeds, actions. and interrelations. New plays are produced now in the context of a living inventory to which they may or not refer, but from which they emerge. In this respect, drama and dramatic characters tend often to bear the imprint of a "post" – not in the sense of postmodernism's tendencies toward quotation, irony, or the parenthetical, but with real debt to some formative influence, such as post-Pirandello or Brecht, post-absurd, or even post-performance. This, too, is contributory to an ancestry, as traditions are reworked and rediscovered even as they are handed down as if generationally.

Despite the many conformities and allegiances to the particular moods and trends of various eras, theatrical characterization has, over time, remained an extraordinarily versatile phenomenon. With allowance even for how rigorously theatrical genre types have been made discrete from one another at times, and how they have directly affected the delineation of character – in the classical, Renaissance, or Neoclassical settings especially – the creation of stage characters has been a consistently inventive and changeable process as well as an adaptive or restrictive one. When the eminence or viability of characterization has been disputed, or when fictive characters themselves have been the targets of antitheatrical prejudice, the impulse and necessity for representing persons through dramatic action and idea has been sustained – even through times when the formal or critical study of dramatic character has abated.[23] Even the "anti" cannot be read only as negative or nihilistic; the commitment to represent ourselves through character is, even at the extreme, an affirmation of sorts – the leaving of a trace, as Beckett might say. At the simplest, yet still remarkable level, fictive theatrical characters are able to stand in for an astonishing range of human endeavors. Further, as our surrogates or as extensions of "fictive" selves, dramatic characters accomplish deeds and discoveries on our behalf, thus creating and enlarging upon a collective experience and knowledge.

The legacy of dramatic literature and of character belongs to many countries, languages, traditions, and epochs. For this discussion, which takes the form of a long view, I have chosen a comparatively few representative works from a lengthy history, mostly ones that are broadly known and particularly illustrative of an aspect of theatrical characterization at a given time or, in some cases, are exemplary of a tradition or are truly seminal – as in the case of *The Bacchae* or *Miss Julie* or *Six Characters in Search of an Author*. While a transhistoric look at the phenomenon of character may run the risk of too broad an embrace of topics that belong more properly to a given setting or time, I have attended whenever possible to commonalities and issues that recur, that have evolved, or that belong to more than a single national or linguistic history. What began as the innovation of a writer and actor in the ancient world and later became Aristotle's "agent" or vehicle for *praxis* and *muthos*, had already turned by the fifth-century B.C. into a means of human representation capable of cosmic as well as personal, philosophic, and political inquiry. The fact that Racine and Corneille, among others, adopted the figures of Greek classicism, along with Horace and the Roman imitators of the Attic theatre, can be seen therefore as unsurprising – despite a connective bridge of over two millennia. The idea that drama can center incisively on interiority or consciousness as against deeds performed or actions taken is one that also spans geography and language together with historic eras. When characters began to be conceived scientifically, with a suggestion of empirical markers for psychological types and behaviors – or, again, for what is formative in a life – a tradition started that continues to this day and will likely persist for as long as fictive models on the stage can stand for what is discovered about our natures. From Antigone or Agamemnon forward, characters in drama have continued to be provocative, not only of what Aristotle might call our sympathy or fright but also of something intriguing or compelling that engages within us a deep curiosity. Dramatic characters, in this long view, have proven over many centuries to be among the most effective impersonations we have for eliciting that curiosity – and, quite possibly, that surprise – about ourselves and the varied circumstances that we continue, very often, to share.

Notes

INTRODUCTION: DRAMATIS PERSONAE

1 In his primer, *Theatre and Mind*, McConachie questions the idea of an audience's "belief" in fictive characters and suggests instead that spectators "multitask" in the observation of performance through an integrated and concurrent perception of character and actor along with other factors, and with several "modes of attention" possible (52–53). McConachie argues elsewhere that in order to understand how an audience reacts, "we need to know how spectators comprehend and negotiate the 'doubleness' of theatre – that is, the fact that a single body on stage can be both an actor and a character, simultaneously existing in both real and simulated time-space" (*Engaging* 7). Compare to Rokotnitz, who writes that, "in a theatre, we are able to observe for ourselves the behavior of the characters embodied onstage. Even if the story it stages is fictional, a live performance enables the audience to witness the events it unfolds as tangibly *as if* they were really taking place. Despite there being a level of symbolic understanding that invites the audience to infer multiple levels of meaning in a play *as a play*, the audience nevertheless also benefits from having embodied knowledge and relies heavily on this knowledge to discern meaning as they watch the play" (McConachie and Hart 135–136).

2 This is not to suggest that all characters in drama are created in like ways, or that all are designed to convey a realistic portrait of a person, but rather to observe that such a perceived completeness is possible despite the abbreviation that is necessary in the theatre. For the reader of a play, the perception of character can be contrasted also with the reading of fiction, in that the dependency of a theatrical text on dialogue and stage directions is conducive similarly to the filling in of absences on the reader's, as against audience member's, part. My purpose here is not to investigate the art and psychology of what is in fact a highly intricate relation of reader and text (of either sort, dramatic or narrative), or to elaborate on theories of audience or reader response, but instead to emphasize this fundamental difference, both practical and aesthetic, in the reception of fictive character by a reader or an observer.

3 While the Aristotelian view (based solely on the *Poetics*) is still widely acknowledged concerning tragedy's beginning with the choral leaders of the

dithyramb, the history is incomplete and is not conclusive. Various findings and interpretations are examined in Chapter 1. See especially Else (*Origin*) for an extensive inquiry into the pivotal importance of Thespis in early tragedy.

4 With respect to Dionysus and the god's associations with the beginnings of theatre, Jean-Pierre Vernant remarks on how "the enigmatic and ambiguous face of the god certainly does smile out at us in the interplay of the theatrical illusion that tragedy introduced for the first time onto the Greek stage" ("The God of Tragic Fiction" 188).

5 Regarding the characteristic forms of Dionysus, see for example Burkert, 166–167. For visual depiction of the god in different guises or on earthenware, see Carpenter and Faroane, 191–195.

6 With respect to a relation of Dionysus and conflict or innate opposition, Otto describes the paradoxical nature of a god who is "the wild spirit of antithesis and paradox, of immediate presence and complete remoteness, of bliss and horror, of infinite vitality and the cruelest destruction" (136).

7 See Green, who remarks on "the separation of the performer we call an actor from the choral group or groups. It was a development which more readily allowed and pointed up discussion and thus difference of opinion within the presentation, so that playwrights were able to create something we recognize as dramatic tension through the interplay of ideas and viewpoints." Green claims that, "we can trace this contrast between group and individual to a date quite early in the fifth century" (16–17).

8 Aristotle elaborates in the *Poetics* (XV) on what constitutes "good," "appropriate," "like," and "consistent" characterization. See Hardison and Golden, 200.

9 I borrow Barish's term and refer here also to Collier's "A Short View of the Immorality and Profaneness of the English Stage" and to Rousseau's "Letter to M. D'Alembert."

10 See States, "Anatomy," for a parsing of these key terms especially.

11 Regarding the Pirandellian reference and phrasing, see Paolucci, "Comedy" (324–325).

12 For an concise overview of dramaturgy as a versatile term with several definitions and associations, see Turner and Behrndt, 17–19.

13 In "The Dual Personality of the Actor," Coquelin describes his approach to a role, emphasizing that an audience must be able to see only the character, not the actor, or the performer's "labor is lost." The approach must begin always with "a deep and careful study of the *character*" (Cole and Chinoy 193). Coquelin takes issue with Irving's emphasis on the "picturesque" (194), while Irving himself insists on the importance of a telling inflection or gestural detail, what he calls "by–play" (354–355). Michel Baron is described by a witness as having "such great truth in his acting and so much naturalness that invariably he made you forget the actor, and he carried the illusion to the point of making you imagine that the action unfolding before you was real" (Nagler 289). See also "Remarks on the Character of Lady Macbeth," by Sarah Siddons, (Cole and Chinoy 142–145).

1 THE ART OF DIONYSUS

1 All quotations from *The Bacchae* are from *Euripides V*, unless otherwise indicated.

2 I note this relation of character and god also in *After Dionysus* (17), with specific reference to Dionysus as what Charles Segal calls the "god of theatrical representation" and "the god of every type of illusion" (*Dionysiac* 298, 330). For Zeitlin, Dionysus is "lord of the theatre" (*Playing* 227, 315).

3 Regarding the female component in the transformation of Pentheus, Zeitlin comments: "In particular, the fact that Pentheus dons a feminine costume and rehearses in it before our eyes exposes perhaps one of the most marked features of Greek theatrical mimesis: that men are the only actors in this civic theater; in order to represent women on stage, men must always put on a feminine costume and mask" ("Playing" 64–65).

4 For elaboration of these precincts of the god, see Easterling ("Show" 45). In her view, all of these aspects pertain to the identity of Dionysus as theatre god.

5 For Henrichs, such complexity results, particularly with the modern (especially Nietzschean) context included, in a Dionysus that "defies definition" (209).

6 Lonsdale is quoted also in Easterling ("Show" 48).

7 In a different context, Padel writes of gods who "are, and are in, wind, storm and fire. In the human world, they send, are, and are in damaging passions: sexual passion, murderous fury" (*Gods* 177).

8 For extended analysis of this sequence in *The Bacchae*, including the robing of Pentheus and its theatrical implications, see Segal's discussion of the play in relation to "metatragedy" (*Dionysiac* 223–228). Zeitlin also singles out the robing sequence for analysis ("Playing" 64–65).

9 See, for example, Nagler: "Greek tragedy had its roots in the choric dithyramb. Aristotle tells us this, and we have no reason to disbelieve his testimony; a Greek philosopher, lecturing on tragedy in the 320's B.C., was much closer to the decisive events than the modern scholar" (3). Pickard-Cambridge, whose inquiry into the dithyramb and its history is arguably the most thoroughgoing to date, notes that the dithyramb's "special connexion with Dionysus throughout its history is sufficiently attested" (1). Characterizing the dithyramb at Athens, he writes: "As a literary composition for chorus dithyramb was the creation of Arion at Corinth, and it seems (like the music of the flute which accompanied it) to have been at first specially cultivated in Dorian lands, but to have attained its full literary development in connexion with the Dionysiac festivals at Athens..." (31). Aristotle's assertion regarding origins is in the *Poetics* (IV) where he observes that tragedy "arose, at first, as an improvisation (both tragedy and comedy are similar in this respect) on the part of those who led the dithyrambs" (Golden, trans. 8). Significant departures include those of Else (*Origin*), who highlights the innovations of Thespis and Aeschylus over a theory of gradual development for tragedy, and Vernant and Vidal-Niquet who offer: "The only origin of tragedy is tragedy itself. The fact

that a protagonist emerges from the chorus chanting a 'dithyramb' in honor of Dionysus or that a second actor (in Aeschylus) or a third (in Sophocles) joins him in his confrontation with the chorus cannot be explained in terms of 'origins' " (305).

10 In Bieber's phrasing: "The Dionysiac religion is an ecstatic religion. The wine, the gift of the god, and religious rapture changed the mortal followers of the god in their frenzy into members of the Dionysiac *thiasus*, the sacred herd of the god" (1).

11 Bieber writes: "Dramatic art requires the actor to lay aside the personality with which he was endowed by birth and to feel himself as one who has abandoned the limitation of his own personality. He must lose his own identity and become a changed being, a demon, a god, or a hero" (9). And further: "Tragedy, the most elevated form of the cult of the god, also presupposes ecstasy and has retained the name for the followers of the god Dionysus. Tragedy, then, is the *song of the holy thiasus in honor of the god.* Hence it was only in the religion of Dionysus that the drama could be fashioned, for only by god-given intoxication could a man be changed into a thiasote, an actor" (16–17). More recently, P. E. Easterling has suggested a similar, if broader, linkage – that through the "capacious" approach that she advocates, by assimilating the multiple faces, appearances, and incarnations of the god, one might "see the interplay between Dionysus' different aspects as providing a particularly strong stimulus for mimetic performance" ("Show" 47–48).

12 For Jane Ellen Harrison: "Surely it is at least possible that the real impulse to the drama lay not wholly in 'goat-songs' and 'circular dancing places' but also in the cardinal, the essentially dramatic, conviction of the religion of Dionysus, that the worshipper can not only worship, but can become, can *be*, his god" (*Prolegomena to the Study of Greek Religion*, 568; quoted by Flickinger, 17).

13 I refer to the *Poetics* (XIII). In Golden's translation, "the best tragedies are constructed about a few families, for example, about Alcmaeon, Oedipus, Orestes, Meleager, Thyestes, Telephon, and any others who were destined to experience, or to commit, terrifying acts" (22).

14 With respect to Thespis as inventor of tragedy, see again Else, who believes that: "Thespis created a new genre, instead of merely tinkering with an old one" (*Origin* 55). Else views the actor/chorus leader relationship differently from how Bieber does, suggesting that Thespis "converted (the exarchon) into an actor by separating him more distinctly from the chorus and giving him set lines to speak" (54).

15 A. E. Haigh imagines or extrapolates an early progression toward this structural alternation as follows, adding or reading in more specificity than is standard in such descriptions: "First of all the actor came forward upon the platform, and delivered a speech containing preliminary explanations of the plot, this speech being called the 'prologue.' Then followed a series of choral odes, sung by the chorus in front of the platform. At each interval in the

choral odes the actor again made his appearance, first in one character and then in another; and his part must have consisted, either in long narrative speeches, recounting events which had taken place elsewhere, or in dialogues with the leader of the chorus. As there was only one actor, this was necessarily the case" (31). Haigh adds that this pattern continued even after the second and third actors were included (32).

16 Hardison, for one, dismisses the idea of Dionysus as earliest character. For him, Thespis introduced a "figure with a set speech who impersonated not the god Dionysus but a legendary or historical character" (101–102). Kerényi, too, disputes the Dionysian character, in direct refutation of Nietzsche, who "believed that in line with an unassailable tradition the oldest forms of Greek tragedy dealt exclusively with the sufferings of Dionysos and that for a long time the sole hero of tragedy was Dionysos. This is false, for there was no such direct tradition" (329).

17 In fact, argues Kerénji, the "oldest stage hero was an enemy of Dionysos," and continues, "Not Dionysos pure and simple, as Nietzsche believed, but Pentheus was the subject and hero of the primordial tragedy. The suffering Dionysos was at one time called 'Pentheus,' the 'man of suffering.' As a hero, only an enemy and victim of the god could bear this name" (324).

18 Haigh, for instance, extrapolates a fully populated dramatic picture from the rudiments of Thespis's innovation, which includes, quite justifiably, the movement from a narrative toward a dramatic means of telling. For Haigh, it was Thespis, or the actor that he introduced, who "played in turn the part of all the prominent figures in the legend, from gods and kings down to heralds and messengers. He counterfeited their appearance, spoke their sentiments, and exhibited their passions." Thespis, offers Haigh, "took the part of the 'actor' himself," and would "appear in several characters in succession, by means of rapid changes of costume" (28–29). While colorful, such a reading of dramatic character in its earliest iteration is unsubstantiated in later scholarship.

19 Butler believes that in developing tragedy, Thespis "drew upon dance, music, epic tales, dithyrambs, lyric poetry, and – most importantly – impersonation. To facilitate his impersonation, he first used white lead to paint his face; later he used a linen mask" (5–6).

20 Expanding on the point, Jones offers this analogy: "The distinction between the composing dramatist who imitates human beings and one who imitates an action rich in human interest is paralleled by a second distinction between the actor who impersonates his mythico-historical original and the actor-mask who appropriates to that original his share of the play's action" (46).

21 For Otto, the mask is symbolic, identified with god as well as actor: "... Dionysus was presented in the mask because he was the god of confrontation. It is the god of the most immediate presence who looks at us so penetratingly from the vase painting. Because it is his nature to appear suddenly and with overwhelming might before mankind, the mask serves as his symbol and his incarnation in cult" (90).

22 Vernant and Naquet characterize this opposition as follows: "What the vision of Dionysus does is explode from within and shatter the 'positivist' vision that claims to be the only valid one, in which every being has a particular form, a definite place, and a particular essence in a fixed world that ensures each his own identity that will encompass him forever, the same and unchanging. To see Dionysus, it is necessary to enter a different world where it is the 'other,' not the 'same' that reigns" (394).

23 For commentary on these four qualities of character see, for example, Hardison (200–201).

24 Goldhill notes that differentiating the ancient from later models of character does "not mean that there is in Greek drama no interest the any internal life of its personae" (174).

25 A fundamental premise in Else's proposition (*Argument*) is that throughout the *Poetics* Aristotle is developing a unified line of argument.

26 This is Butcher's translation (Fergusson 62). Golden translates differently, as "by character that element in accordance with which we say that agents are of a certain type" (Hardison 12). Else renders the passage as "the characters are those indications by virtue of which we say that the persons performing the action have certain moral qualities" (*Argument* 238).

27 Butcher translates the passage in *Poetics* (XV) as follows: "Thus a person of a given character should speak or act in a given way, by the rule either of necessity or of probability, just as this event should follow that by necessary or probable sequence" (Fergusson 82).

28 All quotations of the *Oresteia* are from Lattimore's translation, *Aeschylus I*.

29 The scene of the king's return in *Agamemnon* has, of course, elicited extensive commentary. For discussion of a range of factors that impact the character's decision to descend from his chariot onto the tapestries, see among other sources my own *After Dionysus* (125, 131–132). See also Jean-Pierre Vernant's commentary on Agamemnon's choices in the scene, and reasons for the actions taken (Macksey 287).

30 Jones argues that "Aristotelian man" cannot be like Hamlet because "he is significantly himself only in what he says and does. Instead of 'that within' – Hamlet's omnipresent consciousness – he has the qualities which he owes to his ethos" (37).

31 Easterling speaks to this difference between the ancient play and more recent expectations concerning character: "Modern audiences, brought up on post-Romantic literature with its overwhelming emphasis on the individual, and conditioned by modern psychological terminology, expect a dramatist to be primarily concerned with the unique aspect of each man's experience, with the solitary focus of consciousness which, as John Jones puts it, is 'secret, inward, interesting.' When they first read a Greek play, they are naturally inclined to interpret what the characters say and do as if the ancient dramatist shared their preoccupation with idiosyncratic detail. But closer study soon makes plain that this is an anachronistic prejudice ..." ("Character" 138).

32 I refer to the characterization of Theseus in *Oedipus at Colonus* that is offered by the title character himself (*Sophocles I* 144).

33 Vernant writes, with respect to the historical gap and the character's autonomy:

> This distance must be great enough for the conflict of values to be painfully felt, but the distance must be small enough so that the heroic past is not liquidated, rejected, so that the confrontation does not cease. By the same token, for tragic man to appear, human action must have emerged as such, but the human agent must not have acquired too autonomous a status, the psychological category of the will must not be developed, and the distinction between voluntary and involuntary crime must not be clear enough for human action to be independent of the gods. This is the moment of tragedy. (Macksey 288)

34 See also Easterling, who, with respect to Sophocles especially, urges that "we have to be open to psychological insight in the dramatist's observation." For her, an element of complication or variance of interpretation, introduced by the playwright in connection with character as well as event, can add to the impression of "depth, of a solid individual consciousness behind the words" ("Character" 141–142).

35 With respect to the array of factors that impact Agamemnon's decision and degree of autonomy in this scene, see, for example, my own *After Dionysus* (131–132).

36 Hippolytus is connected intimately with both goddesses, worshipful of Artemis but with Aphrodite holding sway over the play's events through her destruction of Phaedra as well. With Artemis, the intimacy must be severed at the play's end when the goddess cannot behold the dying of Hippolytus first hand – or, as Dunn puts it, she must "avoid being polluted by his death" (92).

37 For discussion and definition of *daimon*, see Burkert (179–181) as well as Vernant and Vidal-Naquet (35–36).

38 Another relation of the commonplace and the divine in the scene of Agamemnon's homecoming is offered by Kitto in relation to Aeschylus's dramaturgy: "The real background that Aeschylus created for this play is not the actual palace, with its retainers and its daily routine, a palace which the temple-haunting martlet might approve; it is the two laws of Hybris and Dike, the activity of the gods; and the physical palace, by a fine stroke of imagination, becomes part of this real background as the home of the Erinyes" (205).

2   CHARACTER, FORM, AND GENRE

1 From William Shakespeare, *Hamlet* I, 2. Unless otherwise indicated, all quotations of the play are from the Folger Shakespeare Library edition.

2 Elaborating on the need for characters to have an essential and individual drama, Pirandello writes: "Every creature of fantasy and art, in order to exist, must have his drama, that is, a drama in which he may be a character and

for which he *is* a character. This drama is the character's *raison d'etre*, his vital function, necessary for his existence" ("Preface" 368).

3 Charney devotes a chapter to the relation of Shakespeare and Pirandello, with emphasis on the theatrical dimension as opposed to the metaphysical: "The Shakespearean and the Pirandellian are two analogous modes of theatrical probing of reality and the ontological status of the play as a fiction, so that the plays of Shakespeare and of Pirandello can be made to comment on each other" (26).

4 In *Shakespearean Neuroplay*, Cook refers to the "blend" that an audience constructs cognitively: "From the rise of the curtain to the bow of the actors, theater prompts for blends. Hamlet walks onstage and the space that is 'Hamlet' has already been blended with the input spaces of the actor playing the role, the character, and the character's role in the play that bears his name" (96). Cook finds that McConachie's "formulation of the actor/character blend is tremendously productive, as it compels a reexamination of the phenomenology of spectatorship and our engagement with fiction. For McConachie, the actor/character is never a fixed and stable entity but a fluid organism created and manipulated by the audience" (106, with reference to McConachie, *Engaging*, 43).

5 Compare Calderwood, who views Hamlet as puzzling "over the fact that as a character he is fully equipped for revenge but that as an actor, or instrument of the plot, he is not allowed to proceed with it" (32).

6 Tragedy's transhistoric purview has been debated extensively. See, familiarly, Steiner *(Death)*, Abel, Krutch, or more recently, Van Laan, States (in response to Van Laan), and Brockmann. In broad outline, the debate over transhistoricity centers typically on the extent to whether it is a genre or a vision or sensibility that may persist over time. In *After Dionysus*, I argue for a Dionysian tragic element in selfhood and experience in life as well as in drama, which in each case is continuous.

7 With respect to the idea of a tragic cosmos that is not bound strictly to one historical era or to particular works of drama or narrative, see, for example, Sewall: "In using the term cosmos to signify a theory of the universe and man's relation to it, I have, of course, made a statement about tragedy: that tragedy affirms a cosmos of which man is a meaningful part" (166).

8 Compare Sewall: "Tragedy is primarily humanistic. Its focus is an event in this world; it is uncommitted as to questions of ultimate destiny, and it is non-religious in its attitude toward revelation. But it speaks, however vaguely or variously, of an order that transcends time, space, and matter. It assumes man's connection with some super-sensory or supernatural, or metaphysical being or principle ..." (166).

9 Sewall comments in this connection that "tragedy contemplates a universe in which man is not the measure of all things" (167).

10 Brockmann summarizes the points of view of Steiner and Abel in this regard, with the focus on a modern theatre that "tends to be self-reflexive and self-conscious, whereas Aeschylean drama did not." Steiner's Hamlet,

in Brockmann's words, is "a fully-depicted, sonorous character whose personality, famously, tends toward indecisiveness, self-reflection, and lack of action: a character, in short, who would have been impossible in Aeschylean tragedy ...." And further, with respect to Abel's standpoint: "Modern drama's search for self-knowledge implies a disjunction between interiority and exteriority that did not exist in the Attic world" (36).

11 Blundell makes this distinction, in regard to the *Poetics*: "A person's *dianoia* is what makes him or her intellectually 'of a certain kind,' but a play's *dianoia* consists of certain types of argument. The derivation of dramatic from personal *dianoia* implies that dramatic *dianoia* will convey the presumed personal *dianoia* of the dramatic figures" (159).

12 Compare Bradley, who refers to *Hamlet* as a "tragedy of moral idealism" (98).

13 States entertains the issue of traits with respect to Hamlet, but is more interested in the means of dramatizing them than the subjective qualities per se (*Concept* 32–34).

14 With respect to what I am calling the "cognitive subplot," compare Fergusson's reference to the play's "movement of ironic analysis, represented by the analogous versions of the main theme which the interwoven plots embody and by Hamlet's monologues and wry jokes: improvisations which are beside the story of the play, in closer relationship to the audience" (119).

15 Bradley refers to Hamlet's "state of profound melancholy" (94), and to a condition that "may truly be called diseased" (104).

16 Compare Frye, who notes that Hamlet "does have the student's disease of melancholy, which means that his actions are apt to be out of synchronization, being either delayed, like his revenge on Claudius, or hasty and rash, like his killing of Polonius" (*Shakespeare* 89).

17 Kenneth Burke posits that Hamlet's deliberate postponements, intended as cautionary with respect to the prospective revenge, actually "threaten to interfere with vengeance. Here Shakespeare nearly dissolved the identity of drama, removing it from the realm of action into a realm of pre-action that would amount to no action" (*Grammar* 247).

18 Regarding a cosmic frame, Fergusson notes that while Hamlet "accepts this order, he does not know where he belongs in it; he is not even sure which way is up" (129).

19 In connection with the Elizabethan sense of a chain of being, I refer especially to Tillyard. With respect to the picture of cosmos and correspondence, including microcosm and macrocosm, see Tillyard (91) and also Fergusson, who situates the "great speech on Man" as follows: "Hamlet sees beyond the tiny involvements of the foreground to the social order indicated by the stage house façade and, above that, to the order in the stars implied by the canopy over his head" (128).

20 In this chapter I emphasize the more unwieldy aspects of Shakespeare's plot structure in comparison with considerations of the tragic genre per se. Hazlitt, by contrast, finds the presentation true to life, with events that "succeed each

other as matters of course, the characters think, and speak, and act, just as they would do if they were left to themselves. The whole play is an exact transcript of what might have taken place at the court of Denmark five hundred years ago, before the modern refinements in morality and manners" (10).

21 Eliot would differ on this identification of a tragic progression, primarily because he finds no correlative of an adequate magnitude between the character of Hamlet and the circumstances, including the relationship with Gertrude (100–101).

22 Aligning the Dionysian with the tragic and identifying both in a rending pattern that can be identified transhistorically provides the thesis for *After Dionysus*.

23 Abel would dispute such an assessment with respect to genre – and, indeed, with the notion of *Hamlet* as tragedy in the first place, a question central to his chapter on this play (40–58). He argues also with the idea that death is "fated" or innate because the play is tragic (51).

24 Compare Abel, who refers to characters in the play as "actors" or as "dramatists," with Hamlet in the latter category (49).

25 I refer to the Burkean "character recipe" in my discussion of dialectic and Shaw's *Candida* (*Irony* 94, 114).

26 While Burke's system of dramatism is not often mentioned in theatrical contexts now, I have referred to the pentad in *After Dionysus* (104–107) and *Irony and the Modern Theatre* (93). See also Calderwood, who considers the ratios in relation to *Hamlet* specifically (105–107).

27 In *A Grammar of Motives*, Burke offers that "any complete statement about motives will offer *some kind* of answers to these five questions: what was done (act), when or where it was done (scene), who did it (agent), how he did it (agency), and why (purpose)" (xv).

28 Bloom writes: "Whatever his precise relation to Shakespeare might have been, Hamlet is to other literary and dramatic characters what Shakespeare is to other writers: a class of one, set apart by cognitive and aesthetic eminence. The prince and the poet-playwright are the geniuses of change; Hamlet, like Shakespeare, is an agent rather than an instrument of change" (412–413). Compare Calderwood on dramatic character generally as "both a source of action, expressing his will, and an instrument of action, dancing to the tune of the playwright and his plot" (31).

3   CHARACTER BY THE RULES: NEOCLASSICISM AND BEYOND

1 Philinte is speaking to Alceste, in Molière's *The Misanthrope*, I, 1 (19). All quotations from the play, and from Jean Racine's *Phaedra*, are from Richard Wilbur's translations.

2 Carlson likens *bienséance* to the English sense of propriety and says that it can be "taken as a synonym for suitability" (93).

3 Calder remarks also that Philinte "has almost no fixed character because he changes with changing contexts. His awareness of the unending cruelty

of man to man inspires not lonely misanthropy, but ironical watchfulness"
(104). I would suggest, rather, that Philinte is consistent in his role as raisonneur he may be a careful observer of the social scene, but he does not deviate
from that philosophy of reasonableness.

4 In Turnell's words, "Eliante minimizes Alceste's peculiarities and by placing
the emphasis on his 'candor' she corrects Philinte" ("Misanthrope" 274).

5 Compare Levin: "Not urbanely amused but sincerely outraged, Alceste
takes an anti-comic attitude, which makes him a suitable target for
fun-making" (124).

6 For overview of the Cid controversy, see, for example, Dukore (211–226) or
Carlson (94–96). Carlson notes that, following arguments over Corneille's *Le
Cid*, the "question of the rules of drama became a concern for anyone inter-
ested in letters or arts, not merely a few specialists. And with this controversy, France replaced Italy as the European center for critical discussion of
the drama; for the next century and a half French critics would largely define
its terms" (96).

7 Regarding contagion among the passions, Rousseau finds also that theatrical depiction of emotion aligns with the particular national character of the
audience. Therefore: "A ferocious and intense people wants blood, combat,
and terrible passions. A voluptuous people wants music and dances. A gallant people wants love and civility. A frivolous people wants joking and ridicule" (18).

8 Barish emphasizes Rousseau's alignment of himself with Alceste and how
"totally this identification rules his analysis" (269).

9 For example, Rousseau insists that in order to please audiences, "there must
be entertainments which promote their penchants, whereas what is needed
are entertainments which would moderate them" (18). And, with respect to
the response of audience at the end of a tragedy: "Do the emotion, the distur-
bance, and the softening which are felt within onself [*sic*] and which continue
after the play give indication of an immediate disposition to master and regu-
late our passions?" (21).

10 Barish describes the Platonic background as follows:

> Artists, says Socrates, owe their allegiance to the inferior principle, which
> trades in fancies and opinions. They depict men divided within themselves,
> torn between passion and reason, and as they do so, instead of helping us
> master our passions they inflame them. They pour fuel on the most com-
> bustible part of our nature. For they aim not to discover the truth but only
> to please, and nothing is easier than to follow the line of least resistance, to
> imitate the passions, which lend themselves to vivid mimetic enactment, and
> which seduce by their very variety and variability. Far more difficult to render
> interestingly or convincingly would be the austerity of a truly temperate soul.
> Artists invite us to sympathize with men racked by emotions we should be
> ashamed to yield to in our own lives. By fomenting our irrational selves, they
> carry us away from the true, the good, and the beautiful. (9–10)

11 Barish characterizes Collier not as an authentic critic but as one who adopts a critical stance in order to "make his diatribe seem a reasoned contribution to debate rather than simply a din of abuse" (225).

12 Gill describes Dorimant in relation to the character type: "An accomplished rake-hero makes assignments, breaks hearts, and converses amiably with equal ease. He seduces women with dazzling self-assurance, enticing some into bed and others to help him, wittingly or unintentionally, with his schemes. The prototype of this beguiling character, the witty, seductive Dorimant of Sir George Etherege's *The Man of Mode*, lives an entertaining life composed of social diversion and private illicit entertainments" (196–197).

13 Barbara A. Kachur refers to the "polar views of *The Man of Mode* as either an amoral and naturalistic comedy or a corrective satire" that still characterize discussion of the play (96).

14 Kachur's view of Dorimant's personality is decidedly grim; for her, the character has a "malicious and vindictive personality" and an "acrimonious and vengeful temperament" (109, 111).

15 For Kachur, "Bellinda's openness affords her a unique relationship with the audience, especially in a play where characters seldom reveal their interior thoughts and feelings" (114).

16 Kachur speaks of Dorimant's "lack of identity," asserting that for him, the "mask has become affixed to his face" (122).

17 Compare Wilbur, in the "Introduction" to his translation of the play:

> Phaedra thus sins by harboring a criminal passion, by avowing it, by conniving at a false accusation which dooms an innocent man, and by desiring the death of an innocent woman. Yet she is at all times an object of sympathy. This is, once more, because she sees her guilt clearly and condemns it, because she struggles against her illicit feelings, and because – in this play which is really a delayed suicide – she wishes to perish rather than pollute the world with her "foulness." (xi)

18 Fergusson remarks on the contrast between Racine's era and the perspectives of more recent times; the "theater of reason," he says, "was a mirror of human life and action formed at a particular time and place, and enjoying a merely mortal life like that of any other real theater. Its rational principles no longer look self-evident and eternal to us; we see that Racine enjoyed a sanction which we have lost; and we are uncomfortable with the perfection of the mind which he achieved" (57).

19 Turnell adopts a Freudian view, interpreting Venus not as goddess of love but of "sexuality." Characters in *Phaedra* are completely in thrall to the goddess, "defenceless [*sic*] against Venus"; and what Phaedra and Hippolytus share is characterized as "sexual appetite" (*Dramatist* 239–240).

20 With respect to "les regles," Turnell argues that "the authority of 'the rules' was not in the main a tyrannical one. The history of authority in the seventeenth century is the history of an authority which was freely accepted because it was felt to be *reasonable*" (*Classical* 7).

21 For Weinberg, the progression is "simple and clearly defined: from an initial state in which Phèdre, because of her sense of guilt, wishes to die, to a final state in which her guilt reaches unbearable proportions and she must die" (256). Compare Barthes, who offers that *Phaedra* proposes "an identification of interiority with guilt" (124).

22 Turnell clarifies:

> The dilemma is plain. Whether one liked it or not – many of the seventeenth-century writers emphatically did not – man is endowed with "reason" and "passion" which are in a state of perpetual conflict. "Reason" is constantly trying to bring more and more of human nature under its dominion; "passion" is continually trying to upset the balance and to drive man to the edge of the abyss, to the *espaces infinis* whose silence was a source of fear to Pascal and his contemporaries. Perfect equilibrium was impossible and would indeed be contrary to nature. (14)

23 Turnell notes that Racine did not depict "violent passion simply for its own sake," but that by "making sexual passion the mainspring of human action, he anticipated some of the more revolutionary findings of contemporary psychologists" (*Moment* 170–171).

24 In the "Preface," Steele confesses that "the whole was writ for the sake of the scene of the fourth act, wherein Mr. Bevil evades the quarrel with his friend, and hope it may have some effect upon the Goths and Vandals that frequent the theaters, or a more polite audience may supply their absence" (McMillan 322).

4 SCIENTIFIC CHARACTER: THE HOW AND WHY OF NATURALISM – AND AFTER

1 Èmile Zola, "Naturalism in the Theatre" (Bentley 356, 361).

2 Zola refers to the "formula" that was the inheritance of ancient traditions, marked by "outlandish situations, improbabilities, dishonest uniformity, and uninterrupted, unbearable declaiming" (352), and characterizes what is "false" and "unacceptable" in the worn-out forms of Romantic and tragic drama (352–356).

3 I base this chapter in part, and with permission, on my essay, "On the Science of Dramatic Character." *Narrative* 19:2 (May 2011): 241–252.

4 For example, see Hardison's commentary on Aristotle's usual methodology, proceeding from general to specific definition (201–205). De Ste. Croix refers to Aristotle's "acumen as a scientist" (26), and also addresses the philosopher's tendencies regarding typology and classification (24–27).

5 Compare, in relation to character in literary narrative, Henry James, who in the "Preface" to *The Portrait of a Lady* cites Ivan Turgenev's prioritization of individual character in the origin of a fictional work: "It began for him almost always with the vision of some person or persons, who hovered before him, soliciting him, as the active or passive figure, interesting him

and appealing to him just as they were and by what they were" (630). For James personally, and with reference to his heroine, Isabel Archer, his "first dim move" in the composition of this novel was "exactly my grasp of a single character" (632–633).

6 From the "Short Organum": "For when we look about us for an entertainment whose impact is immediate, for a comprehensive and penetrating pleasure such as our theatre could give us by representations of men's life together, we have to think of ourselves as children of a scientific age. Our life as human beings in society – i.e., our life – is determined by the sciences to a quite new extent" (*Brecht* 183).

7 Garner refers to Zola's "appropriation of the physiological body within his theory of the naturalist stage" (68), and to the proposal of the "body as the somatic center of an emerging naturalist modernity" (71–72).

8 Consider Brustein's comment, for instance, that "it is incredible that *The Father* could ever have been taken for a Naturalist document" (104).

9 In one version of the "Preface," with translation by Harry G. Carlson, Strindberg refers directly to Darwin in relation to his character: "There are those who find it wrong in modern drama for characters to speak Darwinism" (67).

10 Valency notes that Chekhov "admired Zola, and no doubt thought of himself as a naturalist." By contrast to the phrase "life as it is lived," Valency argues that Chekhov "was no mere observer of 'life as it is,'" being too careful a designer of effects and structure for that to be the case ("Vershinin" 224).

11 Chekhov's correspondence in letters is voluminous, and he wrote often to his wife, Olga Knipper, and other members of the Moscow Art Theatre concerning current rehearsals and productions of his works. With reference to *Three Sisters*, Troyat imagines Chekhov's worry that Stanislavsky was "overloading the production with those naturalistic effects he was so fond of" (256). See especially Karlinsky for letters from Chekhov to Nemirovich-Danchenko and Stanislavsky, among many others. To the former, with respect to the production of *The Cherry Orchard* (1903), he mentions a comparison of Varya to Anya – "Why do you say in your telegram that there are so many weepy people in my play? Where are they?" (459–460). To the latter, he writes about casting: "As I worked on Lopakhin, I thought of him as your role. If for any reason he doesn't appeal to you, take Gayev" (461). Regarding Chekhov's scientific associations, Troyat contrasts the playwright's reputation for warmth with the observation that "in fact Chekhov's art is endowed with the lucidity and impassivity of a scientist" (294).

12 See Goldstein, who reports that Plato "wrote in dialogues, lavishing care on idiosyncratic features of his dialogic characters, many based on real people, and showing us how their entire personalities are brought to bear on their philosophical positions and the way they argue for them" (39).

13 Compare Richardson ("Drama and Narrative") who writes that "performed stories, whether in drama, film, ballet, or video, have an additional enacted dimension that can interact with many of the other elements of

narrative, particularly in the cases of character, time, and space" (142). For Richardson, "enactment gives the concept of character a 'fourth,' performed dimension" (154).

14 See also Phelan's more recent discussion of these same classifications of character, in Scholes (314).

15 Compare Margolin: "Characters are abstract in the sense that they do not exist in real space and time, and are more like concepts in this regard. Consequently they are not open to direct perception by us, and can be known only through textual descriptions or inferences based on those descriptions. In fact, they *are* these complexes of descriptions, not having any independent worldly existence" (68). In "Beyond Poststructuralism," Richardson describes the formalist point of view: "The general premise is that literary characters are not like people at all, but rather ultimately arbitrary verbal constructs within a recognizable narrative structure" (91).

16 Compare Freud, who, in "Psychopathic Characters on the Stage," offers a theory of vicarious experience that might also be understood, like surrogacy, as enlarging the scope of what an audience member or reader has actually lived (*Writings* 88).

17 See also Burke's discussion of "dramatistic analysis" in his *On Symbols and Society* (135–157).

18 See, for example, my chapter on *Arcadia*, which includes attention to ways in which the time frames and scientific principles have an ironic aspect in comparison with what the characters know, or do not, at different points in the action (*Irony* 153–179).

19 Expanding on the integration of science and theatrical form, Shepherd-Barr writes: "The most striking contribution of science plays is that the best ones successfully employ a particular scientific idea or concept as an extended theatrical metaphor. They literally enact the idea that they engage, a performativity that is provocative and innovative and that has occurred so consistently in science plays that it is more than just a trend or a coincidence" (6).

20 For a recent study of the actual lives of scientists in relation to typed or familiar associations, see Shapin, including his reference to post–World War II public conceptions of science (72–73).

21 I give extensive attention to sparagmos and scission within dramatic character in tragedy in *After Dionysus*.

22 Compare to Gary Johnson's perspective on scientific discovery in relation to literary fiction and the "neuronarrative": "As scientists learn more about the general human phenomenon of consciousness, novelists find themselves forced to rethink how that phenomenon manifests itself in their individual narratives" (169).

5 HOW CHARACTERS THINK

1 Halvard Solness, in conversation with Dr. Herdal, imagining the arrival of "youth" just prior to Hilda Wangel's knock at the door in *The Master Builder* (*Ibsen* 800).

2 Freud famously identified neurotic complexes with ancient figures of myth and theatre, but wrote also on pathology and associated "character types" with reference to psychiatry, using in particular the figures of Hamlet, Lady Macbeth, Richard III, and Rebecca West as prime examples (*Writings* 151–175).

3 Suffice to say that Hamlet has been the subject of extensive psychoanalytic assessment. For Freud, he exemplifies the hero who is "not psychopathic, but only *becomes* psychopathic in the course of the action of the play" (*Writings* 92, italics original).

4 Lacan posits Ophelia as "one of the innermost elements in Hamlet's drama, the drama of Hamlet as the man who has lost the way of his desire" (12).

5 Dupin appears also in Poe's "The Murders in the Rue Morgue" (1841) and "The Mystery of Marie Rogêt" (1842). Poe himself referred to "The Purloined Letter" as "perhaps, the best of my tales of ratiocination" (Qtd. McGann 56).

6 For one angle on the story's levels of complexity, see Barbara Johnson's discussion of Lacan's "Seminar on 'The Purloined Letter'" compared with Jacques Derrida's point of view in "The Purveyor of Truth." Johnson introduces her discussion with reference to the story's layers of complication, specifically in relation to Lacan and Derrida, and referring to Poe's story as one that "analyzes itself": "In all three texts, it is the act of analysis that seems to occupy the center of the discursive stage and the act of analysis of the act of analysis that in some way disrupts that centrality, subverting the very possibility of a position of analytical mastery" (149).

7 Translated from the French: "A plan so deadly, if unworthy of Atreus, is worthy of Thyestes," from Crébillon's *Atrée* (Poe 349).

8 Compare the figure of Sherlock Holmes who, in stories such as "A Scandal in Bohemia" (and many others) counts on the power of observation and its difference from mere seeing. Maria Konnikova refers to an encounter in that story in which Holmes, responding to Watson's astonishment at a puzzle solved, remarks: "You see, but you do not observe" (1–4).

9 Compare Edwards, who remarks that "Thomasina is a far more appealing and charming character than her preoccupation with thermodynamics and the irreversibility of time would suggest. She makes her discoveries serendipitously and announces them with a winning, throwaway manner that makes her the perfect foil for her tutor" (180).

10 Carr, like Joyce, Tzara, and Lenin in *Travesties*, was a real historical figure, as Stoppard explains in his acknowledgments (ix–xi).

11 Demastes argues that Thomasina's having a tutor instead of conventional education has allowed her the sort of genius she possesses:

> Stoppard intriguingly instills the spark of chaotics genius to a young nineteenth century woman ineligible for admission to a university leaving her to work alone, unhabituated by university-dispensed knowledge. If Thomasina had been properly tutored and properly educated, would her natural curiosity ever have led to thoughts about chaotics, or would she simply have succumbed

to the alluring indoctrination of Newtonianism that even cluttered such bright
minds as that of her own tutor? ("Portrait" 239)

12 Burke uses the term to signify a bond with a character's antagonist:"True
    irony, humble irony, is based upon a sense of fundamental kinship with
    the enemy, as one *needs* him, is *indebted* to him, is not merely outside him
    as an observer but contains him *within*, being consubstantial with him"
    (*Grammar* 514).

13 Here is Shaw's characterization of Solness, from his review of *The Master
    Builder*: "Also he is daimonic, not sham daimonic like Molvik in *The Wild
    Duck*, but really daimonic, with luck, a star, and mystic 'helpers and servers'
    who find the way through the maze of life for him. In short, a very fascinating
    man, whom nobody, himself least of all, could suspect of having shot his bolt
    and being already dead" (120).

14 I refer especially to "Lukács/Ibsen" and chapter 1, *Irony*.

15 I quote Solness himself in conversation with Hilda (*Ibsen* 825).

16 I focus here on *The Master Builder*, but the relation of Arnold Rubik and
    Irene in *When We Dead Awaken* would also pertain, together with other cast
    members in that play. More broadly, of course, Ibsen's plays consistently
    explore aspects of, and interrelations within, the psyche – as in *Hedda Gabler*
    or *Rosmersholm*, for instance. Fjelde calls Ibsen "one of the great masters of
    human psychology – not least because the psychological questions he raises
    are explored, not for their own sake alone, but as part of a larger world-view"
    (*Ibsen* 494).

17 As, for instance, in the sequence in act three when Aline tells Hilda about the
    loss of her dolls in the fire (*Ibsen* 840–843).

18 By contrast, Peter Nichols's *Passion Play* centers on a variation of the
    two-mind construct, as each partner in a marriage, James and Eleanor, have
    counterparts, Jim and Nell, who are embodied (but unseen, except to the
    audience) alter egos. While Nichols's focus is not on the psychoanalytic aspect
    per se, the alter egos often represent the undisguised desires or thoughts of
    the primary characters, and there is reference to psychotherapy in the play's
    second act.

19 Dysart refers to the "Normal" as "the dead stare in a million adults. It both
    sustains and kills – like a God" (62); near the play's end, the "Normal"
    stands for convention in place of what Alan has experienced in his ecstatic
    worship (109).

20 I refer to mystery in its first definition as "a religious truth that man can know
    by revelation alone and cannot fully understand" (*Webster's New Collegiate
    Dictionary*).

21 Demastes refers to Shaffer's narrator characters, including Dysart, who "can't/
    don't *think* properly" due to "failed epistemologies" that they come to recog-
    nize (*Staging* 137).

22 See also Frye's description of the final act of *Three Sisters* as "about as close to
    pure irony as the stage can get" (*Anatomy* 285). I discuss the ending sequence,

together with Andreev's characterization, with specific attention to the ironic aspect (*Irony* 69).

23 With respect to *The Seagull*, I refer to "the psychic interiority of the play as a whole, as symptomized by the collective participation of several characters who, while retaining their individuality, are nevertheless intimate participants in one another's motives and behaviors" (*Dionysus* 159).

24 Chekhov's depiction of time, and its relation to his dramaturgy, is also well-known, but Gilman is particularly discerning in his conjuring of this factor in Chekhov's drama as also in experience (*Chekhov's Plays* 58–59).

25 William's "Portrait of a Girl in Glass," the prototype for *The Glass Menagerie*, was written in 1943 and features many of the same characters and situations as the play, produced two years later.

26 Also, by focusing on thought especially in relation to dramaturgy, I have not attended to plays or characters where the representation of thinking or its relation to dramatic structure is not pertinent, even as ideas per se may be central. The plays of Shaw – *Candida, Major Barbara,* or *Man and Superman,* for instance – provide a case in point, in which characters can make intelligent, clever, or impassioned observations but where there is no interiority; an actual thinking process is not shown, nor is it germane, even as the playwright's ideas and dialectic are. We are led to know what the Reverend James Morell feels at times toward Eugene Marchbanks, but we are not truly let in on his thoughts. The same might be said of Coward's plays, in which a wonderfully intelligent comedic style is not at all dependent upon the inner life of, say, Judith Bliss or Amanda Prynne. As an elaboration, however, there are many cases where audiences can see that a character has given a good deal of thought to some matter or person, even if an actual thinking process is not dramatized. Regarding *The Misanthrope*, for example, it might be assumed that Eliante has carefully weighed Alceste's qualities and attributes, by way of reaching a considered determination about him – but Molière does not give this process any actual stage time. Similarly, one can assume that Emilia, in *The Country Wife*, has assessed her options with Harcourt by comparison with Sparkish and come to a prudent decision – but her thinking counts much less, for Wycherley, than the integrity she demonstrates by contrast with the perfidy of other characters.

27 Compare Gazzaniga, who says that consciousness has no "exact definition" (61), but proposes that multiple systems in the brain produce it: "I am suggesting that the brain has all kinds of local consciousness systems, a constellation of them, which are enabling consciousness. Although the feelings of consciousness appear to be unified to you, they are given form by these vastly separate systems" (66). For Chalmers, though, consciousness "poses the most baffling problems in the science of mind" (*Character* 3).

28 I refer to Damasio's basic definition of consciousness (*Self* 167–169), in which he aligns the phenomenon with awareness, knowledge, and state of mind, with "a self process added to it" (167); he refers also to consciousness as

represented by writers such as Shakespeare and Joyce (169). In *Consciousness Explained*, Dennett writes that "Our fundamental tactic of self-protection, self-control, and self-definition is not spinning webs or building dams, but telling stories, and more particularly connecting and controlling the story we tell others – and ourselves – about who we are" (418; Qtd. by Lodge, *Consciousness* 15).

29 Young refers to Damasio's "feeling brain, the scientific elucidation of emotion and feeling, and the uncovering of their role in the construction and work of consciousness and culture." She notes also that Damasio "understands emotion and feeling as the bridge between rational and nonrational processes, between cortical and subcortical structures" (25).

30 Lodge describes "stream of consciousness" as the phrase introduced by William James to "characterize the continuous flow of thought and sensation in the human mind." He identifies two primary means of portraying consciousness in narrative fiction, interior monologue and the free-indirect style (*Art* 42–43). In drama, the former can be used as a verbalization of sequential thought, as in soliloquy (Hamlet) or direct address (Dysart, Quentin) or, as noted, Treadwell's Young Woman in *Machinal*. See also Young for the discussion of William James's theories of mind and the necessarily integrated and relational aspect of consciousness (20).

31 Lodge refers to Damasio, who "draws attention to the paradox noted by William James, that 'the self in our stream of consciousness changes continuously as it moves forward in time, even as we retain a sense that the self remains the same while our existence continues.' Damasio calls the self that is constantly modified the 'core' self, and the self that seems to have a kind of continuous existence the 'autobiographical' self, suggesting that it is like a literary production" (*Consciousness* 14–15). Lodge's reference is to Damasio's *The Feeling of What Happens* (217).

32 Toibin emphasizes, with respect to *The Portrait of a Lady*, that "James also wishes to dramatize, to take what happens in the secret chambers of the self, the mind at work in silence as registered by the novelist in sentences, and move this into dialogue, open drama." The scene in which Madame Merle questions Isabel on Lord Warburton and Pansy is, says Toibin, "masterly in its stagecraft, its creation of dramatic illusion, its understanding of the sheer power in a novel of playing it as though there were two actresses on the page, rather than a silent novelist communicating with a silent reader" (*Ways* 20). Lodge contrasts dramatic and novelistic capabilities with reference to cinema: "For those who know and love the novels of Henry James, the movie adaptations will always be more or less disappointing, because of the medium's inability to do justice to what is arguably the most important component of the books – their detailed and subtle representation of the inner life" (*Consciousness* 211).

33 In the modernist context, Gorra compares James's style to James Joyce, Virginia Woolf, and William Faulkner (301–302).

34 In "Lukács/Ibsen," I investigate this passage with attention to "awakening" and a represented "frontier" in particular connection with Halvard Solness and Arnold Rubek.

35 My point here is not to engage with the psychology of reading or reader-response theory, or cognitive studies in relation to narrative, but simply to highlight a fundamental contrast between the apprehension of literary and dramatic character. Compare Gerrig and Allbritton, whose standpoint is that "readers actively participate in the construction of literary worlds, and, thus, literary characters. Rather than being passive recipients of information, readers venture beyond the text to explain and predict aspects of the unfolding story" (380).

6 ANTI-CHARACTER

1 All quotations from *Six Characters in Search of an Author* are, unless noted otherwise, from Caputi's translation (247).

2 Pirandello begins the "Preface" as follows: "It seems like yesterday but is actually many years ago that a nimble little maidservant entered the service of my art. However, she always comes fresh to the job. She is called Fantasy" (363).

3 Dr. Fileno addresses Pirandello as follows, in part:

> No one can know better than you that we are living beings – more alive than those who breathe and wear clothes. Less real, perhaps, but more alive. One is born into life in so many ways, my dear sir, and you know very well that nature avails herself of the instrument of human fantasy in order to pursue her work of creation. And the man who's born as a result of this creative activity, which has its seat in the spirit of man, is destined by nature to a life greatly superior to that of anyone born of the mortal womb of woman. The man who is born a character, the man who has the good fortune to be born a living character, may snap his fingers at death even. He will never die! (99)

4 I refer especially to chapter 4, "Pirandello's Father – and Brecht's Mother," *Irony* (104–124).

5 I have related this logic elsewhere to Valency's assertion that "the essence of irony" was, for Pirandello, "an awareness that being is insubstantial, an illusion peopled by shadows. Thus, what is experienced as tragic is actually comic, and our entire life-experience is a pitiful absurdity" (*World* 101). In this connection, I argue, Pirandello's *sentimento del contraria* "extends from dramatic polarity and opposition to self-nullifying contradiction" (*Irony* 122).

6 Gowing comments further, with reference to the activity of knotting with which Madame is involved in Louis Tocque's "Madame Dangé, Wife of General Francois Balthazar Dangé du Fay" (1753) on "the pretense of purposeful activity" as an increasingly popular component in portraiture of the day (488).

7 Sargent's portraits might be elaborately realistic and detailed, as in the "Portrait of Carolus-Duran" (1879), "Edouard Pouilleron" (1879), or the magnificently

robed figure in "Doctor Pozzi at Home" (1881). By contrast, his "Vernon Lee" (1881) is a study in subjective apprehensiveness or anticipation, while impressionistic abstraction adds an elusive aspect to the characterization of "Robert Louis Stevenson." In each case, the painting's title is a real person's actual name, yet the means of showing and interpreting that person can be very different. Even the famed lushness of "Lady Agnew of Lochnaw" (1892) is a fusion of striking candor – eyes directly on the viewer – united with a nonrealistic blurring of opulent color. References earlier are, respectively, to Ratcliff, 45 (Carolus-Duran, fig. 58); 46 (Pouilleron, fig. 60); 63 (Pozzi, fig. 89); 62 (Lee, fig. 88); 92 (Stevenson, fig. 128); and 160 (Agnew, fig. 239). See also Ratcliff, "Robert Louis Stevenson and his Wife" (1885), 102, fig. 142.

8 With reference to the facets of action in Pirandello's play, Sypher notes that "All these levels of representation are held together in a simultaneous perspective of transparent dramatic planes to be read in many directions at the same time" (69).

9 For one example among many, portraits of actor Henry Irving were painted by Millais, Sargent, Whistler, and Bastien-Lepage, among several artists. There are portraits of Irving with costume and attitude of Mephistophilis, Hamlet, Shylock, and Philip II of Spain, among many of his roles. For one look at the relation of portraiture to acting style, see my "Impression Henry Irving," where I liken the actor's physicalization and gestural behaviors to Bastien-Lepage's methods of portrayal.

10 My reference to the "double" is in specific relation to Wendy Steiner's discussion, and not in connection with other, more familiar, iterations such as the Artaudian (*The Theatre and its Double*) or Denis Diderot's (*The Paradox of Acting*) or Benoit Constant Coquelin's "dual personality" of the actor (Cole and Chinoy 192–202).

11 Wendy Steiner draws a connection among layers of modeling and characterization in relation to Vladimir Nabokov's *Lolita*, in which the figure of Humbert Humbert substitutes the title character for his own lost love, Lolita thus becoming a model for Annabel, who in turn is inspired by Poe's character of Annabel Lee (44).

12 Ionesco reports that "In *The Bald Soprano*, which is a completely unserious play where I was most concerned with solving purely theatrical problems, some people have seen a satire on bourgeois society, a criticism of life in England, and heaven knows what. In actual fact, if it is a criticism of anything, it must be of all societies, of language, of clichés – a parody of human behavior, and therefore a parody of the theatre, too" ("World" 480). I have noted before that there is one sense in which Ionesco's people "signify recognizable human beings, as dramatic characters generally do; in another, they represent 'characters,' the stock figures of genre, beings not of life but of theatre" (*Irony* 141).

13 Lamont notes the pervasiveness of what she calls an "anti-attitude" in Ionesco's drama (5).

14 I make similar points elsewhere, including the idea that "Mr. Smith needs no background, no place or time of birth, no parents, no traumas or telling

dreams, no physiological complaints, no upbringing or influential environment, and no economic worries" (*Irony* 142).

15 With reference to the dramaturgy of absurdist plays generally, Esslin writes that "if a good play is judged by subtlety of characterization and motivation, these are often without recognizable characters and present the audience with almost mechanical puppets" (*Absurd* xvii).

16 Alpaugh notes how in *Happy Days* Beckett creates the "implicit metaphor of a universe and a way of life in which the sense or meaning has been creamed off, leaving style without sense, form without meaning" (Caputi 590).

17 Compare Lawley, who differentiates between the "character" of Winnie and the "*performance* of 'Winnie' by a consciousness not fully constructed or 'centred.' Certainly what we hear and see in the theatre is a performance, but the distinguished actresses who have played the role of Winnie....have been *playing* a performer. Winnie is, of necessity, a virtuoso of the inconsequential. She must improvise through her day, every day with words and her bag as her only resources" (95). For Kenner, Winnie propels herself "though the formulae of cheerful utterance" and makes "the day's project out of being happy" (597).

18 Compare Kennedy on the intrinsic theatricality of the play: "We have here the paradox of an eminently literary/verbal/abstract writer immersing himself in the concrete elements of theatricality, so that almost every speech in the text has the theatre as its context," and Winnie's physical situation "(being buried in a desert-like place, in the blaze of a perpetual noon) is expressed, first and foremost, in the visual sign language of the theatre" (84).

19 For Kenner, *Happy Days* is "a curiously *English* play, English in Winnie's tacit assumption that one has a duty not to lapse into gloom; English in the endless struggle to devalue little annoyances, to cherish small mercies; English in the intent façade of garrulity" (Caputi 597, italic original).

20 My point here is not to engage with dualist or monist standpoints per se, but rather to emphasize that dramatic character can represent a fundamental human concern that remains unsolved by science. For a consideration of the mind-body problem in relation to a specific stage character, from a monist point of view and with reference to Damasio, see Damastes's positioning of Hamlet in opposition to Descarte's dualism ("Hamlet" 34–38). Damasio points to recent scientific thinking that "reveals increasingly persuasively that ineffable stuff like mind/consciousness/spirit/soul has evolved from materialist sources." And further: "Consciousness and mind are stuff of material reality" (35).

21 Chalmers writes that McGinn sees the problem of consciousness as "too hard for our limited minds," and further, that it "may be unsolvable by humans due to deep limitations in our cognitive abilities but that it nevertheless has a solution in principle" (*Character* 16, 119). Searle also points to McGinn as one who "thinks it is impossible in principle that human beings should ever come to be able to understand how the brain causes consciousness" (*Mind* 102). Chalmers differentiates the "hard" questions of consciousness pertaining

to subjective experience from the "easy" (*Character* 4), which have more to do with cognition and information processing. For him, the "really hard problem of consciousness is the problem of *experience*. When we think and perceive there is a whir of information processing, but there is also a subjective aspect. As Nagel (1974) has put it, there is *something it is like* to be a conscious organism. The subjective aspect is experience" (*Character* 5, italics original). The reference is to Thomas Nagel, "What Is It Like to Be a Bat?" *Philosophical Review* 4: 435–450. Compare Lowe, who does not believe that "there are *any* 'easy' problems of consciousness" (117). Lowe disputes Chalmers's relation of consciousness and experience, which he finds "seriously inadequate." To continue the quote, "As regards the notion of experience, it seems to me that he distorts this notion by focusing exclusively upon the *sensuous*, or *phenomenal*, or *qualitative* character of experience (the 'what it is like' aspect of experience, to use Thomas Nagel's well-worn phrase). And this distortion serves, in my view, to obscure the intimate relation of experience and thought" (118, italics original).

22 Searle is in fundamental disagreement with Damasio's conception of self:

> The project is to give an account of consciousness by showing how the interaction between the mind and the self produces it. In order to do that one would have to give an account of the mind and the self that did not already presuppose that either was conscious and then show how their interaction produces consciousness. One would have to explain the mind as a set of ontologically objective biological processes, then do a similar explanation of the self, and then specify the mechanisms by which the structures of the self interact with the mind structures in order to produce qualitative subjectivity. As far as I can tell Damasio does not succeed in doing this. ("Mystery" 51)

23 I refer to Marco Roth's "Rise of the Neuronovel."

24 The reference is to James's "Preface" to *The Tragic Muse* in which he describes the manner of presenting one character (Miriam Rooth) through the perspective of another (Peter Sherringham or Nick Dormer) without reference to the former's interiority: "I never 'go behind' Miriam; only poor Sherringham goes, a great deal, and Nick Dormer goes a little" (9).

25 I quote an e-mail exchange between Richard Powers and myself, May 2, 2011, in which he also references the idea developed by Mikhail Bakhtin among others, that, in Powers's words, "every act of depicting is itself a depiction (of the depicter)." Elaborating upon this point in a later exchange (March 23, 2015), Powers observes that "in a closely focalized novel, apparently descriptive details about 'the world out there' are really embodiments of the interiority of the he-who-sees, dramatizing the filters, anxieties, and obsessions of the protagonist's 'world in here.'"

26 Compare Damasio, who describes the components of a "me" in certain ways similar to Ramachandran, including in his list of four elements "ownership" and "agency" and a feeling of embodiment in particular. Damasio declares that "The aggregate of elements (1) through (4) constitutes a self in its simple

version. When the images of the self aggregate are folded together with the images of nonself objects, the result is a conscious mind" (*Self* 196–197).

27 Miller's deconstructionist point of view is succinctly expressed as: "Character (in the sense of self) is never present. It is always over there, somewhere else, pointed to by characters (signposts) that cannot be followed to reach an unmediated access to what they indicate" (94). Compare Lifton's theory of the "protean" self: "I must separate myself, however, from those observers, postmodern or otherwise, who equate multiplicity and fluidity with disappearance of the self, with a complete absence of coherence among its various elements. I would claim the opposite: proteanism involves a quest for authenticity and meaning, a form-seeking assertion of self" (8–9).

7   DRAMATIC CHARACTER TODAY

1 From Harold Pinter's oft-quoted speech, Seventh National Student Drama Festival, Bristol, March 4, 1962. He continues: "Between my lack of biographical data about them and the ambiguity of what they say lies a territory which is not only worthy of exploration, but which it is compulsory to explore. You and I, the characters which grow on a page, most of the time we're inexpressive, giving little away, unreliable, elusive, obstructive, unwilling. But it's out of these attributes that a language arises. A language, I repeat, where under what is said, another thing is being said" (Quoted in part, Lahr, *Casebook*, xi).

2 *The Homecoming* opened in London on June 3, 1965, produced by the Royal Shakespeare Company with direction by Peter Hall; *Cat on a Hot Tin Roof* premiered in New York on March 24, 1955 at the Morosco Theatre, directed by Elia Kazan.

3 Williams's response to Kerr appeared originally in the *New York Herald Tribune*, April 17, 1955. Relating his characters to persons in the world and to subjectivity with respect to point of view, Williams says: "The truth about character in a play, as in life, varies with the variance of experience and viewpoint of those that view it. No two members of an audience ever leave a theatre, after viewing a play that deals with any degree of complexity in character, with identical interpretation of the characters dealt with" (*Live* 70–71). Kerr begins his review as follows: "*Cat on a Hot Tin Roof* is a beautifully written, perfectly directed, stunningly acted play of evasion; evasion on the part of its principal character, evasion perhaps on the part of the playwright" (Qtd. Chapman 70). By contrast, Eric Bentley's review in the *New Republic* (April 11, 1955) included this: "*Cat on a Hot Tin Roof* was heralded by some as the play in which homosexuality was at last to be presented without evasion. But the miracle has still not happened" (Qtd. Hewitt 472).

4 Maggie's line comes near the end of Act I when Brick is chasing after her, so that her more complete line – "But, Brick?! – *Skipper is dead*! *I'm alive*! Maggie the cat is – *alive*! *I am alive, alive*! *I am – alive*!" – is punctuated by him striking at her with his crutch and finally throwing it across the room at her (45–46).

5 She writes, for example: "Allegory, metatheater, and Brecht's critical dialectics – three methods that lift the spectator's focus from character to the relationship between levels of dramaturgy – became the principal vehicles of this shift" (10).

6 See, for instance, Elin Diamond's critique of realism, especially from a feminist perspective, as "the modern theatre's response to mimesis." She writes: "Realism is more than an interpretation of reality passing as reality; it *produces* 'reality' by positioning its spectator to recognize and verify its truths" ("Mimesis" 60, italic original).

7 Lehmann qualifies this assertion somewhat: "While for good reason no poetics of drama has ever abandoned the concept of action as the object of mimesis, the reality of the new theatre begins precisely with the fading away of this trinity of drama, imitation and action" (35).

8 Compare McConachie, who notes in his primer that "spectators often identify with several different people – some physically present, others imagined – during the course of a performance." And further: "Theatregoing offers spectators the opportunity to put themselves in the shoes of many other people, past and present, in order to understand and judge their actions" (*Mind* 54–55). McConachie refers also, in the context of the spectator's cognitive process, to an audience's "catching emotions from actors as characters" (*Engaging* 7).

9 Martin continues:

> Newspapers, popular magazines, movies and, most of all, television have so flooded modern culture with fictions that many people have difficulty distinguishing between social relations that are real and those that are fantasized. 'Fictive culture' more accurately describes contemporary social life than do such phrases as 'narcissistic,' 'minimalist,' or 'post-modern' culture; for the profusion of fictions is central to the creativity – and the crisis – of our modern condition. (13)

10 Burke writes:

> We shall use five terms as generating principle of our investigation. They are: Act, Scene, Agent, Agency, Purpose. In a rounded statement about motives, you must have some word that names the *act* (names what took place, in thought or deed), and another that names the *scene* (the background of the act, the situation in which it occurred); also, you must indicate what person or kind of person (*agent*) performed the act, what means or instruments he used (*agency*), and the *purpose*. Men may violently disagree about the purposes behind a given act, or about the character of the person who did it, or how he did it, or in what kind of situation he acted; or they may even insist upon totally different words to name the act itself. But be that as it may, any complete statement about motives will offer *some kind* of answers to these five questions: what was done (act), when or where it was done (scene), who did it (agent), how he did it (agency), and why (purpose). (*Grammar* xv)

11 Searle writes:

> ... I am going to accept the conclusion that psychological freedom is real. The purely psychological causes of our actions are often not causally sufficient to determine the actions. However, that still leaves open the deep question, What about the underlying neurobiology? We might have free will at the psychological level in the sense that the psychology as such was not sufficient to fix our actions. But the underlying neurobiology, which also determines that psychology, might itself be causally sufficient to he determine our actions.

And further:

> We really do not know how free will exists in the brain, if it exists at all. We do not know why or how evolution has given us the unshakeable conviction of free will. We do not, in short, know how it could possibly work. (*Mind* 158, 164)

12 Steele, "Preface," 323, and Lillo, "Dedication," 3.
13 Regarding literary genres, Hernadi argues that, "it is not a particular doctrine of three (or four or fourteen) genres that the discerning critic should reject. The fallacy lies in the monistic principle of classification usually underlying such doctrines" (153). While Todorov remarks that to "persist in paying attention to genres may seem to be a vain if not anachronistic principle today," and that it "is even considered a sign of authentic modernity in a writer if he ceases to respect the separation of genres," he advises as follows: "Genres are the meeting place between general poetics and event-based literary history; as such, they constitute a privileged object that may well deserve to be the principal figure in literary studies" (13, 19–20). See Most for discussion of how genre develops and changes over time; with respect to tragedy in relation to philosophy and form, he writes: "In ancient philosophy and literary criticism, there seems to have been nothing whatsoever corresponding to the modern philosophical idea of 'the tragic' as a fundamental dimension of human experience; there were instead only theories of 'tragedy' as a specific genre" (23).
14 *Zoot Suit* premiered at the Mark Taper Forum in Los Angeles, August 1978; in the previous year (1977) the Taper produced *Travesties* and *The Importance of Being Earnest* in repertory.
15 In one such moment, El Pachuco stops the action and calls attention to the relation of performance and audience. He "snaps his fingers. Everyone freezes."

> PACHUCO: Que mamada, Hank. That's exactly what the play needs right now. Two more Mexicans killing each other. Watcha ... everyone's looking at you.
> HENRY: (looks out at the audience.) Don't give me that bullshit. Either I kill him or he kills me.
> PACHUCO: That's exactly what they paid to see. Think about it. El Pachuco snaps again. Everybody unfreezes. (46)

16 Apart from El Pachuco's ability to stop and start the action and to comment parenthetically on events, the play uses banners and songs as part of its narrative; the Brechtian mise-en-scène includes Henry's prison cell and the judge's bench at court composed of bundles of newspapers.

17 Huerta writes that in *Zoot Suit*, Valdez "combined elements of the *acto*, *corrido*, *carpa*, and *mito* with Living Newspaper techniques to dramatize a Chicano family in crisis" (177). Qtd. by Worthen (107).

18 Compare Forster's theory of "flat" and "round" characters in literature, in *Aspects of the Novel*, cited in Chatman (131–132).

19 In her speech, "Women, Where Are We Going?" Heidi concludes: "We're all concerned, intelligent, good women. It's just that I feel stranded. And I thought the whole point was that we wouldn't feel stranded. I thought the point was that we were all in this together" (Wasserstein 232).

20 The reference is to James's phrase and the attention to specificity in "The Art of Fiction," including his reference to the "success with which the author has produced the illusion of life" (*Longman's*, 1884; Repr. *Partial Portraits* 390).

21 See, in this relation, Isaac Butler, who remarks on the persistence of realism in a domestic setting, in spite of continuing efforts to combat the genre:

> Realism and its iconoclastic fraternal twin, in short, have coexisted from the start. If their sibling dynamics are fraught, they're also an essential part of what makes American theatre distinctly American. It's impossible to know what the future will bring, but it's clear that realism and its loyal opposition will be with us for a long time to come, arguing, just like their characters, on a living-room set in a darkened theatre. (42)

22 In John Guare's *The House of Blue Leaves* (1970), for example, when Artie Shaughnessy speaks a line "out front" (3, 4, 5), he is speaking as a piano player in a club, but when speaks "to us" (76), he – along with Bunny, Ronny, and other characters in the play who address the audience – is not just being an entertainer, but is putting himself on a plane with other living people in the theatre. The same is true for, say, the character of Matilde in Sarah Ruhl's *The Clean House* (2004), who opens the play by telling the audience jokes in Portuguese and later in English, but also interacts with other characters in a nonpresentational way. I may be a character, these figures seem to say, but I am like you.

23 The idea of character as a subject for scholarly or critical inquiry has, similarly, shifted between prominence and obscurity. Chatman, in 1978, remarks that, "It is remarkable how little has been said about the theory of character in literary history and criticism" (107), while States, in 1993, observes: "The current neglect of fictional character as a subject of study probably originates in our having had a surfeit of it in the era of psychological criticism" ("Mirror" 452). Gruber (1994) argues that, "There are good reasons to restore character to dramatic criticism, not least of which is that it is practically (hence theoretically) impossible to ignore it" (2). For Gruber, in fact, "studies of character are one of the elements of which

dramatic criticism is made" (4). He attributes the recent "neglect" of character to "a shift in criticism throughout the modern period from studies of character to studies of words," and to the idea that "playwrights, unlike novelists, are not solely responsible for their characters" – referring here to the participation of the actor and the "difficulty of writing about multiple Hamlets" (3).

Works Cited

Abbott, H. Porter. *Beckett Writing Beckett: The Author in the Autograph.* Ithaca: Cornell University Press, 1996.

The Cambridge Introduction to Narrative. New York: Cambridge University Press, 2002.

Abel, Lionel. *Metatheatre: A New View of Dramatic Form.* New York: Hill and Wang, 1968.

Aeschylus. *Oresteia. Aeschylus I.* Trans., intro. Richmond Lattimore. Chicago: University of Chicago Press, 1953.

Alpaugh, Daniel J. "Negative Definition in Samuel Beckett's *Happy Days.*" *Twentieth Century Literature* 11 (1966): 202–210. Repr. Caputi, 585–597.

Andreev, Leonid. "Letters on the Theatre" (1912). Senelek, 223–272.

Aristotle. *Aristotle's Poetics.* Intro. Francis Ferguson. Trans. S. H. Butcher. New York: Hill and Wang, 1961.

Aristotle's Poetics: A Translation and Commentary for Students of Literature. O. B. Hardison, comm., and Leon Golden, trans. Tallahassee: Florida State University Press, 1981.

Baitz, Jon Robin. *Other Desert Cities.* New York: Grove, 2011.

Barish, Jonas. *The Anti-Theatrical Prejudice.* Berkeley: University of California Press, 1985.

Barlow, Judith, ed. *Plays by American Women 1900–1930* (1985). New York: Applause, 2000.

Barricelli, Jean-Pierre, ed., intro. *Chekhov's Great Plays: A Critical Anthology.* New York: New York University Press, 1981.

Barthes, Roland. *On Racine* (1960). Trans. Richard Howard. Berkeley: University of California Press, 1992.

Bate, Jonathan, ed. *The Romantics on Shakespeare.* New York: Penguin, 1992.

Beckett, Samuel. *Happy Days.* Caputi, 403–426.

Bentley, Eric. *The Life of the Drama.* New York: Atheneum, 1972.

Ed. Luigi Pirandello, *Naked Masks: Five Plays.* New York: E.P. Dutton and Company, 1952.

Ed. *The Theory of the Modern Stage.* New York: Penguin, 1968.

Bieber, Margarete. *The History of the Greek and Roman Theatre.* Princeton: Princeton University Press, 1939. 2nd ed., 1961.

Blau, Herbert. *The Audience*. Baltimore: The Johns Hopkins University Press, 1990.

Bloom, Harold. *Genius: A Mosaic of One Hundred Exemplary Creative Minds*. New York: Warner Books, 2002.

Shakespeare: The Invention of the Human. New York: Riverhead/Penguin, 1998.

Blundell, Mary Whitlock. "Ethos and Dianoia Reconsidered." Rorty, 155–175.

Booth, Wayne. "The *Poetics* for a Practical Critic." Rorty, 387–408.

Bradby, David and Andrew Calder. *The Cambridge Companion to Molière*. Cambridge: Cambridge University Press, 2006.

Bradley, A. C. *Shakespearean Tragedy* (1904). New York: Fawcett, 1965.

Brecht, Bertolt. *Brecht on Theatre: The Development of an Aesthetic*. Ed., trans. John Willett. New York: Hill and Wang, 1964.

Brereton, Geoffrey. *French Tragic Drama in the Sixteenth and Seventeenth Centuries*. London: Methuen, 1973.

Brilliant, Richard. *Portraiture*. Cambridge, MA: Harvard University Press, 1991. Rep. London: Reaktion, 1997.

Brockmann, Stephan. "The Death of Tragedy Revisited." *Journal of Dramatic Theory and Criticism* 17:1 (Fall 2002): 23–44.

Brustein, Robert. *The Theatre of Revolt*. Boston: Little Brown, 1962.

Burke, Kenneth. *A Grammar of Motives* (1945). Berkeley: University of California Press, 1969.

On *Symbols and Society*. Ed. Joseph R. Gusfield. Chicago: University of Chicago Press, 1989.

"Othello: An Essay to Illustrate a Method." *Perspectives by Incongruity*. Ed. Stanley Edgar Hyman. Bloomington: Indiana University Press, 1964.

The Philosophy of Literary Form. 2nd ed. Baton Rouge: Louisiana State University Press, 1967.

Burkert, Walter. *Greek Religion*. Cambridge, MA: Harvard University Press/ Blackwell, 1985 (English translation).

Butler, Isaac. "The Death and Life of the Living-Room Play." *American Theatre* 32:4 (April 2015): 38–42.

Butler, James H. *The Theatre and Drama of Greece and Rome*. San Francisco: Chandler, 1972.

Calder, Andrew. "Laughter and Irony in *Le Misanthrope*." Bradby and Calder, 95–106.

Calderwood, James L. *To Be and Not to Be: Negation and Metadrama in "Hamlet."* New York: Columbia University Press, 1983.

Cambon, Glauco, ed. *Pirandello: A Collection of Critical Essays*. Englewood Cliffs, New Jersey: Prentice-Hall, 1967.

Caputi, Anthony, ed. *Eight Modern Plays*. New York: W. W. Norton, 1991.

Carlson, Marvin. *Theories of the Theatre: A Historical and Critical Survey, from the Greeks to the Present*. Ithaca: Cornell University Press, 1984.

Carpenter, Thomas H. and Christopher Faraone, eds. *Masks of Dionysus*. Ithaca: Cornell University Press, 1993.

Chalmers, David J. *The Character of Consciousness*. New York: Oxford University Press, 2010.

The Conscious Mind: In Search of a Fundamental Theory. New York: Oxford University Press, 1996.

"Facing up to the Problem of Consciousness." *Journal of Consciousness Studies* 2:3 (1995): 200–219. See also Shear, 9–32.

Chapman, John, ed. *Theatre '55: Reading Versions of the Golden Dozen Plays of the Year*. New York: Random, 1955.

Charney, Maurice. *Hamlet's Fictions*. New York: Routledge, 1988.

Chatman, Seymour. *Story and Discourse: Narrative Structure in Fiction and Film*. Ithaca: Cornell University Press, 1978.

Chekhov, Anton. *Chekhov: the Major Plays*. Trans. Ann Dunnigan. New York: Penguin/Signet, 1964.

Churchill, Caryl. *Cloud 9* (1979). New York: Routledge, 1984 (rev.).

Clark, Barrett, ed. *European Theories of the Drama*. Rev. ed. New York: Crown, 1965.

Cohn, Ruby. *Back to Beckett*. Princeton: Princeton University Press, 1973.

Just Play: Beckett's Theater. Princeton: Princeton University Press, 1980.

Cole, Toby and Helen Krich Chinoy. *Actors on Acting* (1949). New York: Crown, 1970.

Collier, Jeremy. "A Short View of the Immorality and Profaneness of the English Stage." Abridged, McMillin, 493–506.

Cook, Amy. *Shakespearean Neuroplay*. New York: Palgrave, 2010.

Corrigan, Robert W., ed. *Tragedy: Vision and Form*. Scranton, PA: Chandler Publishing, 1965.

Damasio, Antonio. *The Feeling of What Happens: Body and Emotion in the Making of Consciousness*. New York: Harcourt, 1999.

Self Comes to Mind: Constructing the Conscious Brain. New York: Vintage/ Random, 2010.

Danan, Joseph. "Dramaturgy in 'Postdramatic' Times." Trencsényi, 3–17.

Demastes, William W. "Hamlet in His World: Shakespeare Anticipates/ Assaults Cartesian Dualism." *Journal of Dramatic Theory and Criticism* 20:1 (Fall 2005): 27–42.

"Portrait of an Artist as Proto-Chaotician: Tom Stoppard Working His Way to *Arcadia*." *Narrative* 19:2 (May 2011): 229–240.

Staging Consciousness: Theatre and the Materialization of Mind. Ann Arbor: University of Michigan Press, 2002.

Depew, Mary and Dirk Obbink, eds. *Matrices of Genre: Authors, Canons, and Society*. Cambridge, MA: Harvard University Press, 2000.

De Ste. Croix, G. E. M. "Aristotle on History and Poetry." Rorty, 23–32.

Diamond, Elin. "Identity Politics Then and Now." *Theatre Research International* 37:1 (March 2012): 64–67.

"Mimesis, Mimicry, and the 'True-Real.'" *Modern Drama* 32:1 (March 1989): 58–72

"Refusing the Romanticism of Identity." *Theatre Journal* 37:3 (October 1985): 273–286.

Unmaking Mimesis: Essays on Feminism and Theater. London: Routledge, 1997.

Dukore, Bernard F. *Dramatic Theory and Criticism: Greeks to Grotowski*. Orlando, Florida: Holt, Rinehart, Winston, 1974.

Dunn, Francis M. *Tragedy's End: Closure and Innovation in Euripidean Drama*. New York: Oxford University Press, 1996.

Easterling, P. E., ed. *The Cambridge Companion to Greek Tragedy*. Cambridge: Cambridge University Press, 1997.

"Character in Sophocles." E. Segal, 138–145. 1st pub. *Greece and Rome* 24 (1977): 121–129.

"A Show for Dionysus." *The Cambridge Companion to Greek Tragedy*, 36–53.

Edwards, Paul. "Science in *Hapgood* and *Arcadia*." Kelly, 171–184.

Eliot, T. S. "Hamlet and His Problems." *The Sacred Wood* (1920). London: Methuen, 1972.

Else, Gerald F. *Aristotle's Poetics: The Argument*. Cambridge, MA: Harvard University Press, 1963.

The Origin and Early Form of Greek Tragedy. New York: W.W. Norton, 1965

Esslin, Martin. *Brecht: The Man and His Work*. Garden City, NY: Anchor/Doubleday, 1961.

The Theatre of the Absurd. Garden City: Doubleday, 1961.

Etherege, George. *The Man of Mode*. John Barnard, ed. New York: W.W. Norton (New Mermaid), 1979. Also McMillin, 87–167.

Euripides. *The Bacchae. Euripides V*. David Grene and Richmond Lattimore, eds. Trans., intro. William Arrowsmith. Chicago: University of Chicago Press, 1959.

Hippolytus. Euripides I. David Grene and Richmond Lattimore, eds. Trans. David Grene. Chicago: University of Chicago Press, 1955.

Medea. Euripides I. David Grene and Richmond Lattimore, eds., Trans. Rex Warner. Chicago: University of Chicago Press, 1955.

Felheim, Marvin, ed. *Comedy: Plays, Theory, and Criticism*. New York: Harcourt, Brace, and World, 1962.

Fergusson, Francis. *The Idea of a Theater* (1949). Princeton: Princeton University Press, 1968.

Fisk, Deborah Payne. *The Cambridge Companion to English Restoration Theatre*. Cambridge: Cambridge University Press, 2000.

Flickinger, Roy C. *The Greek Theater and Its Drama* (1918). Chicago: University of Chicago Press, 1960 (Reprint Series).

Forster, E. M. *Aspects of the Novel* (1927). New York: Harcourt, Brace, and World, 1954.

Frayn, Michael. *Copenhagen*. New York: Anchor, 1998.

Freud, Sigmund. "Psychopathic Characters on the Stage." *Writings*, 87–93.

"Some Character-Types Met with in Psycho-analytic Work." *Writings*, 151–175.

Writings on Art and Literature. Forw. Neil Hertz (from *The Standard Edition of the Complete Psychological Works of Sigmund Freud*, 24 vols. Ed. James Strachey). Stanford: Stanford University Press, 1997.

Frye, Northrop. *Anatomy of Criticism*. Princeton: Princeton University Press, 1957.
Northrop Frye on Shakespeare. New Haven: Yale University Press, 1986.

Fuchs, Elinor. *The Death of Character: Perspectives on Theatre after Modernism*. Bloomington: Indiana University Press, 1996.

Garner, Stanton B., Jr. "Zola, Medicine, and Naturalism." Knowles, 67–79.

Gazzaniga, Michael S. *Who's in Charge?: Free Will and the Science of the Brain*. New York: Harper Collins, 2011.

Gerrig, Richard J. and David W. Allbritton. "The Construction of Literary Character: A View from Cognitive Psychology." *Style* 24:3 (Fall 1990): 380–391.

Gill, Pat. "Gender, Sexuality, and Marriage." Fisk, 181–208.

Gilman, Richard. *Chekhov's Plays: An Opening into Eternity*. New Haven: Yale University Press, 1995.
The Making of Modern Drama. New York: Farrar, Straus, and Giroux, 1972.

Goldhill, Simon. *Reading Greek Tragedy*. Cambridge: Cambridge University Press, 1986.

Goldstein, Rebecca Newberger. *Plato at the Googleplex: Why Philosophy Won't Go Away*. New York: Pantheon, 2014.

Gorra, Michael S. *The Portrait of a Novel*. London: Liveright, 2012.

Gowing, Lawrence. Intro. Michel Laclotte. *Paintings in the Louvre*. New York: Stewart, Tabori and Chang, 1987.

Green, J. R. *Theatre in Ancient Greek Society*. New York: Routledge, 1994.

Gruber, William E. *Missing Persons: Character and Characterization in Modern Drama*. Athens: University of Georgia Press, 1994.

Guare, John. *The House of Blue Leaves*. New York: Viking, 1972.

Haigh, A. E. *The Tragic Drama of the Greeks* (Oxford, 1896). New York: Dover, 1968.

Hartman, Geoffrey H., ed. *Psychoanalysis and the Question of the Text*. Baltimore: The Johns Hopkins University Press, 1978.

Hazlitt, William. *Hazlitt on Theatre* (1895). Ed. William Archer and Robert Lowe. New York: Hill and Wang Dramabook, 1958.

Henrichs, Albert. "Loss of Self, Suffering, Violence: The Modern View of Dionysus from Nietzsche to Girard." *Harvard Studies in Classical Philology* 88 (1984): 205–240.

Herman, David, ed. *The Cambridge Companion to Narrative*. New York: Cambridge University Press, 2007.

Hernadi, Paul. *Beyond Genre: New Directions in Literary Classification*. Ithaca: Cornell University Press, 1972.

Hewitt, Barnard. *Theatre U.S.A. 1665 to 1957*. New York: McGraw-Hill, 1959.

Huerta, Jorge. *Chicano Theatre: Themes and Forms*. Ypsilanti: Bilingual Press, 1982. Qtd. by Worthen.

Ibsen, Henrik. *The Complete Major Prose Plays*. Trans., intro., Rolf Fjelde. New York: Penguin, 1965.

Ionesco, Eugène. *The Bald Soprano and Other Plays*. Trans. Donald M. Allen. New York: Grove Press, 1958.
Notes and Counter Notes: Writings on the Theatre. New York: Grove Press, 1964.

"The World of Ionesco." *International Theatre Annual.* No. 2 (1957). Qtd. in Samuel A. Weiss, ed. *Drama in the Modern World: Plays and Essays.* Boston: D.C. Heath, 1964.

James, Henry. "The Art of Fiction." *Longman's Magazine* 4 (September 1884), repr. *Partial Portraits* (1888). Westport, CT: Greenwood Press, 1970.

The Portrait of a Lady (one volume, 1882). Ed., intro., notes, Philip Horne. New York: Penguin, 2011.

"Preface" to *The Tragic Muse* (1890). Ed. Philip Horne. London: Penguin, 1995.

Johnson, Barbara. "The Frame of Reference: Poe, Lacan, Derrida." Hartman, 149–171.

Johnson, Gary. "Consciousness as Content. Neuronarratives and the Redemption of Fiction." *Mosaic* 41:1 (March 2008): 169–184.

Johnson, Samuel. *Samuel Johnson on Shakespeare.* Ed., intro., W. K. Wimsatt, Jr. New York: Hill and Wang Dramabook, 1960.

Johnston, Brian. *The Ibsen Cycle: The Design of the Plays from 'The Pillars of Society' to 'When We Dead Awaken'.* University Park, PA: Pennsylvania State University Press, 1992.

Jones, John. *On Aristotle and Greek Tragedy.* New York: Oxford University Press, 1962.

Kachur, B. A. *Etherege and Wycherley.* New York: Palgrave, 2004.

Karlinsky, Simon, intro., comm., and Michael Henry Heim, trans. *Anton Chekhov's Life and Thought: Selected Letters and Commentary.* Berkeley: University of California Press, 1973.

Kelly, Katherine E. *The Cambridge Companion to Tom Stoppard.* New York: Cambridge University Press, 2001.

Kennedy, Andrew. *Samuel Beckett.* Cambridge: Cambridge University Press, 1989.

Kenner, Hugh. "Happy Days." *Samuel Beckett (Reader's Guides).* London: Thames and Hudson Ltd., 1973. Pgs 147–192. Excerpt repr., Caputi, 597–601.

Kerényi, Carl. *Dionysos: Archetypal Image of Indestructible Life.* Trans. Ralph Manheim. Princeton: Princeton University Press, 1976.

Kitto, H. D. F. *Form and Meaning in Drama: A Study of Six Greek Plays and of "Hamlet."* London: Robert Cunningham and Sons, 1956.

Knight, G. Wilson. *The Wheel of Fire: Interpretations of Shakespearian Tragedy* (1930, 1949). New York: Routledge, 1989.

Knowles, Ric, Joanne Tompkins, and W. B. Worthen. *Modern Drama: Defining the Field.* Toronto: University of Toronto Press, 2003.

Konnikova, Maria. *Mastermind: How to Think Like Sherlock Holmes.* New York: Penguin Viking, 2013.

Krutch, Joseph Wood. "The Tragic Fallacy." *The Modern Temper* (1929). Corrigan, 271–283.

Kushner, Tony. *Angels in America: Millennium Approaches.* New York: TCG, 1993.

Lacan, Jacques. "Desire and the Interpretation of Desire in *Hamlet.*" *Yale French Studies* 55–56 (1977): 11–52.

Lahr, John, ed. *A Casebook on Harold Pinter's "The Homecoming."* New York: Grove, 1971.

"Demolition Man." *The New Yorker*. December 24 and 31, 2007: 54–69.

Lamm, Martin. *August Strindberg*. Ed., trans. Harry G. Carlson. New York: Benjamin Blom, 1971.

Lamont, Rosette C. *Ionesco's Imperatives*. Ann Arbor: University of Michigan Press, 1993.

Lawley, Paul. "Stages of Identity: From *Krapp's Last Tape* to *Play*." Pilling, 88–105.

Lehmann, Hans-Thies. *Postdramatic Theatre*. Trans. Karen Jürs-Munby. New York: Routledge, 2006.

Levin, Harry. *Playboys and Killjoys: An Essay on the Theory and Practice of Comedy*. New York: Oxford University Press, 1987.

Lifton, Robert J. *The Protean Self: Human Resilience in an Age of Fragmentation*. New York: Basic Books, 1993.

Lightman, Alan. *The Discoveries: Great Breakthroughs in 20th-Century Science*. New York: Pantheon, 2005.

Lillo, George. "Dedication" to *The London Merchant*. Ed. William H. McBurney. Lincoln: University of Nebraska Press, 1965.

Lloyd-Jones, Hugh. "The Guilt of Agamemnon." E. Segal, 56–72.

Lodge, David. *The Art of Fiction*. London: Penguin, 1992.

Consciousness and the Novel. Cambridge, MA: Harvard University Press, 2002.

Thinks.... New York: Penguin, 2002.

Lonsdale, Steven H. *Dance and Ritual Play in Greek Religion*. Baltimore: The Johns Hopkins University Press, 1993.

Lowe, E. J. "There Are No Easy Problems of Consciousness." Shear, 117–123.

MacFarquhar, Larissa. "Two Heads: A Marriage Devoted to the Mind-Body Problem." *The New Yorker*. February 12, 2007: 57–69.

Macksey, Richard and Eugene Donato, eds. *The Structuralist Controversy: The Languages of Criticism and the Sciences of Man*. Baltimore: The Johns Hopkins University Press, 1970.

Margolin, Uri. "Character." Herman, 66–79.

Martin, Jay. *Who Am I This Time?: Uncovering the Fictive Personality*. New York: W.W. Norton, 1988.

McConachie, Bruce. *Engaging Audiences: A Cognitive Approach to Spectating in the Theatre*. New York: Palgrave, 2008.

McConachie, Bruce and F. Elizabeth Hart, eds. *Performance and Cognition: Theatre Studies and the Cognitive Turn*. New York: Routledge, 2006.

Theatre and Mind. New York: Palgrave, 2013.

McGann, Jerome. *The Poet Edgar Allan Poe: Alien Angel*. Cambridge, MA: Harvard University Press, 2014.

McMillin, Scott, ed. *Restoration and Eighteenth Century Comedy*. Norton Critical Edition. 2nd ed. New York: W.W. Norton, 1997.

Miller, Arthur. *After the Fall*. New York: Penguin, 1964.

Miller, J. Hillis. *Ariadne's Thread: Story Lines*. New Haven: Yale University Press, 1992.

Miner, Earl, ed. *Restoration Dramatists: A Collection of Critical Essays*. Englewood Cliffs, NJ: Prentice Hall, 1966.

Molière. *Tartuffe and The Misanthrope*. Trans., intro. Richard Wilbur. New York: Harcourt Brace (Harvest), 1965.

Nagler, A. M. *Sources of Theatrical History*. New York: Theatre Annual, 1952.

Nietzsche, Friedrich. *The Birth of Tragedy and The Geneology of Morals*. Trans. Francis Golffing. New York: Doubleday, 1956.

O'Neill, Eugene. *Long Day's Journey Into Night* (1956). New Haven: Yale University Press, 2002.

Otto, Walter F. *Dionysus: Myth and Cult*. Bloomington: Indiana University Press, 1995.

Padel, Ruth. *Whom Gods Destroy: Elements of Greek and Tragic Madness*. Princeton: Princeton University Press, 1995.

Paolucci, Anne. "Comedy and Paradox in Pirandello's Plays." *Modern Drama* 20:4 (December 1977): 321–330.

Parnell, Peter. *Q.E.D.* New York: Applause, 2002.

Phelan, James. *Reading People, Reading Plots: Character, Progression, and the Interpretation of Narrative*. Chicago: University of Chicago Press, 1989.

Pickard-Cambridge, Arthur. *Dithyramb Tragedy and Comedy* (1927). Rev. 2nd ed. T. B. L. Webster. Oxford: Clarendon Press, 1962.

Pilling, John, ed. *The Cambridge Companion to Beckett*. Cambridge: Cambridge University Press, 1994.

Pinter, Harold. *The Homecoming*. New York: Grove, 1965.

Pirandello, Luigi. "Preface" to *Six Characters in Search of an Author* (1925). In Bentley, ed. *Naked Masks*, 363–375.

    Six Characters in Search of an Author. Trans. Anthony Caputi. Caputi, 210–256.

    "The Tragedy of Character." *Short Stories*. Trans., intro. Frederick May. London: Oxford University Press, 1965.

Poe, Edgar Allan. *The Fall of the House of Usher and Other Writings*. London: Penguin, 1986.

Poulet, Georges. "Criticism and the Experience of Interiority." Macksey and Donato, 56–72.

Powell, Jocelyn. "George Etherege and the Form of a Comedy." Miner, 63–85.

Powers, Richard. *The Echo Maker*. New York: Macmillan/Picador, 2007.

Prideaux, Sue. *Strindberg: A Life*. New Haven: Yale University Press, 2012.

Racine, Jean. *Phaedra*. Trans. Richard Wilbur. New York: Harcourt Brace, 1986.

Ramachandran, V. S. *A Brief Tour of Human Consciousness*. New York: Pi Press, 2004.

Ratcliff, Carter. *John Singer Sargent*. New York: Artabras, 1982.

Richards, I. A. *Principles of Literary Criticism* (1925). New York: Harvest HBJ, 1985.

Richardson, Brian. "Beyond Poststructuralism: Theory of Character, the Personae of Modern Drama, and the Antimonies of Critical Theory." *Modern Drama* 40 (1997): 86–99.

    "Drama and Narrative." Herman, 142–155.

Rokotnitz, Naomi. " 'It is required/You do awake your faith': Learning to trust the body through performing *The Winter's Tale*." McConachie and Hart, 123–146.

Rorty, Amélie Oksenberg, ed. *Essays on Aristotle's Poetics*. Princeton: Princeton University Press, 1992.

"The Psychology of Aristotelian Tragedy." Rorty, 1–22.

Roth, Marco. "Rise of the Neuronovel." *n + 1 Magazine* (8): September 2009. Online: http://nplusonemag.com/rise-neuronovel.

Rousseau, Jean-Jacques. *Politics and the Arts: Letter to M. D'Alembert on the Theatre*. Trans., intro. Allan Bloom. Ithaca: Cornell University Press, 1968.

Schlink, Bernhard. *The Reader*. Trans. Carol Brown Janeway. New York: Vintage, 1995.

Scholes, Robert, James Phelan, and Robert Kellogg. *The Nature of Narrative*. Rev. ed. New York: Oxford University Press, 2006.

Searle, John R. *Mind: A Brief Introduction*. New York: Oxford University Press, 2004.

"The Mystery of Consciousness Continues." *New York Review of Books* (Review of Antonio Damasio, *Self Comes to Mind: Constructing the Conscious Brain*). June 9, 2011: 50–52.

Segal, Charles. *Dionysiac Poetics in Euripides' "Bacchae."* Princeton: Princeton University Press, 1982. Exp. ed., 1997.

Interpreting Greek Tragedy: Myth, Poetry, Text. Ithaca: Cornell University Press, 1986.

Segal, Erich, ed. *Greek Tragedy: Modern Essays in Criticism*. New York: Harper and Row, 1983.

Senelek, Laurence, trans., ed. *Russian Dramatic Theory from Pushkin to the Symbolists*. Austin: University of Texas Press, 1981.

Sewall, Richard B. "The Tragic Form." *Essays in Criticism* 4 (1954): 345–358. Also *Tragedy: Modern Essays in Criticism*. Eds. Laurence Michel and Richard B. Sewall. Englewood Cliffs, NJ: Prentice-Hall, 1963.

Shaffer, Peter. *Equus*. New York: Scribner's, 1973.

Shakespeare, William. *Hamlet*. Eds. Barbara Mowat and Paul Werstine. Folger Shakespeare ed. New York: Simon and Schuster, 1992.

Shapin, Steven. *The Scientific Life: A Moral History of a Late Modern Vocation*. Chicago: University of Chicago Press, 2008.

Shaw, George Bernard. "The Master Builder" (1892). *The Quintessence of Ibsenism* (1913). London: Hill and Wang Dramabook, 1957.

Shear, Jonathan, ed. *Explaining Consciousness – The "Hard Problem."* Cambridge, MA: MIT Press, 1995.

Shepherd-Barr, Kirstin. *Science on Stage: From Doctor Faustus to Copenhagen*. Princeton: Princeton University Press, 2006.

Sophocles. *Oedipus at Colonus. Greek Tragedies III*. Trans. David Grene. Richmond Lattimore and David Grene, eds. Chicago: University of Chicago Press, 1992.

States, Bert O. "The Anatomy of Dramatic Character." *Theatre Journal* 37:1 (March 1985): 87–101.

Hamlet and the Concept of Character. Baltimore: The Johns Hopkins University Press, 1992.

"The Mirror and the Labyrinth: The Further Ordeals of Character and Mimesis." *Style* 27:3 (Fall 1993): 452–471.

The Pleasure of the Play. Ithaca: Cornell University Press, 1994.

"Tragedy and Tragic Vision: A Darwinian Supplement to Van Laan." *Journal of Dramatic Theory and Criticism* 6:2 (Spring 1992): 5–22.

Steele, Richard. *The Conscious Lovers.* McMillan 325–383.

"Preface" to *The Conscious Lovers.* McMillan 322–324.

Steiner, George. *The Death of Tragedy.* New York: Alfred A. Knopf, 1961.

No Passion Spent: Essays 1978–1995. New Haven: Yale University Press, 1996.

"A Note on Absolute Tragedy." *Journal of Literature and Theology* 4:2 (July 1990).

Steiner, Wendy. *The Real Real Thing: The Model in the Mirror of Art.* Chicago: University of Chicago Press, 2010.

Stoppard, Tom. *Arcadia.* London: Faber and Faber, 1993.

Travesties. New York: Grove, 1975.

Storm, William. *After Dionysus: A Theory of the Tragic.* Ithaca: Cornell University Press, 1998.

"Impression Henry Irving: The Performance in the Portrait by Jules Bastien-Lepage." *Victorian Studies* 46:3 (Spring 2004): 399–424.

Irony and the Modern Theatre. Cambridge: Cambridge University Press, 2011.

"Lukács/Ibsen: Tragedy, Selfhood, and 'Real Life' in *The Master Builder* and *When We Dead Awaken*." *Comparative Drama* 46:1 (Spring 2012): 17–39

"On the Science of Dramatic Character." *Narrative* 19:2 (May 2011): 241–252.

Strindberg, August. *Miss Julie. Six Plays of Strindberg.* Trans. Elizabeth Sprigge. Garden City: Doubleday, 1955.

"Preface" to *Miss Julie. Five Plays of Strindberg.* Trans., intro. Harry G. Carlson. Berkeley: University of California Press, 1981.

Stynan, J. L. *Modern Drama in Theory and Practice. Volume I: Realism and Naturalism.* Cambridge: Cambridge University Press, 1981.

Sypher, Wylie. "Cubist Drama." Cambon, 67–71. *Rococo to Cubism in Art and Literature.* New York: Random House, 1960.

Tillyard, E. M. W. *The Elizabethan World Picture.* New York: Vintage, 1957.

Todorov, Tristan. *Genres in Discourse* (1978). Cambridge: Cambridge University Press, 1990.

Toibin, Colm. "Happy Birthday, Sam!" *New York Review of Books.* April 27, 2006: 24–25.

New Ways to Kill Your Mother: Writers and Their Families. New York: Scribner, 2012.

Trencsényi, Katalin and Bernadette Cochrane, eds. *New Dramaturgy: International Perspectives on Theory and Practice.* London: Bloomsbury Methuen, 2014.

Treadwell, Sophie. *Machinal.* Barlow, 171–255.

Troyat, Henri. *Chekhov.* Trans. Michael Henry Heim. New York: Fawcett, 1986.

Turnell, Martin. *The Classical Moment: Studies of Corneille, Molière, Racine* (New Directions, 1948). Westport, CN: Greenwood Press, 1971.

Jean Racine: Dramatist. New York: New Directions, 1972.

"Le Misanthrope." Felheim, 268–280.

Turner, Cathy and Synne K. Behrndt. *Dramaturgy and Performance*. New York: Palgrave, 2008.

Valdez, Luis. *Zoot Suit* (1978). Houston: Arte Publico, 1992.

Valency, Maurice. *The End of the World: An Introduction to Contemporary Drama*. New York: Oxford University Press, 1980.

"Vershinin." Barricelli, 218–232.

Vanden Heuvel, Michael. *Performing Drama/Dramatizing Performance: Alternative Theatre and the Dramatic Text*. Ann Arbor: University of Michigan Press, 1991.

Van Laan, Thomas. "The Death of Tragedy Myth." *Journal of Dramatic Theory and Criticism* 5:2 (Spring 1991): 5–31.

Vernant, Jean-Pierre. "Greek Tragedy: Problems of Interpretation." Macksey, 271–289.

Vernant, Jean-Pierre and Pierre Vidal-Naquet. *Myth and Tragedy in Ancient Greece*. Trans. Janet Lloyd. New York: Zone, 1988.

Wasserstein, Wendy. *The Heidi Chronicles and Other Plays*. New York: Vintage, 1991.

Weinberg, Bernard. *The Art of Jean Racine*. Chicago: University of Chicago Press, 1963.

Welsh, Alexander. *Hamlet in His Modern Guises*. Princeton: Princeton University Press, 2001.

Wilde, Oscar. *The Plays of Oscar Wilde*. Intro. John Lahr. New York: Vintage, 1988.

Williams, Tennessee. *Cat on a Hot Tin Roof* (1955). New York: Signet, 1985.

The Glass Menagerie (1945). New York: New Directions, 1999.

"Portrait of a Girl in Glass." *Collected Stories*. Intro. Gore Vidal. New York: New Directions, 1985.

Where I Live: Selected Essays. New York: New Directions, 1978.

Wilshire, Bruce. *Role Playing and Identity: The Limits of Theatre as Metaphor*. Bloomington: Indiana University Press, 1982.

Wilson, August. *Fences*. New York: Samuel French, 1986.

Winkler, John J. and Froma I. Zeitlin, eds. *Nothing to Do with Dionysos?: Athenian Drama in Its Social Context*. Princeton: Princeton University Press, 1990.

Worthen, W. B. "Staging America: The Subject of History in Chicano/a Theatre." *Theatre Journal* 49:2 (May 1997): 101–120.

Wycherley, William. *The Country Wife*. McMillan, 3–85.

Young, Kay. *Imagining Minds: The Neuro-Aesthetics of Austen, Eliot, and Hardy*. Columbus: Ohio State University Press, 2010.

Zeitlin, Froma. *Playing the Other: Gender and Society in Classical Greek Literature*. Chicago: University of Chicago Press, 1995.

"Playing the Other: Theatre, Theatricality, and the Feminine in Greek Drama." Winkler and Zeitlin, 63–96.

Zola, Emile. "Naturalism in the Theatre." Bentley, *Theory*, 351–372.

"Preface to *Thérèse Raquin*." Clark, 376–379.

Index

Abbott, H. Porter, 96, 146
and Beckett's "people", 143
on fictive character in relation to reading,
writing, 94
and real persons, 95
Abel, Lionel, 49
tragedy as transhistoric, 190
Aeschylus, 5, 22, 23, 24, 34, 35, 41, 47
Agamemnon
character and gods relation, 38–39, 47
character of Agamemnon, 32
scene of return to Argos, 32, 34, 38
character of Cassandra, 37
forces at work
and the House of Atreus, 38
and influence of daimon, 38, 39
Oresteia, 48
Allbritton, David W.
on readers and literary characters, 202
Alpaugh, Daniel J.
"negative definition" in *Happy Days*, 142
Andreev, Leonid
panpsychism in Chekhov, 117–118
Aristotle, 6, 14, 34, 49–52, 119, 151, 181
and scientific analysis, 30
Poetics, 21, 27, 28
on character as agent, 31
on character as consistent, good,
appropriate, 29, 133
and *dianoia* (thought), 29, 32, 50
and *ethos* (character), 28–29, 32, 33, 50
and hamartia, 29, 31, 86
and *lexos* (language), 30
and *muthos* (plot), 29, 30, 50, 86, 181
and *opsis* (spectacle), 93
and traits, 28, 86, 167
as functional, 31, 44, 53

Baitz, Jon Robin
Other Desert Cities, 13, 177–179
as family play, 13, 177

character of Brooke Wyeth, 177
character of Polly Wyeth, 177
character of the Wyeths, 177, 178
in relation to dramatic media, 13, 178
and performative character, 178
and acting, 179
and the Reagans, 177
Bakhtin, Mikhail
and focalization, 205
Barish, Jonas
anti-theatrical prejudice, 70
Baron, Michel, 15, 184
and the role of Alceste, 66
Barthes, Roland
interiority and guilt in *Phaedra*, 195
Beckett, Samuel, 11, 141, 146, 160, 180
characters as his "people", 143, 144
Happy Days, 11, 141
character of Winnie, 142–144
and setting, 142, 143
Waiting for Godot, 143, 160
Bentley, Eric, 51
review of *Cat on a Hot Tin Roof*, 206
Bieber, Margarete
and ancient dramaturgy, 24
on Dionysian worship and theatrical origins,
21, 186
Blau, Herbert
on theatrical audience, 2
Bloom, Harold
autonomy of Hamlet, 44, 45, 53, 93
character of Hamlet, 44, 45, 59
reification of character, 46, 53, 95, 96
Blundell, Mary Whitlock, 191
Bogart, Ann
Who Do You Think You Are?
observed behavioral models and mirror
neuron behavior, 102
Bohr, Niels
as character in *Copenhagen*, 97–98
as historical figure, 97, 101

Booth, Wayne
   and the *Poetics*, 28
Bradley, A. C.
   and Hamlet's disease, 53
   and Hamlet's genius, 53
   Hamlet as tragedy, 53
Brecht, Bertolt, 92, 131, 176, 180
   and acting, 158
   character of Mother Courage, 158
   and gestus, 158, 167, 172
   Galileo, 86, 158
   his theory compared with naturalism, 87
   "The Short Organum", 86
   "The Street Scene", 87
   "theatre of a scientific age", 86
Brereton, Geoffrey
   Racinian characterization, 80
Brilliant, Richard
   on lifelikeness, 136–138
   on portraiture, 136
Brockmann, Stephan, 190
Brustein, Robert
   on *The Father*, 196
Buchner, Georg, 176
Burke, Kenneth
   and "character recipe", 58, 60
   and character "motive", 58–59, 165
   and consubstantial characters, 58, 110
   and dramatism, pentad of terms and ratios,
      58–59, 61, 96, 165
Burkert, Walter, 189
   characteristic forms of Dionysus, 184
Butler, Isaac, 209
Butler, James H., 24
   Greek mask, 187

Calder, Andrew, 66, 68
Calderwood, James L.
   and Hamlet's "dual identity" of character and
      actor, 46
   and "metadramatism" in Hamlet, 46
Carlson, Marvin
   and *bienséance*, 192
   and *Le Cid* controversy, 193
Chalmers, David, 124
   consciousness as "hard problem", 146
Character
   and actor, 2, 3, 5, 15, 16, 18, 19, 22–26, 27, 28,
      37, 46, 64, 66, 91, 92, 98, 99, 130,
      133, 135, 137, 139, 150, 151, 158
   and agency, 35, 41, 43–47, 53, 57–59, 92, 96,
      109, 150, 163–167
   and alternative theatre, 13, 160, 180
   ancestry of, 11, 28–32, 52, 141, 159, 168, 169,
      178, 180

and the "anti", 130, 134, 140, 149, 150, 180
and audience, 1–3, 4, 5, 6, 7, 10, 15, 29, 46, 64,
      66, 68, 69, 71, 75, 78, 79, 80, 82,
      94, 97, 99, 104, 109, 110, 114, 120,
      121, 123, 124, 128, 130, 132, 133, 134,
      138, 139, 155, 164
as autobiographical, 121, 123
beginnings of, 3, 4, 14, 22, 23, 24, 25, 26, 90
and "character", 7, 14, 19, 31, 33, 36, 64, 70,
      81, 83, 99, 100, 143, 172
and chorus (ancient), 3, 4, 23, 24, 35, 37,
      50, 114
in cinema, 201
as collective, 12, 60, 77, 116–119, 120, 122,
      123, 174
compared to modeling, 15, 135, 136, 138, 139
compared to portraiture, 135–139
compared with literary or narrative character,
      2, 10, 15, 29, 92, 95, 106, 108, 118,
      126, 128, 147, 149
"death" of, 12, 13, 158–163
and family, 12, 13, 39, 119, 120, 121, 153, 172,
      173, 174, 177, 178
and fictive personality, 163
as formative, 8, 11, 85, 87, 105, 123, 133, 141,
      153, 173, 174, 175, 180, 181
and genre, 12, 41–43, 53, 76, 100, 101, 168, 169,
      170, 171, 178
and interiority, 8, 9, 15, 27, 29, 34, 36, 38, 43,
      46, 49, 57, 72, 79, 104, 118, 119, 123,
      124, 126, 129, 149, 181
and lifelikeness, 1, 44, 63, 130, 131, 156
and mask, 3, 5, 17, 18, 19, 23, 26–28, 30, 34,
      35, 37, 71, 73, 74, 75, 104, 133, 136,
      138, 161, 179
and memory, 9, 12, 105, 110, 114, 120–123, 128,
      145, 170
metacharacter, 11, 12
and mimesis, 13, 91, 101, 102, 133, 136, 138, 141,
      146, 152, 158, 161, 162, 164, 179
and naturalism, 8, 84–87, 92, 105, 153
and neoclassical guidelines, 7, 62, 64, 67, 68,
      71, 73, 75, 76, 78, 79, 171
and performance, performance art, 13,
      162, 180
and personality, 10, 11, 12, 16, 26, 27, 29, 31,
      41, 52, 53, 60, 76, 90, 93, 141, 154,
      155, 163
and plot (ratio), 5, 30, 31, 46, 49, 51, 158,
      162, 167
and the passions, 7, 62, 69, 70, 77, 80, 81
and the "postdramatic", 13, 161–163
and the postmodern, 143, 150, 159, 179
and the reader, 2, 10, 15, 34, 89, 93, 107, 128,
      148, 149, 176

as "real person", 8, 15, 44, 63, 77, 85, 90–102, 130, 131, 133, 139, 146, 156, 174, 178, 179
and realism, 161, 178
in relation to autonomy, free will, 6, 35, 38, 42, 59, 63, 109, 130, 150, 164
in relation to stage time, 1, 200
and reason, 7, 8, 36, 60, 64, 65, 67, 69, 70, 75, 77, 105, 109, 164, 179
and Romanticism, 65, 84
and science, 8, 85, 86, 87–90, 92, 97, 98, 100, 101, 102, 103
and self, 10, 11, 12, 20, 27, 51, 74, 77, 90, 128, 131, 134, 137, 140, 145, 146, 147, 148, 159, 163, 164, 165, 167, 176, 179
and spectacle, 92, 93, 94, 100, 114, 115, 143, 161, 165, 167–168
and spectatorship, 2, 58, 72, 73, 163
as surrogate, 16, 44, 95–97, 99, 163, 180
and suspense, 6, 11, 13, 104, 155, 156, 157, 158, 160
and thought, thinking, 8, 9, 26, 32, 35, 37, 50, 54, 55, 104, 105, 106, 107, 108, 109, 110, 111, 114, 117, 118, 119, 120, 121, 123, 124, 125, 126, 127, 147, 150, 165
as virtual, 139, 163, 180
Charney, Maurice
 Shakespeare and Pirandello, 190
Chatman, Seymour
 character and personality, 93, 94
 character and real persons, 93, 95
Chekhov, Anton, 89, 117, 119, 145
 The Cherry Orchard, 90
  character of Lopakhin, 117, 128
  character of Lyubov, 117, 128, 145
  depiction of time, 90
  and the Moscow Art Theatre and Konstantin Stanislavsky, 90
 The Seagull, 90
  character of Treplev, 117
 Three Sisters, 90
  character of Natasha, 118
  character of Vershinin, 117
Churchill, Caryl, 12, 164
 Cloud 9, 12, 167
  character of Betty, 167
  character of Clive, 168
  and gender, 167
  and stage spectacle, 167
Churchland, Paul and Patricia
 quoted, 103
Cohn, Ruby
 Beckett's characters as "people", 143
 identification with Winnie, 144
 setting of *Happy Days*, 144

Collier, Jeremy
 and anti-theatrical prejudice, 7
 "A Short View of the Immorality and Profaneness of the English Stage", 70, 71
Comedy, comic drama, 6, 7, 15, 168, 169
 ancient, 5
 Neoclassical, 62, 63, 68
 Restoration, 9, 62, 70, 73, 75, 81
  and comedy of manners, 71, 72, 73
  and moral standpoint, 70, 71, 82
  and the performative, 71, 104
Consciousness
 as awareness, 45, 105, 127, 128
 as biological, 9, 146, 166
 and character, 11, 26, 125, 145, 181
 and dramatic portrayal, 10, 54, 124, 127, 148, 149
 and emotion, 50, 102
 and experience, 104, 126, 128, 147
 as a "hard problem" (Chalmers), 146, 179
 and mind-body problem, 146, 149
 and narrative or literary portrayal, 8, 9, 10, 124, 125, 127, 148, 149
 in relation to selfhood, 10, 146, 147, 150
Cook, Amy
 cognitive "blend" of observing actor and character, 190
Coquelin, Benoit Constant, 15
 "Dual Personality of the Actor" on actor and character, 184
Corneille, Pierre, 7, 181
 and *Le Cid* controversy, 68, 193
Cosmos, 55, 56, 99
 ancient Greek, 48
 and chaos, 55
 and character, 39, 47–49
 and the English Renaissance, 5, 48
 and order, 55, 56
 and Racine, 80
Coward, Noel, 90
 and comedy of manners, 171
 Hay Fever, 178
 and performative character, 178
 Private Lives, 178
  character of Amanda Prynne, 200

Damasio, Antonio
 and experience, feeling, 125–126
 and selfhood, 147, 164
Danan, Joseph
 and postdramatic theatre, 162
De Ste. Croix, G. E. M.
 Aristotle as "scientist", 195

Demastes, William W.
  on *Equus*, 115
Dench, Judy, 16
Diamond, Elin, 164
  and *Cloud 9*, 167
  and gender, 167
  and realism, 207
Dionysus, 4, 24, 37, 47, 57
  associations and forms, 4
  and the City Dionysia, 5
  and the dithyramb, 3, 20–22
  ekstasis, enthusiasmos, 18, 19
  as god of character, 17, 18–20, 25, 161
  as god of theatre, 19, 28
  and the mask of character, 4, 18, 26–28, 40
  myths of, 21
  worship of, 21
Dramatis personae, 1, 16, 28, 39, 58, 60, 104, 116,
      119, 123, 134, 147
Dramaturgy
  and "real person" characterization, 7, 8, 15,
      133, 178
  and absurdism, 11, 141
  and aesthetics, 10, 14, 15, 76, 77, 161, 162
  ancient, 4, 23, 26
  and audience, 2, 8, 15, 43, 114, 115, 155, 157,
      158, 172, 173, 174
  as causal, 164, 173, 176
  and character autonomy, 6, 41, 43–47,
      61, 110
  and conflict, 5, 13, 19, 20, 23, 24, 27, 33, 38,
      60, 80, 107, 110, 128, 134, 149,
      157, 173
  definitions of, 14
  as dramatic composition and theatrical
      representation, 8, 9, 12, 14, 98, 168
  and dramatic structure, 5, 9, 10, 11, 13, 14, 19,
      30, 43, 45, 52, 100, 117, 120, 141, 155,
      156, 162, 167
  and English Renaissance, 5, 49, 63
  and genre, 6, 8, 12, 41, 42, 45, 57, 85, 100,
      105, 180
  and mimesis, 13, 101, 102, 152, 161, 162
  Neoclassical, 7, 63, 67, 68, 77, 78
  in rehearsal and production, 14
  and suspense, 11, 156
Dunn, Francis
  Artemis and death of Hippolytus, 189

Easterling, P. E.
  and ancient mask, and actor, 27–28
Edwards, Paul
  character of Thomasina Coverly, 198
Eliot, T. S.
  character of Hamlet, 192

Else, Gerald
  character and plot, 31, 51
  character and speech, choice, 32, 33
  character and thought, 32
  and pathos, 24
  on Thespis, 24
  on tragic origins, 20
Esslin, Martin, 158
  on the absurd, 204
Etherege, George, 85, 171
  The Man of Mode, 82
    character of Mr. Dorimant, 70–75
    character of Sir Fopling Flutter, 71, 73
    and fashion, 73, 74
    and interiority, 72, 74
    mask, uses and definition, 70, 71, 73, 74, 75
    and naturalism, 74, 85
    as performative, 71, 72, 73
    and sexuality, 70, 71
    and the truewit character, 71, 74, 75, 170
Euripides, 4, 5, 34, 35
  The Bacchae, 21
    character of Dionysus, 17
      appearance of, 4, 17
      powers of, 4, 19
    character of Pentheus, 36
      robing of, 17, 18
      and sparagmos, 18
  Hippolytus, 75
    and Aphrodite, 39, 77
    and Artemis, 39, 77
    character of Hippolytus, 39
    character of Phaedra, 35, 39, 75
  Medea
    character of Medea, 29, 30, 35, 41

Faulkner, William, 201
Fergusson, Francis, 46, 50, 86
  on reason and plotting in Racine, 77
Feynman, Richard
  as character in *Q.E.D.*, 98–100
  as historical figure, 98, 100
Flickinger, Roy C.
  on the early dithyramb, 23
Forster, E. M.
  on "round" and "flat" characters, 209
Frayn, Michael, 92
  Copenhagen, 97–98
    character of Niels Bohr, 97
    character of Werner Heisenberg, 97
    in relation to scientific character, 97
Freud, Sigmund
  character types in drama, 106
Frye, Northrop
  on Hamlet and "melancholy", 191
  on irony in *Three Sisters*, 199

Fuchs, Elinor
  and "death" of character, 12–13, 158–160, 161, 162

Garner, Stanton B., Jr.
  the physical body and Zola's naturalism, 87, 196
Gay, John
  The Beggar's Opera
    and characterization, 83
    as anti-sentimental, 83
Gazzaniga, Michael
  on brain and mind, 166
  on free will, 166
Genre
  the family play, 12, 13, 119, 169, 172
  farce, 12, 169, 171
  melodrama, 12, 42, 104, 157, 169
  realism, 178
  satire, 171
Gerrig, Richard
  readers and literary characters, 202
Gilman, Richard
  on character and time in Chekhov, 200
  on Winnie "in time", 144
Goldhill, Simon, 29
  ancient character and mind, psychology, 36
Goldsmith, Oliver, 83
Goldstein, Rebecca Newberger
  on Plato and real persons as characters, 196
Gorra, Michael, 126
  and consciousness in Henry James, 127
  and perception, awareness in James, 127
Gowing, Lawrence, 135, 202
Green, J. R.
  separation of performer and choral group, 184
Gruber, William E.
  on neglect of character in drama, 209
Guare, John
  The House of Blue Leaves
    character of Artie Shaughnessy, 209

Haigh, A. E.
  alternation of character and chorus, 186
  on Thespis, 187
Hazlitt, William
  Hamlet as "prince of philosophical
    speculators", 44
Henrichs, Albert
  on Dionysus, 185
Hernadi, Paul
  and genre, 208
Huerta, Jorge
  on *Zoot Suit*, 209

Ibsen, Henrik
  A Doll House, 149, 157

character of Nora Helmer and Laura
  Kieler, 90
  Hedda Gabler, 157, 199
  The Master Builder, 122
    character of Halvard Solness, 105, 111–114
    character of Hilda Wangel, 105, 111, 112
    and Emilie Bardach, 90
    and consciousness, 9, 110–112
    and the "impossible", 111, 113–114
    as metaphysical, 111, 112
    as tragedy, 114
    and two minds, 110, 111, 114, 117
  Rosmersholm, 199
  When We Dead Awaken, 117, 199
    and consciousness, 128
Ionesco, Eugene, 11, 176
  and anti-character, 11, 139, 140
  The Bald Soprano
    absurdist character, 140
    character of the Smiths and Martins, 140, 141
Irony, 12, 72, 83, 133, 134, 167, 168, 176, 177, 180
Irving, Henry, 15
  artists' portraits of, 203
  roles of, 203

James, Henry, 8, 10, 126
  "air of reality", 177
  and consciousness, 126, 127, 148
  and dramatic, scenic representation, 127, 135
  on film, 201
  on "going behind" character, 149
  The Portrait of a Lady, 135
    character of Isabel Archer, 8, 126, 127, 148
  The Tragic Muse
    "Preface", 205
James, William
  and "stream of consciousness", 126, 201
Johnson, Barbara
  analysis and complexity of "The Purloined
    Letter", 198
Johnson, Gary
  consciousness and the neuronarrative, 197
Johnson, Samuel
  on Hamlet as "instrument" over "agent", 59
Johnston, Brian
  When We Dead Awaken
    tragedy of consciousness, 128
Jones, John
  and Aristotle, 27, 35, 51
  figure of the mask, 27, 30, 34
Joyce, James, 169
  Portrait of the Artist as a Young Man, 135

Kachur, B. A.
  character of Dorimant, 71, 73, 194

Kaufman, George S. (and Moss Hart)
  characters based on real people in *The Man
    Who Came to Dinner*, 90
Kennedy, Andrew, 145
  Winnie's cosmos in *Happy Days*, 144
Kenner, Hugh
  character of Winnie, 204
Kerényi, Carl
  and Dionysus, 21, 187
Kitto, H. D. F.
  on *Agamemnon*, 37, 189
Knight, G. Wilson
  character of Hamlet, 54
Konnikova, Maria
  on Sherlock Holmes and Watson, seeing
    versus observing, 198
Krutch, Joseph Wood
  tragedy as transhistoric, 190
Kushner, Tony, 12
  Angels in America: Millenium Approaches,
    168, 176
  and the Reagans, 177

Lacan, Jacques, 36
  on Hamlet and Ophelia, 106, 198
Lahr, John
  and *The Homecoming*
    personal response to, 154
Lamm, Martin
  character as "case" in *Miss Julie*, 89
Lamont, Rosette
  on Ionesco, 203
Lawley, Paul
  and the character of Winnie, 204
Lehmann, Hans-Thies
  on the postdramatic, 12–13, 161, 162, 176, 207
Levin, Harry
  Alceste's "outrage", 193
Lifton, Robert J.
  and the "protean" self, 206
Lightman, Alan
  adequate language for electron behavior, 101
Lillo, George
  The London Merchant
    character of George Barnwell, 83
    "Dedication"
      on tragedy and the common person, 168
Lloyd-Jones, Hugh
  and will of Zeus in *Agamemnon*, 38
Lodge, David
  and consciousness, 125, 201
  and Henry James
    James on film, 201
  Thinks..., 148
    character of Helen Reed, 148
    character of Ralph Messenger, 148

Lonsdale, Stephen H.
  and Dionysus, as the god *in*, 19
Lowe, E. J.
  and consciousness, response to Chalmers, 205

Margolin, Uri, 197
Marlowe, Christopher
  Doctor Faustus
    and the science play, 100
Martin, Jay
  and fictive personality, 163
McConachie, Bruce
  on audience and cognition, 183, 190, 207
McGann, Jerome
  quotes Poe, 198
Melodrama
  and dramatic structure, 104, 157, 169
  in relation to character traits, 12, 42, 83,
    157, 158
  and suspense, 157
Miller, Arthur, 173
  After the Fall
    character and autobiography, 123
    character of Quentin, 9, 122
    and memory, 9, 123
Miller, J. Hillis
  illusion of self, 150–151
Molière (Jean-Baptiste Poquelin), 7, 85, 131
  Tartuffe, 64, 120
  The Misanthrope
    character of Alceste, 62–68, 72, 81
    character of Eliante, 66
    character of Philinte, 63, 64, 65, 66

Nabokov, Vladimir
  Lolita, 203
Neoclassicism
  and *bienséance*, 63
  guidelines for character, 7, 62, 63, 67, 68
  and instruction, 7, 64, 67, 68
  and *Le Cid* controversy, 68
  and *les regles*, 62, 75
  and reason, 7, 63, 65
  and the passions, 62, 63
  and the raisonneur, 63, 64
  and unities, 7, 68
Nichols, Peter
  Passion Play, 199
Nietzsche, Friedrich
  The Birth of Tragedy
    archetype of Dionysus, 24

O'Neill, Eugene, 9
  Long Day's Journey into Night, 12
    character of the Tyrones, 90, 120, 121, 174
    relation to memory, 120, 121

Otto, Walter F.
  on Dionysus, 28, 184

Padel, Ruth
  and theatre as the god's art form, 19
Paolucci, Anne
  Pirandello and the perception of the
      "opposite", 134
Parnell, Peter
  Q.E.D.
    character of Richard Feynman, 98–100
    in relation to scientific character, 98, 99, 100
Phelan, James
  aspects of narrative character, 94
  and "plausible person", 94
Pickard-Cambridge, Arthur
  and the dithyramb, 23–24
Pinter, Harold, 11, 153, 176
  The Homecoming, 11, 154
    character of Lenny, 153
    character of Ruth, 153, 154
    and mystery, 153, 154, 156
Pirandello, Luigi, 5, 6, 11, 12, 44, 46, 139, 147,
      159, 176, 180
  on the birth and life of character, 42, 43, 130
  and *sentimento del contraria*, 11, 134, 140
  Six Characters in Search of an Author, 42, 131
    character of The Father, 6, 43, 130, 132, 133,
      134, 136, 137, 138
    character of The Stepdaughter, 132, 133,
      136, 138
    relation of Actors and Characters, 43, 130,
      132, 133
Plato
  and real person characterization, 90
Poe, Edgar Allan, 10
  "Annabel Lee", 203
  "The Purloined Letter"
    character and thinking of C. Auguste
      Dupin, 106–107, 110, 111
Portraiture
  of actors, 137
  classical, 135
    and David, 136
    and Gainsborough, 136
    and Ingres, 136
  compared with modeling, 15, 136, 138
  and representation, 135, 137
Poulet, Georges
  on consciousness and reading, 129
Powell, Jocelyn
  Dorimant's "isolation", 75
Powers, Richard
  The Echo Maker, 102, 148
    character of Gerald Weber, 102–103, 148
    and Capras Syndrome, 102

depiction of brain injury, neurology, and
    mental states, 102–103
  and focalization
    and narrative "showing",
      103, 149–150, 205
Prideaux, Sue
  Strindberg's medical apprenticeship, 87

Racine, Jean, 7, 63, 68, 85, 181
  character of Phaedra, 7
    and interiority, 79, 80
    and passion, 75, 80, 81
    and reason, 75, 80
    and sexuality, 76, 81
  Phaedra
    and dramatic structure, 77, 78
    power of Venus, 77, 78
    relation to Euripides, 77
    as tragedy
      Neoclassical tragedy, 75, 76, 77, 104
Ramachandran, V. S.
  on selfhood
    components of, 150, 164, 205
    problem of, 150
Renaissance, English
  and cosmos, 5, 48
  Elizabethan Age
    chain of being, 55
  revenge tragedy, 47, 52, 55, 59, 168
Richards, I. A.
  and tragedy, 128
Richardson, Brian
  character and the dimension of
    performance, 196
  character as verbal construct, 197
Rokotnitz, Naomi
  and observation of characters in live stage
    event, 183
Rorty, Amélie Oksenberg
  characters aggrandized in tragedy, 34
Roth, Marco
  and the neuronovel, 148
Rousseau, Jean-Jacques, 7
  "Letter to M. D'Alembert on the
    Theatre", 68–70
  on *The Misanthrope*, 68, 69
  on Alceste, 69
Ruhl, Sarah, 12
  The Clean House, 209

Sargent, John Singer
  individual works of, 202
  and portraiture, 136
Schlink, Bernard
  The Reader
    character of Michael Berg, 175

Searle, John R., 166
  on consciousness, 146, 147
  differs with Damasio, 147
  on mind, 110
  on self, sense of self, 147, 164, 179
Segal, Charles
  and Dionysus, 37
    as fusion with nature's energies, 20
    as "patron god of theatre", 20
Seneca, 110
  Shakespeare's debt to, 47
Sewall, Richard B.
  and tragic cosmos, 190
Shaffer, Peter
  Equus
    character of Alan Strang, 114
    character of Martin Dysart, 114, 115
    as Dionysian, 114, 115
    and memory, 114, 122
    and two minds, 114, 116, 122
Shakespeare, William, 12
  Hamlet
    and Aristotle, 51, 53
    and cognitive subplot, 51, 104, 147
    and cosmos, 48, 55
    and genre, 47, 55, 60
    as revenge tragedy, 47
    and the supernatural, 56, 127
    as tragedy, 48, 53
      tragic "sense", 56–57
    and "world character" (States), 60, 116
  Hamlet, character of, 5, 6
    and agency, 43, 53, 58, 59
    and autonomy, 6, 43, 44, 45, 59
    and interiority, 43
    and pathology, illness, depression, 52–53
    as performative, 5, 44, 46, 57
    relationships, 56, 58
      to Gertrude, 56
      to Ophelia, 54
    and thought, consciousness, 5, 9,
      43, 45, 48
  King Lear, 47, 92, 149
    as tragedy, 128
  Macbeth, 47, 95, 120
Shapin, Steven
  scientific figures and typed
    associations, 197
Shaw, George Bernard, 131
  Candida
    and character thinking, 200
  reviewing *The Master Builder*, 199
Shepherd-Barr, Kirstin, 100
  form and content in the science play, 98
  science and theatrical metaphor, 197

Sheridan, Richard Brinsley, 83
Siddons, Sarah, 15
Sophocles, 5, 22, 29, 34, 36, 157
  Antigone
    character of Antigone, 33, 34, 35, 39,
      52, 106
    character of Creon, 52
  Oedipus at Colonus
    character of Theseus, 35
Stanislavsky, Konstantin, 90
  acting theory, 92
  and truth of character, 161
States, Bert O.
  anatomy of character, 92
  and "completeness," jealousy regarding
    character, 95
  components, levels of dramatic character, 94
    in relation to *opsis*, 93
  differs with J. Hillis Miller, 152
  on identity, personality, 93, 94
  individual and group character, 116, 147
  and "world character" in *Hamlet*, 60
    relation to Burke, "character receipe", 60
Steele, Richard
  on comedy, 168
  The Conscious Lovers
    "character" of Bevil, Jr., 82
    "Preface" to, 83
    and "Providence", 83
Steiner, George
  "absolute" tragedy, 48, 57
Steiner, Wendy
  modeling and character, 138
  and the virtual, 139
Stoppard, Tom, 12, 92
  Arcadia
    character of Septimus Hodge, 97, 109
    character of Thomasina Coverly, 97,
      108–110
    and two minds, 110
    relation to Oscar Wilde, 169
  Travesties
    character of Henry Carr, 110, 170
      as metatheatrical, 12, 170
      as real person, 169, 170
    and genre, 169, 170
    and historical characters, 169
    as metatheatre, 170, 171
Strindberg, August, 8, 86, 87, 89
  and Darwinism, 89, 101
  Miss Julie, 85, 86, 87
    character of Miss Julie, 88, 89, 100, 102,
      105, 124
    "Preface" to *Miss Julie*, 88, 89, 100, 159
    and Siri Von Essen, 90
    and tragedy, 88, 100, 101

Stynan, J. L.
  on Zola and characterization, 85
Sypher, Wylie
  "cubist" drama in Pirandello, 137

Terry, Ellen, 16
Theatrical illusion, 1, 4, 6, 11, 13, 17, 28, 130, 139,
    161, 184
Thespis
  as actor, 3, 22, 26
  in relation to character, 22, 24, 26
  roles of, 3, 23, 25
  as writer, 22
  and tragedy, 3, 22, 23, 24
Tillyard, E. M. W.
  and Elizabethan chain of being, 55
  and world picture, 191
Tocque, Louis, 135
Todorov, Tristan
  on genre, 208
Toibin, Colm
  on Samuel Beckett, 141
Tragedy, tragic drama
  "absolute" tragedy (George Steiner), 48, 57
  ancient, 3, 4, 5, 15, 20, 22, 23, 24, 31, 34, 39, 44
  and cosmos, 39, 48
    microcosm, macrocosm, 48
  as Dionysian, 20, 21, 24, 56, 100
  in English Renaissance, 5, 45, 47, 60,
    100, 168
  and genre, 7, 41, 57, 78
  and modernism, 100
  and naturalism, 84
  and sparagmos, 57, 101
  as transhistoric, 47
Treadwell, Sophie
  Machinal, 9
    character of the Young Woman, 123
Troyat, Henri
  Chekhov and Stanislavsky, 196
  Chekhov as scientific, 196
Turnell, Martin
  on Molière
    The Misanthrope
      on Alceste, 66, 67
      on Philinte, 64
    and Neoclassicism, 194
  on Racine
    Phaedra
      character of Phaedra
        sexual desire, 81, 194
      and passion, 78, 195
      on reason versus passion, 80, 195

Valdez, Luis, 12
  El Teatro Campesino, 172

in relation to Brecht, 12, 172
  Zoot Suit, 168
    character of El Pachuco, 171
    character of Henry Reyna, 171
    as family play, 172
    and historical events, 171
    as metatheatre, 12, 171
Valency, Maurice
  on Chekhov and Zola, 196
  and irony in Pirandello, 202
Van Laan, Thomas
  tragedy as transhistoric, 190
Vanden Heuvel, Michael
  alternative theatre and realism, 160
Vernant, Jean-Pierre, 35, 184, 188
  with Pierre Vidal-Naquet, 28, 39, 185

Wasserstein, Wendy
  The Heidi Chronicles, 168, 176
    and formative experience, 174
    character of Heidi Holland, 174
Webster, John
  The Duchess of Malfi, 49, 120
Wedekind, Frank, 176
Weinberg, Bernard
  interiority in *Phaedra*, 79, 195
Wilde, Oscar, 171
  The Importance of Being Earnest
    and comedy of manners, 169
    relation to *Travesties*, 169, 170
Williams, Tennessee, 86, 90
  Cat on a Hot Tin Roof, 11, 30, 155
    character of Brick Pollitt, 155, 156
    character of Margaret ("Maggie the Cat")
      Pollitt, 156
  The Glass Menagerie, 12
    and memory, 120, 121, 122
    character of Amanda Wingfield, 122
    character of Laura Wingfield, 122
    character of Tom Wingfield, 122
    on mystery, 155, 156
    "Portrait of a Girl in Glass", 122, 135
Wilshire, Bruce
  character of Hamlet and theatricality, 58
Wilson, August, 176
  Fences, 12
    character of Troy Maxson, 173–174
    as family play, 173, 174
    and formative experience, 173
Woolf, Virginia, 201
Wycherley, William, 9, 85, 171
  The Country Wife, 82
    character of Horner, 9, 70

Young, Kay
  on the "feeling brain" (Damasio), 201

Zeitlin, Froma
  Dionysus as "lord of the theatre", 185
  robing of Pentheus, 18
    and feminine costume, 185
Zola, Emile, 8
  "Naturalism in the Theatre"
    character and "truth", 84
    dispute with Romanticism, 84
    dispute with tragedy, 84
    on environment and character, 85
    and naturalistic character, 84, 87
    and scientific character, 84, 85, 87